Good Sex

Good Sex

Feminist Perspectives
from the World's Religions

Edited by
Patricia Beattie Jung
Mary E. Hunt
Radhika Balakrishnan

Rutgers University Press
New Brunswick, New Jersey, and London

Third paperback printing, 2005

Patricia Beattie Jung's essay was previously published in *Theology and Sexuality* (March 2000): 26–47. Reprinted here with the permission of the editors of *Theology and Sexuality.*
Ayesha Imam's essay was previously published in *Dossier* 17 (1997): 7–25. Reprinted here with the permission of the editors of *WLUML Dossier.*
Part of Pinar Ilkkaracan's essay was originally published in "Exploring the context of women's sexuality in eastern Turkey" in *Reproductive Health Matters* 6, 12 (November 1998), and is reprinted here with their permission.
Dorothy Ko's essay was first published in a slightly modified version under the title "Rethinking Sex, Female Agency, and Footbinding," in *Research on Women in Modern Chinese History* 7 (August 1999): 75–105.

Library of Congress Cataloging-in-Publication Data

Good sex / edited by Patricia Beattie Jung, Mary E. Hunt, Radhika
Balakrishnan
    p. cm.
  Includes bibliographical references and index.
  ISBN 0-8135-2883-6 (alk. paper) — ISBN 0-8135-2884-4 (pbk. : alk. paper)
  1. Women and religion. 2. Sex—Religious aspects. I. Jung, Patricia
Beattie. II. Hunt, Mary E., 1951– III. Balakrishnan, Radhika.

BL458 .G647 2001
291.1'78357—dc21

00-039033

British Cataloging-in-Publication data for this book is available from the British Library

For young women,
for whom we wish power, pleasure, and justice

Contents

Acknowledgments

We are deeply grateful to the Religious Consultation for Population, Reproductive Health, and Ethics for its gracious sponsorship of this project. We thank its president, Daniel C. Maguire, for wise counsel and cheerful support. We appreciate the work of S. Jamakaya, the consultation's administrator, during the development of the project. Her tireless efforts in coordinating our communications as an editorial trio, both with each other and all the participants, her attention to the myriad practical details that surrounded our international meetings, and her careful preparation of early drafts of this manuscript were carried out with efficiency and aplomb. We thank as well MaryAnne Walter, our travel agent, for all her work in helping us to gather together as a team from many parts of the world. We acknowledge with thanks the Ford Foundation for funding and especially our program colleague there, Marjorie Muecke, for her active involvement in this work. We are grateful to Dr. John McCarthy and Dr. Robert Di Vito, chairs of the Theology Department and Graduate Program in Theology at Loyola University Chicago, respectively, for their encouragement and provision of graduate research assistants who contributed to this project. Thanks go to Edward Peck, now an assistant professor at Neumann College in Philadelphia, who as a doctoral student helped develop a list of bibliographic resources distributed to participants in the early stages of our work, and to Timothy Sever, a doctoral student at Loyola University Chicago, for his careful proofing. We appreciate as well the work and hospitality of Carolyn Farrell of the Gannon Center for Women and Leadership for sponsoring early public discussions of the book at Loyola University Chicago. Warm gratitude goes to the staff of WATER (Women's Alliance for Theology, Ethics, and Ritual) for their support of this project, especially to Carol Scinto, whose editorial judgment improved the final product.

We are most grateful, of course, to all those who contributed directly to this project as scholar-activists. Thanks for your hard work writing your essays, reviewing the work of others, and making the time to participate in this unique international conversation.

Finally, special thanks go to our respective "good sex" partners, Shannon Jung, Diann Neu, and David Gillcrist, for their patience while we were busy enjoying Good Sex with others.

Introduction

What is good sex in a globalized world in the twenty-first century? What do feminists have to contribute to the understanding and embodiment of good sex? In this volume, we present the work of an international, interreligious group of feminist scholars who began to probe these issues together with attention to religion and a priority on women's well-being.

Constructions of sexuality, as well as notions of what is good, involve many experiences and interpretations. Religions have been the traditional guardians of sexual norms and practices. In fact, patriarchal religions are infamous for their taboos and proscriptions with regard to women and sex. Remarkably little feminist work has been done to probe women's sexual experiences. But the interreligious, multidisciplinary feminist perspectives that make up this conversation intend to change that.

We consciously constructed our process to reflect our commitment to interreligious, multidisciplinary feminist work as the most adequate starting point for new insights. We realized that mutual illumination, as well as mutual criticism, would result. We understood the many pitfalls of such work, especially since it was formulated in the West and structured according to our ever expanding but always limited horizons. Most important, the work was designed to promote conversations between and among participants, as well as between them and their colleagues at home. This volume is one more extension of that process.

Our team of feminist scholars and activists worked without the expectation of consensus or agreement. Rather, we worked with the hope that our efforts might broaden women's sexual options and develop more subtly shaded understandings of sexuality that will lead to women's participation in the world with greater safety and dignity. The process of coming together as a dozen women from eight countries and seven faith traditions provided us with an opportunity to get to know one another and participate in an intercultural feminist conversation, something we agreed was all too rare in our individual experience.

Most anthologies of this sort are collections of essays written by individuals who do not know one another. This book, however, was forged through face-to-face discussions involving both the thorough critique of each essay and, above all, careful attention to the hegemonic constructs that condition our words. We learned in the doing and came to appreciate the value of engaged, collective scholarship that is consistent with feminist goals and commitments.

The idea for this project was sparked at the charter meeting of the Religious Consultation on Population, Reproductive Health, and Ethics in 1994 in Washington, D.C. Jose Barzelatto, M.D., then the director of the Reproductive Health and Population Program of the Ford Foundation, pointed out that religion remains a powerful cultural force that shapes people's lives and their prospects for health and well-being. He observed that because religions can arouse such passion, scholars of religion can be helpful to activists and other professionals in identifying and expressing the various religious grounds for promoting fair population policies, just economic measures, and responsible reproductive health programs. He suggested that scholarly and popular materials on these topics need to be prepared and disseminated to and through nongovernmental organizations in order to bring progressive religious voices into the public policy conversation.

Given the complexities of feminist/womanist/*mujerista* and other women-defined challenges to hitherto patriarchal religions, Jose Barzelatto's suggestion is even more compelling on issues relating to women's well-being. The consequences of some religion-based policies, especially those regarding birth control and abortion, have been very costly to the social fabric, especially for women. One of the questions that remains is: if sex is not exclusively, primarily, or necessarily for procreative purposes, as some religions, for example, Catholicism, have argued for centuries, then what is it for? If it is for pleasure and/or relational purposes, how can this be articulated in different moral contexts in ways that are women friendly, safe, religiously faithful, and culturally appropriate across a range of traditions?

Patricia Beattie Jung left that meeting enthusiastic about doing scholarly work on sexual ethics with a direct service link. She submitted a project proposal to Daniel C. Maguire, president of the Religious Consultation on Population, Reproductive Health, and Ethics. The Consultation's board of directors responded by inviting her to work with its members Radhika Balakrishnan and Mary E. Hunt on such a promising project. The Consultation gathers interreligious, cross-cultural, and interdisciplinary teams that work in tradition-specific ways to collaborate on central ethical concerns with an eye toward activism. Ours was to be a feminist version of that model.

We, the project coordinators and editors of this volume, made the safe assumption that women's religious wisdom regarding sexuality had not often been incorporated into male-dominated religious and ethical accounts of what constitutes good sex. We decided that women might best begin to give voice to their insights in a women-only environment. We searched the globe for women who might contribute to such a conversation, polling friends and colleagues, and identified well over eighty feminists with expertise on the topic of women, religion, and sexuality.

We selected thirteen women whose participation in this process we had funds to sponsor. (We hoped that additional colleagues might collaborate in other ways, including the use of this book in their own work.) We chose women who worked either as scholars or grassroots activists and, in a few cases, as both. We resigned ourselves to the unfortunate but practical reality of choosing English as the working language, a constant reminder of the problems associated with overcoming hegemony.

Our group members came from eight countries—Brazil, China, India, Nigeria, Thailand, Turkey, the United Kingdom, and the United States— and from a range of religious traditions—Buddhism, Chinese religions, Christianity (both Protestant and Catholic), Hinduism, Islam, Judaism, and capitalism, for in this project, we came to see capitalism, a global economic system, as the functional equivalent of a world religion. Participants had the privilege of meeting for two working periods, each several days in length. Some of us had a third opportunity to gather, at the 1998 Annual Meeting of the American Academy of Religion in Orlando, Florida, where we focused as a panel on our methodology as a useable model of feminist scholarship.

At our first meeting, in Philadelphia in October 1997, we agreed on guidelines for producing scholarly essays. We designed a process whereby we could cooperate in the development and refinement of one another's work without consensus, closure, or certainty. The aim was to learn how to learn with one another to reshape our own perspectives and move toward—even if we never reached— some common understandings, ethical thresholds, and action steps.

On the basis of our discussions, we collaborated on informal guidelines we would use to work through some of the cultural and religious issues on which we had differing perspectives. We decided not to search for a common mind among us, as some of our Consultation colleagues had found useful, nor to try to reduce each quite distinct perspective at our table to one that might be projected as commonly representative of our group. Because women have traditionally been allowed so little voice in the formation of their traditions, the threat of the continued suppression of these perspectives loomed large. Rather, we agreed to live with the ambiguities associated with our differences. We embodied as teammates the varying ways women struggle every day to survive in environments hostile to their particularities.

At the end of the first meeting, we shared with one another a sketch of the topic we each planned to research. We left with the commitment to shape our individual essays in light of our discussions, taking into account the differing definitions, assumptions, and interpretations among us. We also shared a common commitment to add to the discourse on sexuality and to try to say something helpful, each from our own perspective. The U.S., English-language, and Christian dominance in the world and at the table made us accountable for screening at every turn the ways in which we might unwittingly replicate hegemonic discourses and practices.

At our second meeting, in Amsterdam in July 1998, we focused on our essays, each of which had been critiqued beforehand by two colleagues. This meeting was even richer than the first, as we knew so much more about one another by then. We knew better how to ask questions, what vocabulary to choose for productive discussion, and how to listen more acutely. It was amazing to name a theme and have expertise emerge around the table, to ask a question and be given several helpful answers. We became a team in a real sense, a rewarding experience for feminist scholars used to working alone. On a personal level, we found that sharing meals and recreation, sightseeing, and evening discussions helped us to deepen our appreciation for one another and lent an energizing dimension of fun, so often absent from scholarly work

The chapters in this volume are grouped in three sections to highlight some of the most important themes that dominated our conversations: creation of desires, prices of sex, and reconstruction of sexualities. Gathered in each section are writings that focus on a signal element—one common to and traceable in many of the other chapters essays—of special concern in this group.

Chapters in the section on creation of desires explore the problems of the historical construction of women's sexuality, critiquing dominating forms of inclusivity and blanket generalizations. The chapters in the section on prices of sex specify some of the high costs of sexuality for many women and make concrete suggestions for social changes, so that women may come to experience and, we are hopeful, celebrate good sex. Chapters in the concluding section on reconstruction of sexualities further uncover the problems of the interpretive process, highlighting in broader analytic terms some of the ways women might faithfully resist normative constructions of their sexuality. These writers offer constructive alternatives based on women's religious wisdom that hold promise for a just future.

A major insight from this project is the value of expanding the company we keep. In a global economy in which people of diverse backgrounds come closer together and connections grow stronger, we submit that adequate and meaningful ethical and religious reflection on sexuality needs to be done in ways that resemble those we have tried here. The company we keep as scholars and activists must include voices from outside our disciplines as well as within them. Exclusive reliance on one's own cultural or religious tradition, or even common understandings of the meaning of those traditions, will prove insufficient.

Tradition remains a problematic concept. In our group, every scholar identified a tradition from which she came. Women coming from the same tradition demonstrated such diverse ways of being within that tradition that virtually nothing could be taken for granted, the dynamism of traditions being what it is.

Even in the case of the most repressive of traditions, there was, perhaps surprisingly, both an appreciation for the tradition and a healthy disdain for its shortcomings. This kind of love-hate relationship allows women to function effectively as bona fide members of traditions that argue against women's existence or well-being (for example, Catholic lesbians and Muslim feminists), as well as change agents within those traditions. This was equally the case for capitalism, in some ways the common faith that all of us critiqued even as we live it, however differently.

Every tradition inclines its faithful adherents to the uncritical acceptance of its biases and its partial truths, something we seek to avoid. Traditions, whether religious, disciplinary, or otherwise, do not ask whose voices are privileged and whose are silenced within their own parameters. The point is not that any particular tradition is without significant insight. Rather, no tradition is a completely trustworthy resource, nor is any tradition comprehensive. This reality compels us to recommend interdisciplinary, intercultural work as a norm.

There are practical reasons for thinking about what makes for good sex interreligiously and cross-culturally. While it is true that religious intolerance and theocratic tyranny are on the rise in many places around the world, there is also unprecedented challenge to dominant interpretations of traditions and a marked increase in religious pluralism in many places. These phenomena make interreligious work an obvious and necessary methodological shift from approaches based on a single tradition. In many parts of the world—for example, in Brazil, parts of Western Europe, and the United States—pairings of people from different traditions, indeed whole families made up of a rainbow of religions, argue for thinking interreligiously about sexual ethics. The most compelling practical reason rests with the need to understand in global terms the relationship between the economic and political damage inflicted by corporations, governments, and patriarchal religions.

As we sought increased clarity, we found the need to be self-conscious of the ways in which we use terms such as *the autonomous self, pleasure,* and *human rights.* It quickly became apparent that we did not all mean the same thing by these terms, nor did we value or prioritize them in the same way. For example, we evaluated globalization from our various perspectives, admitting its contributions to this project, namely, fax, e-mail, air travel, and the like. Yet we also agreed on its downside, especially the structures of economic inequality that assure that some will profit and others will be disadvantaged for generations as economic globalization puts decision making in the hands of fewer and fewer people. We learned from one another that globalization made this conversation both possible and necessary.

We shared as a team stories of women's experiences—poor women whose reproductive options are circumscribed by laws rooted in religion, women for whom sexual pleasure is practically unheard of, lesbian women who fear that coming out may cost them their reputations, in some cases their lives. These stories pushed us to ask questions about how our religious and ethical reflections might contribute to social change.

Although it is true that we came to no common conclusions, produced no manifestos for action, we did approximate what we have come to think of in retrospect as shared ethical understandings and thresholds. These concerns motivate us in different contexts to diverse actions. Nonetheless, women's sexual safety, dignity, and well-being are the primary foci of our attention and work.

Our time was limited, our scope narrow. But as we looked ahead, we saw ways in which our insights could be useful in efforts to bring about justice in such areas as sexual tourism and trade, sex work, sexual slavery, sexually transmitted diseases in the midst of the global HIV/AIDS pandemic, the revalorization of female sexual delight, female circumcision, breast implants and cosmetic reconstructive surgeries, pornography, child marriages, arranged marriages, marriages by capture, antilesbian activities, marital rape, dowries, the domestic confinement of women and girls, domestic violence, honor killings or other socially legitimated ways of murdering wives who prove unsatisfactory, unequal access to and terms of divorce, rape in war, compulsory motherhood, the devaluation of child care, the overemphasis on female parenting, and unequal educational and economic opportunities for women.

The pluses in a process of interreligious and cross-cultural collaboration are many, as this volume illustrates. All of us gained new perspective on the assets and limitations of our own ways of thinking. We confronted the gap between the accessibility unto overload of printed and preserved information about some traditions and the dearth of information on others. This pattern mirrors global power and accounts for the disproportionate influence or hegemony of Western sources. It is the unjust legacy of colonialism.

The Buddhist, Chinese, and Hindu women commented that one of the things they shared when participating in an interreligious dialogue was being Other to the dominance of monotheistic discourses. Part of the colonial pattern has been to dismiss the colonized Other's construction of sexuality as perverse. This understanding made the specter of Western hegemony loom large. A similar problem arises when Christian and Jewish scholars have abundant feminist resources in their respective arenas, whereas colleagues from non-Western traditions are among the pioneers in their work.

We recognized the partial and limited character of all scholarly work. We admitted that not all women around the table shared certain fundamental discursive categories. For example, even the meaning of the notion of good (as distinct from bad) sex proved controversial. Likewise, there was no common understanding of the individual *self,* or even a shared idea of *religion* or *traditions.* That lack hampered our ability to come to common thresholds, an occupational hazard in the method we chose. We concluded with a sense that when we work on future projects, this process and experience will keep resonating in ways that will make us pay much closer attention to our discursive presumptions and limits.

Everyone's consciousness of how the celebration of women's sexual pleasure might collude with the colonization of others in the now globalized sex trade and in industries spawned by the development of new reproductive technologies was greatly heightened. Because we were committed to working with each other, the questions of whose pleasure was to be celebrated and at whose expense could not be dodged. This raised for some participants a certain ambivalence about the approach to collaboration we adopted, lest we might have, however unwittingly, reinforced oppressive patterns.

This work is not unflawed. There remains on the part of some a concern that we deferred too much to the admittedly very real and deep differences among us. No one wanted to flatten out important differences, make false generalizations, ignore the significance of our particularities, revive cultural imperialism, or resuscitate essentialism. But the notion that women cannot recognize anything in one another's experiences or problems is also dangerous. It springs from the belief that no connections across cultural and religious boundaries can or should be made. This supports a form of relativism that we rejected in this project.

Another concern was the real costs involved in this kind of work. We grappled with whether we are proposing an even more elitist approach than the one we seek to replace. Although there is privilege in our way of working, we see value in the model. Now that we are used to this method, it is hard to go back to a more parochial way of doing things. It makes one uneasy to talk only with colleagues in religion if one is a theologian, only with social scientists if one is a social scientist, and so on.

Not all of us had much expertise in the kind of interreligious and international collaboration that this project invited. But as a result of this collaboration, we see how crucial it is to test our work in a global crucible. We now see our scholarly accountability to more than our own traditions and our own countries.

Part I
Creation of Desires

Sexual desires are constructed within very specific socioeconomic, cultural, and religious contexts. These factors—colonial hegemonic power, legal and religious regulations and taboos, capitalism, religious images and symbols, technological advances, and many others—taken together make up the framework, the cultural backdrop, that fuels and shapes desires. In these essays, that framework is acknowledged insofar as it conditions women's choices and challenged insofar as it prohibits women from exercising them.

Grace Jantzen, an English philosopher, in "Good Sex: Beyond Private Pleasure," argues that British colonialism has meant that British attitudes about sex have had an inordinate influence in shaping what counts as good sex throughout the world. She traces the roots of those attitudes from early Christian sources through contemporary liberal feminism's hard-won emphasis on women's personal pleasure. She warns that good sex characterized solely in terms of pleasure without reference to wider issues of justice may serve those who wish to promote oppressive reproductive policies and practices. Feminist emphasis on good sex cannot rest content with the individualism and hegemony promoted by the Western market economy.

Ayesha M. Imam, an anthropologist from Nigeria, in "The Muslim Religious Right ('Fundamentalists') and Sexuality," argues that colonial discourse led to the ability of fundamentalists to essentialize women's sexuality under the rubric of monolithic Islam. She details the problematic results of conflating

Islam with Muslim attempts to practice it. Her richly detailed analysis of the diversity of discourses about and regulations concerning sexuality provides a valuable road map for distinguishing religious from more broadly social, cultural, and historic forces in this process, thus creating the potential for the transformation of certain gender roles.

Rebecca Alpert, a U.S. rabbi and women's studies scholar, in "Guilty Pleasures: When Sex Is Good Because It's Bad," posits that the regulation of sexual desire and behavior is a common factor both in most religious systems and in the creation of desire. She examines the role of such regulation in Judaism with attention to women's experiences. She suggests that while such a system may inhibit sexual pleasure, it also has unintended liberating and eroticizing consequences for the sexual lives of its adherents. Implications of this dynamic for other religious traditions and for other than sexual aspects of Judaism are provocative and suggestive.

Radhika Balakrishnan, a U.S. economist born in India, in "Capitalism and Sexuality: Free to Choose?" addresses the ways in which notions of the self both influence and are determined by the conditions of production in various societies. She examines the way the capitalistic expansion of market forces functions like a religion for many peoples, transforming traditional social relations and structuring new ones. She argues that it is necessary to pay attention to the ways in which this religion's effects on women are simultaneously liberating and exploitive. Only then will feminists be able to develop a sufficiently nuanced criticism of global capitalism and a more accurate, albeit complex, appraisal of its effects on women's lives.

One

Grace M. Jantzen

Good Sex

Beyond Private Pleasure

When is sex good? For whom is sex good? Western Christendom has throughout its history been obsessed with sex and its regulation, an obsession that continues in Christendom's modern secular modulations. Everything from toothpaste to fast cars is sold with the help of advertisements appealing to and promoting sex, usually between young, glamorous, heterosexual partners. It seems a far cry from the suspicion about sex in early Christian writings. Yet I suggest that from another point of view it can be recognized as the same preoccupation, turned inside out: sex pervades the Western social and symbolic order from (at least) late antiquity to the present.

I write from a position within that Western symbolic and social order as a white, privileged, academic feminist. Yet I write also as one whose life work is a challenge to the structures of Western modernity. As a lesbian feminist, I first learned to identify the masculine and heterosexual bias of these structures; struggles for justice quickly opened my eyes to issues of racism, colonialism, and capitalism as well. These strands intersect in many ways with connections and tensions among them. Part of the motivation for my essay is my belief that whereas Western feminists have rightly learned to celebrate sexual pleasure, we have not always been as quick to discern the wider issues of justice involved. By making sexual pleasure a private issue, we have colluded with ideals of Western individualism, and our work

3

has therefore sometimes been unhelpful to women in other parts of the world or positioned differently in the West. I therefore want to overcome the implicit opposition of pleasure and justice. While delighting in pleasure, we need also to be clear about whose pleasure we are celebrating, and at whose expense. The celebration of pleasure, I suggest, should not collude with Western modernity's attempts to turn pleasure into a privately owned commodity (especially for Western feminists who can afford it) bought at the expense of reproductive justice for all.

In this chapter, I examine some of the transformations of what has counted as good sex, paying particular attention to the Western feminist celebration of women's sexual pleasure. Important as this celebration is, I suggest that these feminist interventions are themselves in grave danger of supporting a bourgeois focus of attention solely on personal fulfillment and enjoyment, abandoning the public and political arenas to those who would be only too glad for feminists to be so preoccupied. I argue that we need to question feminist emphases on sexual pleasure and reconnect them with issues of justice and morality, not to reinvoke the repression of pleasure, lest the celebration of private pleasures distract attention from new public policies. Such policies are being formed around new reproductive technologies, genetic engineering, and other public practices of sex with potentially devastating consequences; often they reintroduce Western domination.

The Best Sex Is No Sex

From its early history, Christianity formed its thinking by weaving with its own distinctive contributions major threads from Jewish thought on the one hand and Platonism on the other. In the case of sex, these two were sharply at odds. Whereas Jewish thought promoted sex (at least married, heterosexual sex) partly for making babies but also for conjugal pleasure, Platonism was suspicious of the body in general and sex in particular: the life of wisdom was the life of the mind. This view was, moreover, misogynist: the female was conceptually linked with matter, sex, and reproduction, the male with mind, spirit, and the divine.[1]

As Platonism became a dominant force in the development of Christendom, many of these attitudes were adopted by the early Church. For instance, all the major fathers of the early Church wrote at length on the topic of virginity, and they were unanimous on its being the best possible state:

the best sex was no sex. This was not quite as repressive as it might at first seem, however. In late antiquity, with its rigid social expectations tied to family and reproduction, the rejection of sex could be a path of radical freedom, especially for women.[2] Moreover, unlike some of the sects that Christians branded heretic, Christendom never quite condemned sex altogether. Sex was good, only it must be contained within heterosexual marriage and be intended to lead to reproduction. Then it would further God's creative purpose and fulfill the divine command to "increase and multiply and replenish the earth" (Genesis 1:28). Any other use of sex was bad sex, "a hissing cauldron of lust."[3]

There were, of course, many variations on the Christian presentation of sex. Roughly speaking, however, this view had three main consequences. In the first place, the pleasure of sex was suspect. Sex was meant to produce babies, not sensual gratification.[4] A theme found in Augustine and repeated through the Western Middle Ages was that if humankind had not sinned, reproduction could take place without desire, man and woman lying together side by side, "and they would gently perspire as if sleeping. Then the woman would become pregnant with the man's perspiration, and, while they lay thus sweetly asleep, she would give birth painlessly from her side . . . in the same way that God brought Eve forth from Adam, and that the Church was born from the side of Christ."[5] Although this suspicion about the pleasure of sex was applied to men as well as to women, in fact the pleasure of the heterosexual male was privileged (it was, after all, necessary for procreation), while (with exceptions) female pleasure was apt to be categorized as a foul trap for men, a "devil's gateway."[6]

The second consequence of the Christian construction of sex was that it could be good only within heterosexual marriage. Same-sex coupling, autoeroticism, and heterosexual coupling outside marriage were all forbidden, with varying degrees of intensity.[7] All of these, after all, would occur only for sensual gratification. Thomas Aquinas, in the thirteenth century, argued that masturbation and even coitus interruptus were worse than rape or incest, since the former could not lead to reproduction while the latter could.[8]

The third consequence was that, for women, sex was equated with compulsory motherhood. Women were to a far larger extent than men defined by their reproductive function. The only alternative sanctioned by Christianity (and now we are back to the beginning) was virginity, often coupled with religious life in a convent. Men could enter a monastic order, of course. But whereas men could be defined in many ways without explicit reference to sex—monk, soldier, knight, merchant, and so on—respectable women were either virgins or mothers.

Good Sex, Secular Sex

In the modern West, there have been major shifts in the configuration of what counts as good sex. Although today's configurations are ostensibly secular, it is not hard to discern in them many of the attitudes of traditional Christendom. I shall mention four aspects of the way good sex has been construed in the modern West, all characteristic of English-speaking countries and, through their imperialism, influential also in other parts of the world.

Sex in the secularizing world of seventeenth- and eighteenth-century northern Europe continued to be seen in terms of procreation. In the countries most closely aligned with Roman Catholicism, this was, of course, most pronounced; the official teaching of the Church—that good sex must be intended to produce a baby—had not changed. The direct result for women was that abortion, contraception, and often even sex education were unavailable or illegal. This remains the case in some European countries where the Catholic Church retains great power, such as Ireland. In Protestant and increasingly secular countries of Europe and North America, however, procreation itself came to be seen more and more in terms of the inheritance of property, first among the upper classes and landed aristocracy and then, with the rise of capitalism, among the middle classes as well.[9] Good sex in such a context is not about love or relationship but about ensuring succession. Once there was a male heir, further procreation was not necessarily desirable. Families continued to be large, partly to ensure succession should the eldest son die—child mortality rates were high—and partly because of the lack of effective contraceptive measures, yet there was a gradual shift from emphasis on procreation to emphasis on property. Another effect of this shift, of course, as Lawrence Stone points out, was more prostitution and the blatant double standard for husbands and wives. Wives had to be absolute in their sexual fidelity because if they were not, their husbands could not be sure that the presumptive heir was their own. Husbands were under no such obligation.[10]

Along with the emphasis on property and inheritance, sexual pleasure became much less suspect. Promoted first by a Protestant emphasis on the human and the individual and then by the increasing rejection of religious sexual morality, good sex might be pleasurable; and as long as the requirements of inheritance had been met, it did not have to be intended to produce children. The idea of companionate marriage began to take hold. All of this, however, became part of the widening split between the public and the private (a split that is specifically Western, and not characteristic of countries such as China or India except insofar as Western values have been imposed on them). Property, inheritance, laws of primogeniture, and virtually all the professions were part of the public realm, which was largely a male preserve. Women, at least in the ideal of the upper classes, were increasingly confined to the private realm, to domesticity, homemaking, and the reproduction of children.[11] Sex too was increasingly seen as a private matter, sexual pleasure the most private of all matters. The genitalia came to be known as "private parts." Although the churches continued to try to dictate what was and was not permissible in the bedroom, and although the consequent religious guilt should not be underestimated, the tide was turning. Good sex (and bad) was private sex, and nobody else's business.

Although private pleasure might be good, public laws created by men and for men put strict limits on the sorts of pleasures that could be tolerated. Adultery by women was severely punished, since it threatened the certainty of lineage and thus the legitimate inheritance of property: a man had to be sure that the children his wife bore were really his. Homosexual acts between men were, in many places, proscribed. Discovered, they could bring imprisonment or even death. Lesbian sex was hardly recognized: sex could not properly be said to have taken place without a penis involved.

In practice, good sex for women was still sex within heterosexual marriage, and the ideal of motherhood was reinforced. Marriage, with motherhood, was a woman's main prospect, especially in Protestant countries where the convent was no longer an option. Economic policies and educational practices favored men and were closed as avenues of self-support for women. A woman was to a great extent at the mercy first of her father and then of her husband. If she was mistreated in marriage, she had nowhere to turn; if she left her husband, their children remained in his custody. A woman was not legally a person in England until toward the end of the nineteenth century.

Although the centuries after the Enlightenment in Europe are seen as increasingly secular, they coincided with waves of missionary activity, especially in the African, Asian, and American countries that Europe was busy colonizing. The self-abrogated right of Europeans to dominate derived to a considerable extent from the sexual practices of the colonized. Over and over, the inferiority of non-Europeans was rhetorically established by portraying them as nonmonogamous, sexually promiscuous, and of vast sexual appetite.[12] The obverse of their bad sex was the good sex of white Europeans, with its emphasis on chastity (at least for women), monogamy, and idealized motherhood. As Wanda Deifelt has pointed out, it is to a great extent because the colonizer's own sexuality is promiscuous that sexuality in the tropics is constructed as promiscuous. In fact, the colonizer's mistress or prostitute and her children were often much worse off, for example, than the colonized's second, third, or fourth wife and their children, whose rights were assured.[13] The European views justified colonization and even the slave trade, sexually exploitative as they were: it is a classic case of rationalizing evil by projecting the evil that is being done onto its victims. Good sex (read: European sexual ideals) was the measure of humanity and progress. Whatever the actualities of colonization and the barbarities of the slave trade, they were made more palatable to the wider European/British public by the insistence that they were necessary for the "progress of civilization," a phrase that was often code for British versions of idealized sexual morality.[14]

Colonization was regularly accompanied by armies of missionaries, many of them sincere in their beliefs, who taught the "natives" to pray to the Christian God and to wear Western clothing that covered their shameful nakedness. Yet mixed with their humanitarian efforts in education and medicine lurked Western sexual ideals, which formed a major part of their agenda.

Yet while the purity and danger theme protecting European womanhood was ubiquitous, it was played out in ways as different as the Spanish Catholic colonization of Latin America and the construction of British India in the nineteenth century. Likewise, the forms of resistance were specific, different in Muslim Africa, for instance, than among the native peoples of North America, and different again among Confucian cultures.

Nevertheless, painting with a broad brush, we can see two major effects of colonization. On the one hand, projecting the colonized people as the sexually perverse Other confirmed European ideals of good sex. And on the other hand, to the extent that the West was successful in its bid for hegemony, European ideals of good sex (Christian; and then secularized from Christian roots) were imposed on the colonized countries and even internalized by their peoples, though they might be in considerable tension with home-grown values, and there was much creative resistance.

Feminist Interventions

The public-private division on which much of Western modernity's understanding of good sex relies has been challenged by feminists and others in ways that have had a huge impact on how good sex is construed. In this reconstruction, the reliance on changes brought about by the Romantic movement are often not sufficiently credited. One of the effects of the Romantic movement was a shift from the idea of marriage as primarily serving to ensure patrilineal inheritance to the idea of companionate marriage. In such a marriage, wife and husband form not just a practical alliance but an intense relationship in which each is of paramount emotional significance to the other. Here, good sex is not merely sex that will ensure the family line but the very glue that cements the marriage bond. Good sex is therefore loving sex and pleasurable sex. Good sex unites the partners at levels of emotion and passion beyond those required when good sex was primarily about making babies. In the West (as contrasted, for instance, with Tantric traditions), pleasure is tied to the individual, who bonds with another in romantic relationship. This ideal of intense bonding between two people still assumed a heterosexual and permanent monogamous marriage, and within that marriage women were still disproportionately identified with reproduction and child rearing. Nevertheless, the stage was set for divesting women of some of these expectations.

With romantic love, however, went fixed ideas about gender roles and the ways in which sexuality could be expressed. Its ideal was a woman who would be an angel in the household, separate from the outside world. The home was still to be the private haven to which public man would return from his bruising forays in the outside world. In fact, its havenlike aspect might be more apparent to the man than to the woman, since within the home she was still subordinate to her husband. Beating was not unusual, and it is only in very recent years in most Western countries that rape within marriage has been recognized as a legal offense. In the meantime, men could frequent prostitutes or keep mistresses with impunity, though the women thus involved were by those very relationships considered degraded.

Still, the ideals of romantic love together with the increasing influence of women helped to bring about a sexual revolution. As Anthony Giddens has demonstrated, men had long depended on women to regulate their emotional and sexual lives; thus it was women who were able to bring about many of the changes in patterns of intimacy in the twentieth century.[15] The rise of feminism, of course, gave the changes added impetus. With the small family size encouraged by changes in capitalism, the development of reliable contraceptive methods, and new reproductive technologies, sex can be to a very large extent uncoupled from making babies. Marriage today depends more on the "satisfaction of intimacy than on the property bond or on children."[16]

Once sex is unlinked from reproduction, it becomes much less obvious why it should be restricted to marriage. Within marriage or not, good sex is negotiated between its participants for their own reasons or desires. Good sex thus becomes pleasurable sex that is fully consensual, and that takes place between individuals who can decide what part of their relationship it shall occupy or indeed whether they will have a continuing relationship at all. This means that there is no good reason why persons of the same sex should not also enjoy good sex, intimacy private to themselves with no goals beyond their own choices. And feminists have long advocated that women can claim as much right to good sex as men can, and that they can stand against the double standard of sexual morality.

Yet it would be foolish to pretend that things are really that easy, even in the West, and even in those areas of the West most influenced by feminism. There is still plenty of prejudice against lesbians and gay men, and there are still far too many women subordinate to their husbands economically and sexually. It would be a bad joke to say that such women are now free to choose good sex for mutual pleasure and intimacy. Moreover, it is important not to romanticize these changes as moral progress of the human spirit or to overstate the importance of feminism in bringing them about. A more realistic, if also cynical, appraisal recognizes that the changes in late capitalism mean that in economic terms it is less important to regulate women's bodies and reproduction than it is to commodify sex, so that sex can be put to the services of advertising, consumerism, and other sorts of vested interests about which I shall have more to say.[17] For sex to be a commodity, it must be seen as pleasurable: indeed, we are pressured now to find sex pleasurable, to get it right every time, to suppose that intimacy depends on perfect sex. Celibacy is viewed as weird and probably unhealthy. Once again, sex, this time pleasurable sex, serves a function that is not likely to be on the minds of the people engaging in it.

All of this is of great importance, and some of it is explored elsewhere in this volume. What I wish to do is to probe a little further in the direction of this functional construction of good sex and the role of feminism. Feminist interventions have critiqued and challenged much of what has counted as good sex in Western history, not least the public-private division. Feminists have been concerned in this critique to lift up and celebrate that which was ostensibly private, to demand the transformation of intimacy, and to delight in women's sexual pleasure. Feminists have been leaders in working for liberation from compulsory motherhood and compulsory heterosexism. All of this I applaud. Yet it seems to me that feminists are in grave danger of colluding with some of the most dubious of Western capitalism's practices.

What I perceive is that feminist interventions, perhaps recuperated for capitalist and consumerist purposes, are too often staying at the level of private pleasures.[18] The celebration of sex, openly talking about what was heretofore hidden, can of course be enormously liberating. Yet I think that the focus—even the fixation—on good sex as pleasurable sex has generated a new variety of compulsion, this time for achieving pleasure. Moreover, this compulsory pleasure is intensely private, nobody else's business. Even feminists hardly challenge the idea that sexual pleasure is one of the most private aspects of contemporary life. And this easily clears the way for those who are only too happy to have attention, including feminist attention, directed toward private sexual pleasure and not toward its political and economic construction and consequences.

Good Sex and Public Policy

Given this turn of events, those with antiprogressive vested interests are free to form public policies in areas that would have been much more carefully scrutinized were the current understanding of good sex not identified with private pleasure. I shall touch on four examples. First, the pharmaceutical companies and beauty industries can use the emphasis on intimacy to foster, for their own commercial ends, a desperation for private sexual pleasure. They can market any number of products, from diets to shampoos, that claim to increase attractiveness and intensify pleasure. Feminists are well aware that ideals of female beauty have been constructed by and for men, but perhaps less aware of how easily feminists' own ideals of good sex can be co-opted for this construction. Even more sinister is the fostering, especially among infertile women or couples, of a desperation for motherhood. Fertility drugs and new reproductive technologies such as in vitro fertilization (IVF) promise enormous financial gain for pharmaceutical companies and IVF clinics. With the focus on sexual morality now turned toward pleasure and intimacy and away from reproductive consequences, it is easy to celebrate good sex and ignore the shaping of public policy in relation to these new reproductive technologies and their construction of women and motherhood.

Second, it is entirely possible for Western middle-class feminists to celebrate good sex as pleasurable sex and ignore the ways in which poor women, or women and children from poor countries, are sexually exploited. There is, for example, the exploitation of women as prostitutes, both in Western countries and elsewhere. If good sex is constructed simply as pleasurable sex, then what could be objectionable about sexual adventure or tourism, at least in situations where women (and young men) voluntarily offer themselves for the sexual pleasure of wealthy Westerners? But this question leads to others—How is this "voluntary" self-offering arrived at? What other choices are available, and with what consequences? And what about the very young children (who are most sought after by Western sex tourists) sold into prostitution by desperately poor families? What of AIDS and other sexually transmitted diseases, and how do they affect prostitutes and their families and friends? Feminists have, of course, been aware of the evils of sex tourism, but again there is less awareness of how the changing ideals of good sex play into the hands of those who would promote or participate in these practices.

Third, and even more worrying, are the persistent rumors of women and children of poor countries exploited for fetal tissue or for organs for experimentation. Largely unprovable are the rumors of street children disappearing in parts of Latin America, of prostitutes who service military bases being paid extra for producing fetal tissue, of biomilitary or biomedical experimentation on material thus procured. Yet they are rumors every feminist should be worrying about. If we made a collective effort either to disprove these rumors or to confirm them and put a stop to such activities, we could be more confident that our celebration of good sex is not at the expense of those for whom sex is anything but good.

Fourth, the uncoupling of sex from reproduction and the advent of genetic engineering have opened the way for developing ideals of perfection or desirable characteristics, especially in babies, and for avoiding "defects" or "deviance." Some genetically determined characteristics, especially gender, are already obtainable by technology, either by manipulating the embryo before implanting it or by the much cruder method of genetic testing of the fetus and selective abortion. Many more characteristics will soon be obtainable by one or other of these methods. Just as disturbing as the idea of designer babies, however, is the whole rhetoric of defect and deviance, which is all too likely to have repercussions for people with disabilities, or for lesbians and gay men, and to be available for every kind of racist and oppressive purpose. It is not part of my agenda to condemn all genetic engineering or to suggest that feminists should try to stop it: some of this science is trying to eliminate severe congenital conditions that one could hardly wish on any child or family. But great vigilance is called for. And to the extent that feminists take our eyes off public policy formation around issues of reproduction, we are giving a gift to those who would like nothing better than to be left in peace to pursue questionable ends. At whose expense is the current Western feminist construction of good sex?

Inconclusive Remarks

Feminists have rightly worked to uncouple sexual pleasure from compulsory motherhood, compulsory heterosexuality, and the double standard that has for centuries accompanied sexual experience. We enjoy good sex; we celebrate sexual pleasure. These are not issues that feminists should go back on. However, the celebration of private sexual pleasure has become such a preoccupation in the West that insufficient attention is paid to public policy formation in areas of life that once would have come under the purview of sexual morality. This is a gift to those whose vested interests lie in the commodification of reproduction and the use of organic or genetic material for purposes that, at the very least, should be closely scrutinized. It is thus also a betrayal by Western affluent feminists of poor women in the West and of people—especially women and children—in materially deprived parts of the world, who often are the ones most immediately affected by Western public policy.

The solution to the problems that may arise from feminists' preoccupation with good sex as private pleasure certainly does not lie in parading in public what is properly intimate. This would in any case do nothing to focus feminist attention on public policy. I think it important however, to remind ourselves of the hard-won value of the insight that led to the slogan of second-wave feminism, "The personal is the political." When we remember how we gained the right to our intimate pleasures, and how and in whose interests good sex has been variously constructed, we are more likely to call to mind the present construction of sexual pleasure and the way it serves the purposes of late capitalism.

Sexual pleasure is not neutral, nor is it a biological given or a natural essence. Sexual pleasure, as Foucault has taught us, is, like sex itself, socially and discursively constructed.[19] Our attitudes toward sexual pleasure can be constructed to work for justice or against it, to enhance and empower or to demean. Rather than focus exclusively on the private pleasures of sex, we need to combine the energy of our sexual pleasure with the power of our passion for justice.

Two

Ayesha M. Imam

The Muslim Religious Right ("Fundamentalists") and Sexuality

The point has been made more than once that there is a tendency in the study of Muslim societies to "[reduce] everything to a given set of doctrines, with a given set of edicts on women [or anything else], and [to attribute] the practices and ideology of Islamic movements to the implementation of these doctrines," that is, to essentialize them.[1] One reason for this is the conflation of *Islamic* and *Muslim*.

The Confusing Conflation of Islamic and Muslim

Islam is the religion or faith (the way of Allah); Muslims are those who believe in Islam and attempt to practice it. Islam is an issue of theology. However, what Muslims (human fallible people) make of Islam is an arena open to social scientific inquiry. In other words, how human beings understand and apply Islam in their contemporary realities and daily lives is often contentious (or at the least an area of debate). This is so not only in the present but throughout the history of Muslim communities. The recognition that *Islamic* and *Muslim* are not synonyms helps avoid essentializing not only Islam but the histories of Muslim communities, for it refuses to favor the dominant discourse—the formal expression of thought and behaviors—of any Muslim community over all others.[2] This essentializing dynamic occurs, of course, in other faith traditions also, for example, in Judaism, as evidenced in Judith Plaskow's chapter in this volume.

15

But Muslim societies do have commonalities. An acceptance of the Qu'ran as the holy book of Islam and of the *hadith* as exemplary sources of knowledge of Islam is one.[3] (The historical experience of being colonized and the present experience of being postcolonial subjects are probably others.) As a direct revelation, the text of the Qu'ran is not questioned. Nonetheless, interpretations of what the message of the Qu'ran means in the daily life of Muslims are examined—and always have been. There are debates on the reliability of particular *hadith* themselves, as well as on their implications for the everyday lives of Muslims. The development of various schools of *Sharia* testify to the diversity of understandings about how Islam should be practiced.[4] The Hanafi, Hambali, Maliki, and Sha'afi schools of Sunni Islam, as well as the Shi'a schools, provide differing understandings of Islamic legal opinion, all of which are Muslim. They vary, for instance, in their opinions about the permissibility of the use of contraceptives and abortion.[5]

Essentializing Muslim societies ignores reality: there are many ways of being Muslim. Among all the possibilities, who can authorize the essential Islam? This question directs attention to the power relations in Muslim communities—Who has the power to define and enforce particular ways of being good Muslims, including dealing with the sexualities of Muslims?

Muslim *and* Islam *Are Not Synonymous with* Arab *and* Middle East

A second common conflation is to make *Muslim* and *Islam* synonymous with *Arab* and *Middle East.* Despite Islam's historical origin in Arabia and the honorable status accorded by it to the Arabic language, there are far more non-Arab and non-Arabic-speaking Muslims than there are Arabs or Arabic speakers. This is evident in Asia. Indonesia is the largest Muslim country, with a population of nearly 200 million, which outnumbers Arab Muslim populations. Pakistan and Bangladesh between them account for another 100 million or so Muslims.

Africa, too, has a large Muslim population, less evident for a number of reasons. First, there is the habit of referring to much of North and East Central Africa (all the way from Morocco on the far northwest coast of the continent, to Sudan and Somalia on the east of the continent down as far as the equator) as part of the Middle East. Second, there has in these countries been a process of Arabization. This began with the early Muslim expansions in the first two centuries of Islam (the seventh and eighth centuries of the Gregorian calendar), during which time, for example, the indigenous languages of Lower Egypt disappeared. The process moves on, more recently, to the periods of nationalist independence in the 1960s—as in Algeria, where state policy deliberately ignored other Algerian languages, such as Berber, in favor of Arabic. Arabization also includes the increasing influence of fundamentalist movements in the 1990s, as in contemporary Sudan.

Even in less Arab-dominated areas, there have been many Muslim communities for a long time. Parts of East Africa have been under Muslim influence since the seventh century, and particularly since the eleventh century. In some areas of West Africa, Islam has been recognized as a state religion since the eleventh century. In fact, there are almost as many Muslims in West Africa as in the whole of the Middle East (Nigeria alone has about 50 million), and Islam remains the largest growing religion in Africa.

The geographic and historic spread of Islam points to the fact that its practice in Muslim communities is neither identical nor static. Each community has its own history, and hence there is the need also to identify Muslim discourses by period and location as well as to refer to broad similarities. The lives of women and men in Muslim societies show not only similarities but also enormous differences from one time period to another, between different communities, and within the same societies at any point in time. For instance, in very many countries in Africa and Asia (as in Egypt and in Nigeria), the past shows elite women recognized and esteemed as scholars.[6] Yet often in the contemporary world, schooling for girls is resisted on the grounds that Muslim girls should marry early and not waste time studying.

Divorce and polygyny are very common and unremarkable in Muslim communities in Nigeria, but uncommon and currently regarded as shamefully embarrassing in India and Bangladesh.[7] Similarly, women's seclusion practices are generalized in Bangladesh, in northern Nigeria, in Mombasa, Kenya, and in northern Sudan, where they are regarded as intrinsic to Islam.[8] Yet seclusion is virtually unpracticed in Indonesia, Senegal, the Gambia, Burkina Faso, and Niger.[9] Further, the very forms of seclusion and the strata of women and men implicated in seclusion practices in both northern Nigeria and in Bangladesh have changed in the last fifty or sixty years—but for different reasons and in different ways.[10] Evidently, a reference simply to "Islamic seclusion" in discussions of sexuality may obscure more than it clarifies.

Muslim Discourses of Sexuality

The issues of divorce, seclusion, and even access to education all have implications for considerations of sexuality. That they vary points to the need to recognize and distinguish different Muslim discourses of sexuality. There is a dominant stereotype of Islamic sexuality that presents Muslim women as always both submissive to and tightly controlled by men, who may marry four wives. Sexuality in this discourse is, of itself, neither good nor bad, but an elemental and natural force that should be suitably channeled in society. Both men's and women's sexuality are seen as naturally active, and while men's arousal pattern is often faster, foreplay is enjoined as a religious duty on men, as women also have a desire for and right to sexual pleasure and satisfaction. Compared to men, women are thought to have nine times the potential for sexual desire and pleasure. It is women's passive exuding of sexuality, however, that provokes the vulnerable men, who then deliberately arouse and fulfill desire in women. Thus women's sexuality is seen as naturally both greater and more passive than that of men. The idea of natural sexuality here is not solely reproductive, but it is definitely heterosexual, with masturbation, homosexuality, and bestiality condemned as unnatural.[11]

Muslim patriarchs conspire with the salacious gaze of the West at the Other to present this as the single and typical discourse of sexuality in Muslim societies—but the realities are different. The honor-shame complex, in which a man's honor lies in controlling the bodies and sexual practices of women in his family, is widespread in the Mediterranean area, Arabia, and parts of South Asia.[12] The range of this complex also includes non-Muslim communities, as in Greece.[13] But it is virtually unknown in sub-Saharan Africa and much of Southeast Asia. For instance, in Hausaland, "honor killings" are unknown. Men marry prostitutes eagerly, and women may be known to be prostitutes by their families. It is not a favored profession, but neither are women killed for it—much less for suspicions of non- or extramarital affairs.[14]

The view of women's sexuality as threatening to the social order, over-whelming, impossible for women to control, or impure (and therefore in need of purification and control to protect women's virtue) is behind the practice of clitoral amputation.[15] This is the norm in some countries, such as Egypt, Sudan, Mali, and the Gambia. Clitoral and labial amputation and labial closure make sexual intercourse painful and difficult for women—sometimes the closed labia must be reopened with a knife, razor blade, or other sharp instrument.[16] In all these countries, these practices are defended as requirements of Islam. Yet they may also be practiced in non-Muslim communities (in southeastern Nigeria or in Sierra Leone, for example). Further-more, in other countries with Muslim communities, such practices are wholly unknown (e.g., Algeria, Tunisia, Pakistan, and Singapore) or (as in northern Nigeria) not common among Muslims and considered pagan.[17] In fact, by contrast, in northern Nigeria a baby girl may be made to undergo hymenectomy in order to ensure she can be easily penetrated, although this is apparently a disappearing practice.[18]

Muslim discourses of sexuality vary not only by community but also over time. For example, northern Nigeria has been predominantly Muslim at least since the eighteenth century (some argue the fourteenth century). But even in the last sixty or seventy years, there have been changes in the dis-course of sexuality. *Tsarance* (a Hausa term meaning institutionalized pre-marital lovemaking or sexual play that stops short of actual penetration), a common and unremarkable practice up to the 1940s and 1950s, is now con-sidered unIslamic and "rural."[19] At the other extreme, girls are frequently now not allowed even to dance at the *kalangu* (Hausa: drumming and danc-ing held each market day).[20]

The Nature of Sexuality and Subjectivity

The analysis of different discourses of Muslim sexuality—their con-ditions of possibility, their histories, their implications in daily life—depends, of course, on our understanding of the nature of sexuality. In general terms, one needs to understand the processes by which selves (always gendered, always sexual) are formed, in order to investigate the ways in which people realize themselves in, resist, or support particular ideologies and practices of sexuality. This historical and comparative approach to sexualities clearly rules out biologistic premises. But what is sexuality? A fundamental component of identity is our sense of being not simply human, but male or female in sex and with particular gender formations. Juliet Mitchell argues that this is a relational difference, based on the necessity of heterosexual reproduction.[21] However, she, along with many others, stresses that the contents of sexuality are social, rather than a matter of reproductive biology, since what masculinity or femininity entails is not the same universally.

Although we may feel our sexuality as emanating from and personal to each of us, it is constructed and regulated publicly in many different ways. These include customs or laws that define who may marry or engage in sexual practices with whom, in which ways, and in what circumstances. They also include policies (formal or informal) about the control of fertility and so forth. Sexuality is not restricted to physical sensual gratification either but informs, for instance, one's sense of self-worth (indicated in statements like "I'm only a woman") and modes of self-fulfillment (such as that Hausa men may feel their virility is bound up in economic control of their households but not in domestic labor, or Arab men that their manhood is expressed in control of the sexual conduct of wives and sisters). Sexuality also has to do with how one relates to people of one's own or other genders, regardless of any intent to seek sensual gratification with them (for instance, with avoidance, contempt, deference, competition, or bonding). Finally, it is structured also into the organization of social space and relations of production, for example, in gender divisions of labor in agrarian societies, and occupational sex segregation and the "woman's wage" virtually worldwide.[22]

Subjectivity (including sexual gender identity) should be seen as constructed through taking positions in a number of (often intersecting) discourses.[23] Thus, subjectivity entails sexual identity, but also ethnic, religious, and other forms of identity.

Foucault suggests the importance of looking at the constitution of the subject "at the level of those continuous and uninterrupted processes which subject our bodies, govern our gestures, dictate our behaviors etc."; subjugation to the how of power operations itself constitutes the subject.[24] Our subjectivities and sexualities are partly constituted by the ways we ordinarily act, according to the dictates that govern gender divisions of labor, daily dress, behavior toward spouses, and so on.

Discourses are themselves historical products, however. The conditions of their existence and the historical terrain they construct are not static.

Yet new ideological terrain are not so much completely new fields but the reordering, disarticulation, and rearticulation of pre-existing ideological elements in new ways, as well as of new elements.[25] And, I might add, so that they intersect other ideological terrains at different points or in new ways. Further, some ideological elements are more crucial and stable than others in making up the fractured and unsecured subjectivity—not around the phallus alone, as Lacan suggests, but certainly around key questions of sexual, ethnic, class, and other forms of identity. The work of Gramscian intellectuals can be seen as transforming subjectivities to the extent that they can combine these key elements with new-forged articulations of others.[26] And this is where we can begin to consider the discourses of sexuality being (re)constructed and (re)invented by contemporary religious and other movements and their implications for changing ideas about and practices implicated by sexuality.

Fundamentalism?

First, a caveat on the term *fundamentalism,* which has come to describe all sorts of conservative right-wing movements, and particularly Muslim fundamentalism. *Fundamentalism* is a term from Christian history that is not particularly appropriate to other religions. The common usage also causes political difficulties, as many Muslims have no objection to being referred to as people who are concerned with the fundamentals or the roots of the faith. Many of these are not otherwise supporters of the types of movements referred to as "fundamentalist" but have declared an affinity with them by accepting the nomenclature. In addition, the term is a misnomer because what the fundamentals of a faith are depend very much on who is doing the defining—they are not a simple or uncontested issue. Furthermore, it is necessary to distinguish between general moves toward increased religiosity and cultural assertions—such as Muslim renaissance or revivalism—and what many of us prefer to term the "religious Right" or "religious conservatives," who are only one strand of a broader phenomenon.

Muslim religious-right movements share a number of characteristics with all religious-right movements.[27] First, they claim to have returned to the fundamentals of faith and to a tradition unsullied by modern excesses. Subjected to inspection, this is actually a creative vision (re/construction) of Muslim society and not a return to any known historical past or literal interpretation of *surahs*. There is selection and interpretation always. Second, they claim to own the only true vision and are intolerant of all other views, whether or not also Muslim. Muslim dissenters are denied with the argument that Islam is in danger, and therefore all protesters against their views are traitors to Islam—here is the excuse for forcible suppression.[28] Third, they seek power to impose their own vision forcibly on others. Fourth, they focus on the Umma as the community of identity, the community of Muslim believers, and consider irrelevant all other forms of identity (national, ethnic, and occupational). Fifth, they excoriate "Western feminism" and attempt to brand all forms of women's assertion to autonomy as foreign, Western, and anti-Islamic. Finally, there is the objective of the control of women (including women's sexuality) by men and the wish to legislate what women can or cannot do and to punish nonconformers. It is this view of sexuality that I will discuss.

Common Concerns of Muslim Religious-Right Views on Sexuality

In keeping with their vision of a boundaryless Umma, Muslim religious-right movements—from Afghanistan to South Africa, and Iran to Bangladesh, and including Muslim minority communities in countries like Britain and France—have a remarkable consistency of vision regarding gender relations and sexuality. They share a central concern with women, an asceticism about the body, a focus on women's sexuality in particular as a source of immorality, the increase in means for men to satisfy heterosexual desires, and the reconstruction of patriarchal control over women and their sexuality.

At the heart of Muslim religious-right groups is their concern with women.[29] Where logically one might expect a focus on the (gender-neutral) five pillars of Islam—the profession of belief in Allah and the prophet, the five daily prayers, the annual month-long fast, the giving of a tenth of one's goods for charity each year, and the pilgrimage to Mecca—there is instead a preoccupation with women. It is women's dress and behavior that are frequently made symbols of new "Islamic" orders from Iran to Sudan and now in Afghanistan. When women refuse to conform, by violating the movements' prescribed dress code or by continuing to go to work or to school, they are the subjects of threats and violent attacks.[30] As a huge literature has pointed out with regard to nationalism also, women are made the repositories of culture, as opposed to participants and cocreators.[31] Therefore, to ensure a proper next generation, the investment in the control of women's reproductive powers and of women's influence in social transmission to children grows. And authentic Muslim culture becomes the (re)invention of customs that decrease women's autonomy—in Algeria, for instance, men are empowered to vote in place of their wives and daughters—while all other practices are made illegitimate or ignored. The objective is the increased domesticity of women, their identities and sexualities restricted to women's supposed primary roles as wife and mother.

Asceticism (one hesitates to say Puritanism) about the body, particularly for women, is another characteristic of religious-right movements, in which it is generally referred to as the requirement of modesty. In Muslim religious-right groups, modesty is expressed through the imposition of dress codes—most particularly for women, though the Taliban in Afghanistan is requiring presently that men grow beards. Muslim women's dress codes are often misleadingly referred to generically as veiling or the *hijab*. This stereotyping obscures both historical changes in modes of dress and cultural contexts and the possibility that people may be referring by these terms to quite different modes of dress. The black loose cloak that covers the body from head to ankles known as the *chador* in Iran is not the same as the loose swathe of sometimes diaphanous cloth draped around the body and called the *tobe* in Sudan. Both are unlike the headscarf and *maiyafi* (a cloth covering head and shoulders) of modest women in Nigeria. Nor are any of these identical with the headscarf (sometimes worn with jeans) that is acceptable in South Africa. All signify a control of women's sexuality, however, and indicate that women need to be covered in some way to prevent their exuding sexuality. Increasingly, Muslim religious-right groups are taking the most restrictive dress codes, homogenizing them, and imposing them on varied Muslim communities. The Bashir regime in Sudan, for instance, attempted to impose the Iranian *chador* on Sudanese women in the early 1990s.

In addition to increasingly restrictive dress codes, this modesty is often also seen as requiring a denial of sensuality or openness in body care. The wearing of makeup, jewelry, or perfume is frowned on in many places. *Hammans* (bathhouses) even for single-sex use, and massages, despite the long historical and cultural traditions of their use and enjoyment, are now not licit or at least questionable in Iran and Turkey. It has been suggested that this unwillingness to see or touch the unclothed body is resulting in unease in touching oneself and thence in lower standards of personal hygiene in Iran, particularly where households do not have private bathrooms (Homa Hoodfar, personal communication). It certainly has implications for the control of sexuality and the permissibility of open enjoyment of bodily sensations.

Muslim religious-right groups focus on sexuality as a source of immorality. There is the commonly stated assumption that if unrelated women and men are together, they must be engaging in (illicit) sexual acts. This unrestrained sexuality is dangerous to morality and social order. However, it is women's sexuality that is peculiarly responsible and culpable. It is women who must abide by restrictive dress codes that signify asexuality. It is women who must be segregated or secluded so as not to tempt men. Thus, it is women's very presence that is so powerfully sexual that men's restraint fails. And it is women who are most at fault in any situation that suggests immorality, because they should have avoided it. Thus, this discourse finds women's sexuality to be naturally and unconsciously powerful and, simultaneously, blameworthy. Female sexuality must therefore be constrained, controlled, and punished in Muslim religious-right practices.

In Nigeria, local state decrees penalize girls who hawk goods on the street, rather than the men who harass and molest them.[32] In areas where the honor-shame complex is found, women are killed by fathers and brothers, sometimes on the mere suspicion of having engaged in nonmarital sex. Yet neither female nor male relatives of the men who are suspected of immorality find it incumbent upon them to kill their sons or brothers. Honor killings of women are condoned by the communities in which they occur (in the Arab-speaking Middle East, for instance). Often enough, honor killings are also condoned by the state, for example, in Iraq and Israel, which accept suspicion of immorality as a defense that precludes murder charges.[33] In Bangladesh, there has in the past few years been a surge of completely extralegal decisions by village *salishes,* or councils, to stone and burn women they charge with immorality (see the award-winning documentary "Eclipse" made by Ain-o-Salish Kendra). The Sudan Women and Law Project's 1996 interim report notes that in Sudan, since the 1990s, a woman can be legally stopped and questioned by any man who feels she is not wearing appropriate attire. Or she can be harassed, picked up, and held by the police until her husband, father, or brother arrives to guarantee her suitable dress in the future.

This control of women's sexuality is particularly clear in the stances concerning women's fertility management. Most typically, all practices that relate to managing fertility are removed from women's control and handed over to men and the state. These range from decisions over whether or when to have intercourse, to decisions over knowledge of and access to different types of contraception, to the permissibility or impermissibility of pregnancy termination. Neither women nor men are expected to have intercourse before marriage, although, as I have mentioned, the penalties for women who do are far more severe than for men. Wives may never refuse to have sexual intercourse with their husbands; it is their husbands who have the right to decide. Muslim religious-right groups also frequently at first refuse to permit any form of birth prevention (whether pregnancy prevention or abortion). This stance ignores the fact that there are different positions on permissibility within Sharia over fertility management; even concerning abortion, there the decision often hinges on when the soul is infused into the fetus and hence at what stage of development abortion is permissible. Muslim religious-right groups instead postulate the most restrictive conditions for abortion—a complete ban or abortion only to save the mother's life. New restrictions may also be instituted in Sharia, such as that the woman must have been raped and in the first trimester of pregnancy (e.g., Sudan in the 1990s), before it is defensible to carry out an abortion. Attitudes to pregnancy avoidance can nonetheless vary. In the early days of the Iranian revolution, contraception was considered antithetical for good Muslims. Recently, though, the Iranian religious right (still in state power) has started to encourage family planning and to list acceptable forms of contraception. Even so, in either case it is not women themselves who may judge and decide whether and how to manage their fertility.

Men's sexuality is also channeled, but in a way that gives them more control than women are permitted. The religious-right discourse gives men more means and avenues of satisfying desires—if heterosexual. Polygyny frequently becomes an unbridled right of Muslim men, in some cases (such as Nigeria's) almost an obligation. Marrying girl children is defended and promoted as a man's right and as a preventive of immorality. There is a growing lack of concern for the consent of the bride to marry. Women's right to choose their marriage partner is increasingly whittled down or removed altogether, as in Sudan, where there has been a shift from allowing women to make the choice to enabling her *waliyi* (guardian, always male) to enforce his choice on her. *Mut'a* (temporary marriage permitted in Shiite Sharia) is on the increase, including in Sunni communities in which it was previously unknown or condemned as Shiite apostasy, such as in Algeria and Sudan.[34] The treatment of rape militates against women. The religious right not only refuses categorically to recognize rape within marriage but also poses such severe conditions for proof (such as the eye-witness testimony of four upright men) that a woman who charges rape or who becomes pregnant as a result of rape may well find herself, rather than her rapist, punished on the grounds of "self-confessed immorality" or "unfounded charges," as has happened in Pakistan (see Shirkat Gah News Sheets).

In general terms, one might say that the Muslim religious right (like Christian and Hindu religious-right groups) has been reconstructing patriarchal control over women and their sexuality. The locus of control has been shifting from the patriarch proper (the father as household or family head, with control over the women and men of his household/family) to the state (control of women and men), to state-sanctioned control of all women by all men (i.e., any man, anywhere). Thus, any man may enforce his idea of appropriate dress on any woman he sees in Sudan. There is the use of *salishes* to condemn a woman for alleged adultery or bigamy in Bangladesh, even when the act in question is done with her father's permission. There has been tacit state toleration of acid throwing when a woman in Algeria refuses intercourse with a man, even if that refusal was in the name of modesty and chastity, or of women's abductions in Nigeria for being in public spaces. There has been increasing violence against women who refuse to conform in Algeria, Sudan, Bangladesh, and Afghanistan, among other countries.

Finally, there is the issue of same-sex relations, about which there is still little literature or research. Muslim establishments converge with religious-right groups in condemning "unnatural deviations" (homosexual relations of men or women, transvestitism, transsexualism, and so on). There seems always to have been a loud silence on women's same-sex relations. However, in many Muslim communities in the Middle East, the eastern coast of Kenya, or northern Nigeria, for example, there has been a centuries-long history of quiet toleration of male same-sex relations (including sexual intercourse and forms of cross-dressing). The condemnation of these practices, often now explicitly including women's same-sex relations, has become increasingly strident. They are denounced as not only unnatural, but also anti-Islam and due to the corrupting influence of the West, feminism, or both (feminism is viewed as a solely Western construct).

Specificities of Muslim Religious-Right Discourses of Sexuality

Despite the many commonalities of rhetoric, religious-right discourses are not all the same. The internationalizing of the Muslim religious right (in political links; money circulation and donations; printed, audio, and visual matter; scholarships) is an important topic not yet well researched.[35] Where and how the ideologies and programs are decided, passed on, and shared, and what the links are between religious-right groups in different communities, are issues yet to be elucidated. Even so, how ideologies are reconstructed, transformed, influenced, and construed in the practices of specific communities is extremely important. It makes a real and crucial difference if exhortations for women's modesty are couched in terms of men's lack of culpability in killing women on the ground of honor (Iraq) or relatively lightly in terms of wearing a headscarf outside one's home (South Africa). There are substantively different effects on women's and men's lives and sexuality when the religious right says in one place that any form of contraception is anti-Islamic (immediate postrevolution Iran), and in another place or at another time that Allah has provided certain safe and legitimate means for spacing births (contemporary Iran).

At the end of this chapter is a table of practices and claims of the Muslim religious right in different countries. It is incomplete, but it serves to illustrate the point that, despite the commonalities and similar rhetoric, these groups are not identical. Nor are the contexts in which Muslim religious-right groups operate, the ideological-political state and content of hegemony in each community, or the arrangement and power of groups who are not part of the religious right. It behooves us to remember that Muslim is not the only identity that groups (even religious-right groups) may choose to inflect in particular circumstances. Other identities—postcolonial, ethnic or regional, professional, gender—may be also drawn upon. In every community, these and probably other issues have a recurrent effect on discursive practices at ideological levels and in behaviors.

There is also a need to look at the impacts of religious-right discourse according to social relations in communities. In Pakistan, for instance, the *hudood* ordinance affects mostly poorer women who have not the social and economic resources to avoid being entangled in it. Restrictions on formal sector work affect mostly middle-class women (for instance in Algeria, Sudan, and Nigeria). Segregation and seclusion and the lack of work outside the home most affect poorer women in Bangladesh and in Sudan, where women street food sellers are being picked up, harassed, and fined. There are reports that female genital mutilation is on the increase in refugee camps, which affects the poor and displaced of both Somalia and Sudan.

Finally, women's and men's relations with religious-right discourses of sexuality (or other) are likewise diverse. As mentioned, Muslim-imposed modesty may lead to a dislike of undressing or touching one's body. But dress codes may also be rejected, even in the face of death threats, as in Algeria and Sudan, or resisted in favor of a modesty of demeanor demanded from both women and men (northern Nigeria), or adopted for a whole parade of different rationales. These could include acceptance of the view that women's sexuality must be hidden and controlled as a symbol of one's faith in minority communities, as a means of protection from harassment, as a means of asserting mobility outside one's home (i.e., achieving some freedom of movement), or for fear of the consequences if prescribed clothing is not worn. Restrictive dress codes have also been adopted in ways that subvert any hope of making women socially invisible or diminishing their sexuality—there are women's magazines that advise how to wear *hijab* in an attractive manner, as well as fashion parades and designer *chadors* in countries as varied as Egypt and Nigeria.

Similarly, the adoption of seclusion or acceptance of segregation may be the expression of a view that sexuality is uncontrollable in the presence of nonrelated women and men. Or it may be a result of the renegotiation of the patriarchal bargain, so that men take the responsibility of household maintenance,[36] or because there are no work options outside the home, or because of social pressure, or a mixture of all of these. Each of these situations has different implications for sexuality. Conforming behavior alone is not sufficient to establish conforming sexualities.

Practices and Claims of Religious-Right Groups in Five Countries

Iran	Sudan	Nigeria	Bangladesh	Pakistan
Religious right in state power	Religious right in state power	Religious right not in power, but increasingly vocal and influential	Religious right not in power, but very vocal and influential	Religious right not in power, but has been able to influence state
Legal imposition of dress code	Legal imposition of dress code; won battle of *tobe,* but noncompliance is grounds for sack or lack of promotion	Social imposition of dress code, which also affects non-Muslim women in multireligious state		Women must wear "Islamic dress," but men national dress
Iranian women may not marry non-Iranian men; Rafsanjani now talking of more open relations between women and men	(1994 revival of 1959 law) Sudanese men students abroad may not marry non-Sudanese women (unless Egyptian) without diplomatic permission.	In principle, women should not marry non-Muslim men but it is done and accepted.		
Woman cannot give self in marriage	Rejection of Hanafi law that woman can give self in marriage in favor of Maliki, under which it is more difficult	Both women and men have *waliyi,* who often seek their consent; father has right to compel virgin		
Women first eliminated from urban work outside home (especially formal sector); gradual return in some areas	Women being eliminated from urban work (especially public sector and in judicial system)	Increasing pressure for dress code, calls for gender-segregated work; failed attempt to ban women from civil service	Attacks on nongovernment organizations working on issues of women's economic autonomy (tree planting now "un-Islamic") or education	
Contraceptive use/ abortion "un-Islamic" first, now permitted. Both positions with *fatwas* to support	Abortion legal only if in first trimester *and* woman was raped	Abortion legal if mother's life threatened. Dislike of contraceptive use; coitus interuptus and safe period okay	Development of extrajudicial practices of *salishes* accusing women of adultery, bigamy	Jamaati-Islami resolve that family planning un-Islamic; abortion illegal (10 years)

(continued)

Practices and Claims of Religious-Right Groups in Five Countries (continued)

Iran	Sudan	Nigeria	Bangladesh	Pakistan
Mut'a on increase, polygyny on increase	*Mut'a* introduced in 1990s; house of obedience legalized 1992 (state enforcement of wife's obedience to husband)	Stress on men's right to polygyny and to child brides		*Hudood* ordinance does not distinguish nonmarital sex from rape; evidence rules favor men, but punishment is same for both
First women's sports discouraged; now females do sports and swim covered up; not televised or open to men spectators		Girls not encouraged to do sports, dancing increasingly considered not licit		Music and dance banned in girls' schools

Three

Rebecca T. Alpert

Guilty Pleasures

When Sex is Good Because It's Bad

Although my formal education ended before the second wave of feminism took hold in the academy, and well before the postmodern era, the insights of both have been crucial to my writing and thinking for many years. One might even say that I learned them, albeit in nascent forms, during my graduate education in religious studies. There, I carefully noted the missing perspectives of women, but I also studied in an interreligious context that made me aware of the multiple perspectives through which the world may be viewed and consequently of how very partial my own truth was. I think I have learned those lessons well. I write only from my own (Jewish and feminist) perspective, and I make every effort to name that perspective and make it clear how particular a viewpoint it is.

These lessons came to me again in the course of working on this project with women from many religious and cultural perspectives. I can write only from my particular context: the privilege of living as a North American Jew at the turn of a new century, influenced by the feminist movement, supported by the presence of a gay and lesbian movement, trained to be a rabbi in a seminary that ordains not only women but gay men and lesbians as well. I thus live under conditions that permit me to write as an autonomous self. Comfortably located in the secular academy, I can afford to challenge the authority of the Jewish community; I can live openly as a lesbian and as a committed Jew and rabbi, inside and outside the community simultaneously.

Without the oppression experienced by Jews at other times and places, and by women in many places today, I can both honor and critique my tradition and live with the ambiguity that such a position requires. I preface my work here with the acknowledgment of the privilege of being able to, as a rabbi, "say the darnedest things" as my colleague in the project Suwanna Satha-Anand pointed out. I offer my comments about Judaism at the turn of the century in light of what I learned from my cocontributors and from those about whom they write, many of whom do not live with such privilege.

The Regulation of Sexuality

Regulating sexual behavior is a significant dimension of most religious systems, and Judaism is no exception. Throughout its long history, Judaism has defined licit and illicit sexual desires, relationships, and behaviors. Over time, the form and content of what has been permitted and prohibited have changed, but a system of regulation has remained a constant. While some might wish to challenge the need for such a system, I am suggesting that some such system will always be in place, that even in times when regulations have undergone changes, new ones have arisen to take their place. Although these regulations have often been oppressive, they have also had unintended liberating consequences. My goal here is to examine the criteria for the regulation of sexual behavior in Judaism and the consequences in terms of their potential to redefine good sex from a Jewish feminist perspective.

Let me be careful to note that I am not using the terms *good* (and *bad*) in relation to ethics, but in relation to law. Sexual ethics are indeed important (as are the ethics of all relationships), but it is my contention that a system of regulation that defines sexual desires and behaviors as permitted or forbidden does not necessarily also define right and wrong. In this context, good sex will always be ethical, but it may also be forbidden.

Of course, I understand that it is inaccurate to make sweeping generalizations about Judaism. Judaism is not by any means a monolithic tradition, and it is an oversimplification to suggest that there is one Judaism. Rather, we are looking at a complex entity whose values vary by historical era and geographic location. Furthermore, Judaism is often defined based on passages from the Talmud, the main text of rabbinic Judaism, compiled and redacted around 500 CE, which itself is a complex document reflecting traditions of several hundred years and of several different communities. The voices of later thinkers and texts, medieval, modern, and contemporary, are often seen only as reflections of that work, while the biblical culture of the Israelites is viewed only as a precursor.

Often, the complexity of the Talmud itself is glossed over. Additionally, feminist insight reminds us that the texts that have been preserved reflect the traditions of the elite group of men whose thought represents only one fragmentary perspective of the world in which the Jews lived. We have no idea of the extent to which the rulings of this elite were taken seriously or put into practice even by the societies in which they lived. What we do know is that portions of those texts, usually taken out of context, are often used to serve some contemporary rhetorical purpose.

Given this complex reality, we must be extremely careful when making generalizations about Judaism's perspective about sex. It is accurate to describe Jewish teachings on sexual desire as complex and ambivalent, containing both positive and negative elements, and changing perspective with time and location.[1]

Still, it is of value to look for strands in Jewish thinking (whether or not they are representative or widespread) that could help us understand how sexuality was regulated in ancient Judaism. My goal is to take into account some of these ancient strands, viewing them through a lens of contemporary feminist thinking about sex in order to create a dialogue between those perspectives, with the hope that what emerges will become one more strand of Jewish thought.

How Sex is Regulated in Jewish Teachings
Connecting Sex, Kinship, and Procreation

Jewish texts generally encourage sexual activity that will result in procreation in a marital relationship. Sexual desire is valued because it drives the reproductive impulse. A rabbinic teaching suggests that it is because of sexual desire that men marry, build houses, and have children.[2] To this end, physical acts of heterosexual sex between people who are obligated to reproduce are encouraged in ancient Jewish texts. Sex acts are broadly permitted within any union that has or had (or even in some cases will have) reproductive potential, which is understood as potential for Jewish continuity. There are traditions that explicitly permit sex in licit relationships which no longer are fertile: sex between infertile wives and husbands, sex with postmenopausal wives, and anal and oral sex within a marital relationship. In the biblical stories of Tamar and Ruth, it is obvious also that laws about sexual boundaries can be transgressed for the sake of procreation. Both of these biblical heroes commit sexual acts to ensure the continuity of the ancestral line—Ruth with a stranger, and Tamar with her father-in-law.

The corollary of this perspective is the prohibition of sexual acts that would in any way interfere with reproduction. One need only examine the biblical ritual for the *sotah,* the wife suspected of adultery, and the rabbinic adumbrations of that text, to see the negative attitudes toward sexuality that might interfere with appropriate procreation.[3] The *sotah* (and to a lesser extent, the man with whom she is accused of committing adultery) is to be publicly humiliated. Although the *sotah* ritual was not practiced, certainly after the destruction of the temple, the rabbis' rhetoric about it shows their serious approbation of sex that counters procreative possibilities.

Sex and Order

Ancient Judaism also regulates sexuality as part of a larger system of creating an orderly universe. Many sexual activities are prohibited as a way to define boundaries between what is permitted and forbidden behavior for a Jew. What distinguishes these regulations is their arbitrary nature. They fit into the paradigm of "purity and danger" suggested by Mary Douglas. These activities do not necessarily interfere with procreation but are part of a system of containing sexual desire. For the purposes of procreation, sexual desire is understood as useful, but it is still called *yetzer hara,* an evil inclination, and must be controlled and limited.[4] Therefore, activities such as masturbation that might cause someone to be tempted to break the rules are prohibited.[5] Male homosexual behavior is also prohibited.[6] The same logic prohibits sex with people with whom one is not supposed to marry (and therefore procreate), such as certain relatives or non-Jews. This system also creates prohibitions of certain sexual activities within the marital context, such as sex during (and in rabbinic Judaism, one week after) a woman's menstrual period or during daylight hours or completely naked.[7]

Regulation by Gender

Sex is regulated differently for men and women. Because the rabbis thought that women were unable to exercise sexual control, rabbinic Judaism mandates that men are obligated to satisfy their wives' sexual desires, described as the obligation of *onah*. The conditions of satisfying that desire are the subject of much debate in ancient sources and by contemporary scholars.[8] Their main goal is to limit women's sexual desire by making sure that it has a regularly moderated outlet.

Men on the other hand must control their sexual desire. Men are understood as having the duty (and the right) to give sexual pleasure, but not to satisfy their own sexual needs. Sexual control places men on a higher spiritual plane than women, as described by Michael Satlow: "For the rabbis, both Palestinian and Babylonian, Jewish piety was linked to self-control. At its (relatively rare) extreme, piety could manifest itself as asceticism. More commonly, however, self-control was exercised through adherence to the law, and above all, through moderation even in legally permitted activities."[9] Manliness is expressed in terms of piety and control. Men were to subdue their powerful sexual desires through adherence to the law and the study of Torah. Women's sexual desires were controlled by men.

Adultery and marriage laws were also different for men and women. For a man, adultery was defined as having sex with another man's wife, tampering with the lineage and possession of another man. The Hebrew Bible is replete with stories of men with multiple wives and concubines. Ashkenazic Jewry did not outlaw polygamy until the year 1000, and it was never officially outlawed by Sephardic Jewry.

The question of homosexuality is also treated differently by gender. Male homosexuality was punishable by death during certain biblical periods (Leviticus 20:13), while female homosexual behavior was considered a minor offense.[10] Male masturbation is discussed at length in the Talmud, while female masturbation is mentioned only once.[11]

Sex and Commitment

Contemporary Jewish thinkers perpetuate these regulations by connecting them to the higher purpose of love and commitment. Orthodox discussions about sex strongly advocate for procreation. But they also explain regulating sex as a way of enhancing love and commitment. Norman Lamm celebrates the restrictions of *niddah*. Lamm suggests (and many Orthodox Jews testify to the fact) that being required to abstain from sexual relations for half the month increases the desire experienced when permitted to engage in sexual encounters and enables couples to prolong the romance of their marriage, thus helping to sustain long-term, committed, monogamous relationships.[12]

Liberal thinkers may disagree with many of the activities that ancient Judaism sought to regulate, but they too construct a system of regulation based on an ethic of relationships that highlights consent and mutuality. Rather than trying to find reasons for the ancient rules, this system creates its own criteria for sexual behavior (love and commitment) and then regulates behavior on that basis. This perspective of Jewish ethics is certainly well grounded in Jewish values about relationships, and the commandment to love your neighbor as yourself.[13] This perspective is supported in ancient Jewish texts where wife beating and rape within marriage were generally viewed negatively.[14] These approaches create a hierarchy that privileges long-term, committed relationships, suggesting that other forms of desire, while valid, are less valued. But they do remove most arbitrary prohibitions, creating room for young people to experiment with sex (provided that they are moving toward commitment), for sex during menstruation, and for the recognition of gay and lesbian relationships.

The Problems with Regulating Sex

Regulating sexuality has both positive and negative dimensions. Looking at both dimensions enables us to begin to create new approaches to defining good sex from a Jewish feminist perspective. The various dimensions of sexual regulation in Judaism bring different problems that must be brought to light before we can imagine what benefits a system of regulating sexual desire and behavior might have for the promotion of good sex.

Sex As Instrumental to Other Values

Making sex an instrument to achieve other values like procreation and love is problematic because it does not allow for the possibility that sexual pleasure is a value in its own right. As we have already seen, sex was only acceptable if it was for a higher purpose. In most ancient texts, that higher purpose was procreation. Desire in the service of procreation had few constraints, even when it transgressed other norms.

Linking sex to procreation does not fit in contemporary society. Times have changed, and more sophisticated contraception, the possibilities of adoption, fertility treatments, alternative forms of insemination, and acceptance of the validity of gay and lesbian relationships have severed the automatic connection between sex and reproduction, even in sexual encounters within marriage. Making sexual pleasure instrumental to other values shifts the focus from looking for the meaning and value of sex itself. There is a strong need for the focus to shift from regulation of sexual behavior to the discussion of sexual pleasure.

In contemporary Jewish sexual ethics, the higher purpose of desire is love and commitment. Sex is understood as a vehicle for intimacy and closeness, for the creation of a couple, as a primary value. This has the negative effect of creating hierarchies of sexual behavior, suggesting, for example, that committed monogamous relationships are the most valued, serially monogamous relationships or relationships before marriage less so.[15] But there is not any place to locate a Jewish understanding of desire for its own sake, for the pleasure of sexual and sensual feelings, for touch and for physical release.

Differentiation by Gender

Regulating sex differently for men and women also limits the value of Jewish teachings on sexuality. As sexual power dynamics have changed, it is hard to imagine maintaining the idea that women as a group have less ability to control their sexual desire than men do. Contemporary male scholars of Jewish sexuality like to ask what might have been different if women had the power to write these texts. They urge contemporary feminists to construct a system of sexual desire that is good for women.[16] But these requests miss the point. A reconstructed Jewish feminist view of sexual desire should be based not on defining a new erotic for women, but on the removal of gender as a defining characteristic of desire.

Recent theorists of bisexuality suggest that gender need not be the defining characteristic in choosing a sexual partner.[17] Desire can be constructed around many other issues or pleasures. According to this theory, we are not necessarily attracted to someone because of their gender; we may be more attracted to their eye color, intellect, humor, or height. Sexual desire is not necessarily predicated on the gender of the object of that desire, so we should not assume rigid differentiation according to gender when we are looking at the agent of desire. There is no reason to assume different abilities to control desire, or to create different ways of constructing desire based on gender. So we are left with the idea that men and women have strong sexual desires and that men cannot be viewed as carrying the obligation of controlling women's desires for them. Both men and women need to work at finding a balance between limiting and enhancing sexual desire.

Making Sex Seem Bad, Dangerous, and Shameful

Another difficulty with a system that regulates sexuality based on arbitrary notions of order and chaos is that it connects illicit sexual behavior with shame. The rabbinic exhortations to the *sotah* are a blatant example of this connection, as are contemporary Orthodox commentaries about male homosexuality.[18] Even contemporary ethical writings tend to devalue sex that is not oriented toward the goal of love and commitment. Sex for pleasure, even autoerotic stimulation, is not examined for its possibility to enhance life. People choosing to be involved in sex for its own sake rarely find support within Jewish circles. People who are not in committed relationships are marked as suspect, or in need of being "fixed up" with someone. The language itself implies discomfort with a person whose sex life is not publicly visible and appropriately regulated.

Such a system is also harmful because it is punitive. In the Hebrew Bible, death is the punishment for many sexual transgressions, including adultery and male homosexuality. Although throughout most of Jewish history corporal punishments were not carried out, sexual transgressors suffered communal approbation and scorn.

This negative valuation of sex for pleasure or without the goal of procreation or commitment forces people to lie and hide their sexual desires. This consequence of the regulation of sexuality is particularly negative, because it additionally compels people to break other important relational values. Jewish practices for regulating sexual behavior are problematic because they differentiate desire by gender and thereby make assumptions about how men and women are; devalue sex for its own sake rather than to achieve some higher goal; make sex appear to be negative and shameful, requiring people without licit relationships to lie and hide; and misuse Jewish texts for the purpose of controlling sexuality.

The Value of a System of Control

Given these negative dimensions, how can we find value in a system that controls sexuality? Despite the problems inherent in this system, it also provides some advantages and possibilities for good sex.

Acknowledging the Power of Sexual Desire

What is the purpose of a system to control desire? A system based on controlling desire starts from the assumption that desire is overwhelming and chaotic and will disrupt otherwise orderly lives. Forbidding people to act out on sexual desires affirms that sexual desire is dangerous. Acknowledging that everyone has sexual desire, and that desire is a powerful, dangerous, and chaotic force in need of regulation, is helpful within the context of such a system. Sexual desire has the potential to disrupt the order of society, and controls are important in moderating its effects.

Making room for the incredible power of sexual desire is valuable. Sexual desire is irrational and unpredictable. We do not know what creates and stimulates desire within an individual. Love may be gentle and kind, but passion isn't always, nor is it always wise to express or act on it. Recognizing the dangerous dimension of sexual desire can enable people to find creative ways to work with it.

Forbidden Sex

Ironically, a system that seeks arbitrarily to limit and control sexual desire unwittingly enhances the power of sexual desire. The efforts to control desire make it more desirable.

A look at the creation story will help to illustrate. In ancient rabbinic interpretations, this was not a story of forbidden sex. The rabbis assume that Adam and Eve had sexual relations in the garden—to be sure, in the service of procreation. But a Jewish mystical text from the Middle Ages suggests another interpretation: Adam and Eve had sexual relations but did not experience sexual desire until Eve ate from the tree.[19] Eve disrupted the order of creation through her act and brought knowledge to humans. Part of this knowledge was that what is forbidden may be erotic because it is forbidden. This insight may also be apprehended in the Song of Songs, which graphically describes the power of secret love. In her commentary on the Song of Songs, contemporary interpreter Marcia Falk describes the ways in which this text presents lovers in covert, nighttime rendezvous, away from public censure.[20]

Illicit sex is appealing because it is an opportunity to do what is forbidden, to test the rules. The erotic is connected to wildness, chaos, and disorder—just what the rabbinic tradition wishes to tame and make orderly. Part of the appeal of desiring the wrong person at the wrong place or time is precisely that they are wrong, that this desire breaks norms. Let me be careful again to make the point that wrong is not the same as unethical—sex that is bad or wrong can still conform to ethical standards. That is why setting up an arbitrary system of licit and illicit sex is helpful. One can break norms without performing acts that are harmful and still derive the pleasure that attends what is forbidden.

A system that regulates sex encourages people to lie about and hide sex that is not acceptable. While in many instances this is troubling, it is also true that the pleasure of illicit sex is enhanced through secrecy. This is not necessarily a bad thing. Not being able to talk about the sexual encounters you are having may serve to make them more exciting. This is clearly illustrated in the rabbinic text from the *baraita* literature, which suggests that when a man has a strong sexual desire he cannot control he should go to another town, dress in other garments, and fulfill his need, rather than doing so at home or among acquaintances.[21] There was also something quite powerful about "the love that dared not speak its name"—before gay sex became something that could be discussed in public, the closet was sexy, even if oppressive.[22] Gay people developed coded language with which to communicate. The need to be secretive was turned into an erotic of its own.

This kind of guilty pleasure may require no action. There is no need to assume that refraining from acting on these desires diminishes them—the desire itself may suffice to provide sexual pleasure. Forbidding sex in these cases may serve to heighten the desire to experience what we cannot. This kind of desire is guilty pleasure; it can be enjoyed for its own sake but enhanced by its transgressive nature.

Autoerotic sexual desire, having sex with animals, using inanimate objects as stimulation, cross-dressing, or having fantasies about other people when one is involved in a committed relationship that is defined as monogamous are all ways of transgressing the norms of sexuality. Sexual behavior or desire that in most cases harms no one and whose only goal is self-pleasure may be experienced with greater joy and intensity because it is forbidden.

Experiencing desire for the "wrong" person is another form of desire that must be kept to oneself and so is erotic because it is forbidden. This could include an unrequited love or attraction to someone who is married, to someone who would be an unacceptable partner (because of sexual orientation, class, religion, race, age, or familial relationship), or to a total stranger. Sex with the right or wrong person at the wrong place or time enhances erotic pleasure. Those who break the laws of *niddah,* who begin sexual encounters when time is limited to complete them, who have sex in public places, who visit porn shops or consume erotica on the Internet all indulge in guilty pleasures. While these activities might lend themselves to providing pleasure in any event, that pleasure is enhanced by the illicit nature of the act.

Assuming that forbidden sex is powerful because it is forbidden does not assume that licit sex without limitations cannot also incorporate desire, that forbidden sex cannot also take place within licit relationships, or that sex is automatically wonderful because one has acted on a forbidden desire. But forbidding certain sexual partners or situations can make them seem more attractive. Operating within a system that controls desires may serve ironically to enhance those desires and to contribute to the pleasure one experiences when acting on (or even thinking about) those desires. And it has the potential to challenge the privileged status of licit relationships.

Sex Talk and Sublimation

Talk about prohibiting sex invites discussion of sex and so can be most valuable. There are extensive discussions of licit and illicit sexual behavior in the Hebrew Bible and in rabbinic literature, as well as in later mystical and philosophical literature.[23] As Michel Foucault has suggested, talking about sexual behaviors and their prohibitions can be erotic for some and at the least sexually educational for others.[24] This is an unintended consequence of a system that regulates sexuality.

When sexual desire and behavior is controlled and limited, it may go underground as illustrated earlier, or it may take the form of sublimation. Even the rabbinic ideal of sublimating desire through the study of Torah can be a vehicle to guilty pleasures, albeit unconscious ones. Recent scholars have suggested the homoerotic nature of the house of study for men.[25] The exclusion of women from this site produced an environment presumably devoid of sex, but in fact full of sexual energy, as many same-sex environments tend to be. Furthermore, sexual topics were freely discussed in the houses of study, and these conversations themselves may have stimulated sexual desire. Proceeding from the assumption that sexual desire is not determined by gender, bringing women into the house of study would not necessarily change the environment.

Rabbinic Judaism gave positive reinforcement to men for controlling their sexual desires through the study of Torah. One dimension of this activity of sublimation is to substitute God for the male and the people of Israel for the female erotic partner, such as is often demonstrated in prophetic literature. The Song of Songs, an erotic love poem, was interpreted as an allegory by the ancient rabbis, a description of the relationship between God and Israel, and the literal reading was ignored or denied. The sexual meaning attributed to the chanting of *L'cha dodi* certainly brings erotic energy to that ritual. It is a medieval poem recited every Friday evening in synagogue at the beginning of the Sabbath that uses imagery of marriage to describe the relationship between the people of Israel (groom) and the Sabbath (bride). Rather than eliminating the human dimension of the erotic, sublimation only connects Torah more deeply to eroticism. These allegorical moves are also helpful in creating possibilities for guilty pleasures, for those who are open to interpret them that way.

Employing the strategies of control and sublimation are effective means of dealing with sexual desire. They enable guilty pleasures, while at the same time providing moderating influences on powerful feelings and restricting actions that have the potential to violate ethical standards of relationships. And they connect Torah with the erotic so that the people of the book can also experience ourselves as the people of the body.

Broader Implications of Transgressive Sex

I have argued so far that the option of transgressing these restrictions may produce guilty pleasures, thus enhancing our sexual experiences. But having these experiences may have broader implications. The model of transgression entailed here is a model of resistance to power and to conforming to group norms. If gay men and lesbians had not persisted in transgressing Jewish rhetoric against same-sex relationships, those relationships might still be considered illicit by all of the Jewish community. Transgressing those laws enabled lesbian and gay relationships to be perceived as licit by at least some segments of the Jewish community. The same may be true for other sexual acts and desires that have the potential to be moral, but that are still considered forbidden. To set up a system that invites transgression teaches people that they can question the values of the societies in which they live, and the results may be dramatic in bringing about the possibility of social change.

To begin to think about good sex from a Jewish feminist perspective, we need to understand the power of regulating sex, even if those regulations are enforced only through discursive means. The rhetoric of regulation is problematic because it validates sex only when it is an instrument of procreation or commitment, links sexual differences and capacities to gender, makes sex for its own sake both less valued and shameful, and encourages people to develop secret sex lives. On the other hand, a system of regulation helps us recognizes the powerful nature of the erotic and ironically invites transgression, which at the least is seductive and at most transformative. It is a flawed system, but one from which we can benefit if we question it wisely.

Four

Radhika Balakrishnan

Capitalism and Sexuality

Free to Choose?

The world's fastest growing religion is transnational capitalism. As David Loy states, "The Market is becoming the first truly world religion, binding all corners of the globe more and more tightly into a world view and set of values whose religious role we overlook only because we insist on seeing them as 'secular.'"[1] Just as all other religions are gendered, so too is transnational capitalism. It transforms existing social structures and produces new ones. It is imperative in a discussion on women's religious wisdom on sexuality that the many ways capitalism influences our lives be better understood.

As capitalism increasingly penetrates all areas of life and livelihood, becoming a more firmly integrated global economy than ever before, what are its consequences for women's lives? I am particularly interested in untangling the effects of capitalism on women's agency, autonomy, and sense of self. Capitalism emphasizes individual responsibility and mediates self-determination in and autonomy through market relationships. As a consequence, capitalism undermines old scripts that assigned self-determination to some people and denied it to others on the basis of race, caste, gender, and property. Capitalism was aptly characterized by Marx as a system that "overthrows the narrow parochialism of earlier society, destroys tradition, and disrupts personal dependence in favor of the impersonal connection of the 'cash nexus.'"[2] Although class, race, gender, and ownership of assets other than one's own labor power do continue to intersect with capitalism, affecting the nature and extent of autonomy, capitalism has engendered new forms of autonomy for some groups, including some groups of women. The expansion of market forces is transforming the structure of social relations within which many women live and is producing new structures. I am interested in exploring some of the contradictory ways changes brought about by capitalism affect women's lives.

Capitalism has changed gender relationships in ways that have increased women's assertion of autonomy and at the same time exploited women as sexually objectified commodities. This increase in autonomy and sexual exploitation has triggered criticisms of the Westernization of society by the religious right in a number of Third World contexts. I believe that *Westernization* is a key term in these critiques because it facilitates what appears to be an anti-imperialist and nationalist resistance to some of the advances of transnational capitalism, even as it permits the religious right to focus many of its anxieties and agendas on resisting local changes in women's social status.[3] I think that many of these criticisms of Westernization are influenced more by changes in women's status, choices, and ways of life than by the growth of transnational capitalism itself. The religious right's critique of capitalism as Westernization makes a feminist countercritique imperative, since feminists do not necessarily share the view that these changes are entirely negative. Feminists need to pay attention to the ways in which capitalism's effects on women are simultaneously liberatory and exploitative.

Such a feminist countercritique of capitalism and its effect on women is also likely to differentiate itself from certain radical critiques of transnational capitalism.[4] While these radical critiques do not share the religious right's explicit opposition to changes in women's social relationships, they share a certain dogmatism that includes a negative interpretation of transnational capitalism. As a result, these "radical critiques" also fail to attend to and praise some of the more "liberatory" effects of capitalism on the lives of several groups of women. A feminist countercritique can, I believe, challenge part of the radical critique by calling attention to the mix of liberating and exploitative effects that contemporary transnational capitalism has on the lives, choices, and agency of some groups of Third World women.

The growth of transnational capitalism has been accompanied by a religious ideology that not only shapes our world but promises secular salvation in the form of increased production and consumption. It promises increased wealth for a nation, and improvement in the standard of living of its citizens. A sense of one's own value, as well as the value of others, increasingly depends upon the market's monetized valuation of one's labor and its products. In addition, people who live in the shadow of capitalist market relations find that "it is not always easy to know when decisions come from within and when they do not, when people want what they want and when they only think that they want or are interested in what actually they only believe they should want or be interested in."[5] These seemingly contradictory notions of autonomy and self-esteem connected to market relationships are key to the ways capitalism transforms gender relations.

In this chapter, I present five vignettes, four of which are based on my own experiences. I use my own experience because I find this exploration integrally related to my own biography, location, and contradictions. As an immigrant to the United States, I have a fundamentally contradictory relationship to both the country of my birth, India, and the country of my citizenship, the United States. My feelings about both places are inextricably tied to being a woman; the freedom and oppression that both places represent are part and parcel of my understanding of the relationship between sexuality and capitalism. I will reflect on the questions that arise out of these experiences, and on the implications that they have for the ways we might understand the changes in women's sense of self and in their relationship to others that have arisen from these five particular encounters with global capitalism.

Women enter into capitalist relationships both as producers and as consumers, and both roles affect women's agency, sense of self, and sexuality. The way in which I use the term *sexuality* is fairly broad. I refer by it not only to women's choices over sexual relationships and sexual activity in the narrow sense, but also to ways in which women experience themselves as constellations of desires and powers. Some of the powers I have in mind are the powers of producing within a market economy, powers connected to the control of wages and of conditions of work, and power to renegotiate roles in the family and the everyday micropleasures they enjoy in these roles as part of the production process. Some of the desires I have in mind are consumer desires for products, whereby women begin to experience themselves as entitled to these desires and to the products meant to satisfy them.

I would also like to consider women's desire for sexual knowledge and opportunities that shape their self-identity as sexual subjects free from certain kinds of surveillance and constriction. In short, I am interested in the ways in which women's roles as both workers in the production process and as consumers can positively affect their own sense of self and their relationships to others.

Vignette 1

This story is based on conversations with a colleague about her research on women factory workers in Bombay. These women were all from Kerala, a state in South India, and were brought to Bombay to work in a factory. In Kerala, they were landless agricultural laborers who had no work or had worked under semifeudal conditions, as had many generations of their families. They now lived in a women's dormitory in Bombay, away from their families; they earned and kept their own wages, went to movies, and bought lipstick and colorful clothes. These small luxuries represented a space for themselves and their own desires that they would not otherwise have had. These women worked long hours for little money. They were not a part of the organizing effort of other workers, primarily because they were women and were kept linguistically and spatially separate from other workers in Bombay.

This story shows both the production and consumption sides of the implications of being brought directly into work under capitalism. As laborers in the production of commodities, these women had access to and control over their own wages, however meager. The value of their human capacity was based on the market's value and demand for their labor. Their sense of self was no longer predicated on their relationship to the local landowner, but rather to an amorphous marketplace based on the wages they received. These women now claimed a sense of individuation. The liberatory moment that the commodification of labor brought is important to note. In a capitalist economy, the worker's laboring capacity is a commodity owned by the worker and sold for a wage.[6] In this context, it is difficult to ascertain whether these workers were free to look for other buyers for their laboring capacity. But assuming some level of mobility, it is in theory possible for these women to leave this factory and find other work. "Transnational capital therefore simultaneously undermines the reproduction of patriarchies by moving women from one sphere of social control to another."[7] The contradictory forces of capital that present themselves here pose some questions. Is the exploitation of these women within this structure somehow better than the exploitation from which they came? Is the sense of individualism that comes from not only the structure of labor but the women's physical removal from their familial and social structure liberatory?

As women's participation in the paid labor force increases, it changes the gender construction of society. As Beneria points out: "As women become continuous participants in the market, it is likely that this will have an influence on their motives and aspirations, adopting patterns of behavior so far observed more frequently among men. . . . Thus the market can have a positive [effect] such as the breaking up of patriarchal traditions like arranged marriage that limit individual autonomy. It can also have negative consequences for those who suffer from the insecurities created by the market."[8]

The combination of wage labor and physical separation from family and place of origin also affects women's role in the family. Rather than being dependent on their parents and therefore burdens, these women not only supported themselves but most often remitted wages to their parents.[9] Aiwa Ong describes the relationship between sexuality and the life of the factory workers in China and Malaysia that parallels the experience of the workers in Bombay: "Separated from their families, working women did enjoy such new freedoms as living in singles' dormitories, having more buying power, and postponing marriage. These personal choices, including premarital sex, were already available to working women in Hong Kong and Taiwan, in recognition of their filial contribution to the family economy."[10]

Another aspect of their expression of autonomy was as consumers with the ability and responsibility to want what they want. They could go to the movies, explore being a sex object, buy lipstick, reject the confines of previously proscribed sex roles, and feel that they could want what they want. In Malaysia, factory women were criticized for bad behavior, Western outfits, for deferring marriage, and for indulging in the pleasures of the consumer society; they were the target of Islamic revivalists who opposed industrial development.[11] It is precisely these kinds of choices on the part of women, though mediated and mitigated by the market, that threaten the gendered social structures that the religious right wants to control. These women were removed from the family, community, caste, and other existing social structures that had mediated their relationship to the world. They could now work within the larger context of a disembedded global economy whose rules change to keep the accumulation process undisturbed.

These contradictions call for a feminist reconceptualization of the oppositional narratives of nationalism and of the universal critique of transnational capitalism. It is important to take into account the individuation and sense of self and of control one can get when a tube of lipstick can transcend the confines of a particular life, based on what one can consume.

Vignette 2

When I was studying the implications of subcontracted, home-based work for women workers in Sri Lanka, I visited a wooden toy manufacturing industry outside of Colombo. I first met with the owner, who took me on a tour of the factory that had once produced the toys on an assembly line that had employed both men and women. This facility is now used only to check the quality of the work that has been subcontracted to small shops and to package the final products shipped to stores in Europe. He told me that he found this a better alternative to producing in a factory, because the in-factory workers often organized to slow down production during busy seasons and advocated for higher wages and better working conditions. This, he explained, made him lose control over his ability to fill his orders and made him more vulnerable to the demands of the global economy. He now contracts out the work to women who run small work stations at their homes, employ their neighbors to produce these goods, and receive a piece rate for the work they deliver. The women pay for the supplies they use, such as paint, but are provided the wood to make the toys. The manufacturers do not pay for any goods that do not meet their standards. Any increase in the price of supplies is borne by the women. If there were a downturn in the demand for the product or if the women complained about the rates they receive, they would not be given any more work.

After visiting the factory, I went to visit one of the work sites an hour away. A woman ran a small workshop behind her house, where she employed five of her neighbors on a piece-rate basis. (To start her business, this woman had saved some money as a contract worker somewhere in the

Middle East). The women worked together, both old and young, with their children around them so that they could all keep an eye on them. I arrived in the afternoon and at first did not find any workers there; they had gone home to take care of household work. The woman who ran the shop told me of some of the problems she faced having to bear the brunt of the uncertainty of the market and the increase in the price of the paint, which reduced the piece rate that she and the rest of the workers received. They were generally happy with this factory employer because he had always paid them on time and the work was generally regular, a condition they had heard was not always true with other employers.

I spoke with the rest of the women when they returned. One woman who was older, possibly in her fifties, was very happy to have this job. She had been working as a rubber-tree tapper and found the work physically difficult. She also found this work much more convenient, since it allowed her to go home to cook for the family and work late into the night for extra money. When she worked in the rubber plantation, she was still responsible for the work at home but had to do it before and after her paid work. She also said that it was much more enjoyable to work with her neighbors, though for less money, and be able to talk to them and often share their household work as well.

Another woman, much younger, said that this work saved her having to travel an hour to get to work. Travel was considered undesirable and not safe for young unmarried women. She also had control over the money that she earned, and, since it was piece rate, no one in her family really knew what her income was. She had started a bank account and had just bought herself a gold chain that all the other women pointed to with a smile.

Subcontracted work that moved the location of work closer to or actually into the home made it easier for women to carry the double burden of paid and unpaid work. In places where social taboos limit women's public mobility, this kind of subcontracted work permitted women to earn wages and stay at home, or at most go to their neighbors' houses and work with other women. It also allowed an unmarried young woman money and security that otherwise often only marriage could bring.

In this scenario, unlike that of the workers in Bombay whose lives had been changed by moving away from their families, gender-based social structures were changed by workers staying in the vicinity of home. Here, capitalism's need for cheap labor allowed women a certain flexibility and control over their wages. They were more vulnerable to the forces of the market both in terms of demand for the product as well as inflation, but they had easy access to their homes, and the company and help of the community of their neighbors. In other countries, where the market had suffered a serious downturn and men had lost their factory work, subcontracted home-based work, still controlled and managed by women, became the principal means by which the family maintained itself.

Where social constraints on public mobility or when religious prohibitions prevent women from leaving their community, such subcontracted work gives them a way to earn wages and change the power relations within the household. The forces of transnational capitalism simultaneously maintain and subvert the existing social structures: they uphold patriarchal constraints on women's mobility and change the gender dynamics in the family.

Vignette 3

For a few years, I worked for a U.S. foundation in a regional program that supported work on reproductive health in Asia. In Bangkok, I visited agencies that were organizing workers in the sex industry, especially around HIV/AIDS. At that time, both the clothing industry and the tourism industry (which is inextricably connected to the sex trade) were being promoted by the Thai government as part of its growth-oriented economic policies. At the same time, the Thai government was officially committed to encouraging women to leave the sex trade for other sectors of the economy, the garment industry in particular. There were government programs that trained women to use sewing machines and then found them employment in the garment factories outside Bangkok. As a result of the economic crisis in Asia, many of these garment factories closed, and anecdotal evidence suggested that an increasing number of women were entering the sex trade for the first time. Though the domestic demand for sex workers decreased as a result of the economic crisis, the devaluation of the Thai *baht* made sex tourism even cheaper for foreign tourists; the government had a serious stake in promoting the sex trade, which brought hard currency into the country.

As a money economy depends more and more on a wider set of actors and a complicated set of relationships, its economic dependence on particular persons decreases while its economic dependence on international society as a whole increases. This larger dependency changes the embedded notion of an economy based on family or community and therefore changes the existing social structures. These local dependencies become replaceable; their worth is based on the objectivity of the contribution that is expressed in money.[12] This brings about a certain level of self-sufficiency: one is not dependent on a specific actor but on a principle of accumulation based on an overall international interdependence.

The structural ways in which a given society may shape these dependencies—particularly when the money contributions are unequally distributed in the world—are gendered, when one examines sex work. The economic inequalities of global capitalism make it expedient for a country to sell the sexual services of its women to attract foreign currency; the same inequalities give consumers in other countries enough money to buy sexual services as recreational commodities.

Given this economic context, it is interesting and paradoxical that the Thai government was not alone in its effort to convert sex workers into factory workers. I visited a nongovernmental organization (NGO) in Chiang Mai that also sought to get Thai women to find alternative forms of employment and to leave the sex trade. The problem was that these women would run away from the factories and return to the sex trade in Bangkok.[13]

In light of social structures and women's agency as they operated in the manufacturing sector and the sex industry, transnational capitalism had in fact made stemming the rise of HIV infection among sex workers very complicated. With the feminization of the international labor force over the past quarter century, the number of women in the paid labor force has increased a great deal, even in countries where women's paid work was low or socially not acceptable.[14] Yet the alternatives to working in the sex industry for young women in East and Southeast Asia (where the growth in the clothing industry has caused a dynamic change in women's roles) are often characterized by harsh working conditions, as Dickens points out:

> In the rapidly growing textile and clothing industries of developing countries the labor force is similarly distinctive. Employment in the industries

tends to be spatially concentrated in the large, burgeoning cities and in the export-processing zones. The labor force is overwhelmingly female and predominantly young. Many workers are first-generation factory workers employed on extremely low wages and for very long hours; a seven-day week and a twelve to fourteen-hour day are not uncommon.[15]

Given these conditions, constant supervision, and low wages, many women rejected the factory work in favor of the more lucrative sex trade in order to help support their families. Though exact figures are difficult to come by, primarily for political reasons, estimates of the number of people in the Thai sex industry before the economic crisis range from a hundred thousand to a million, a substantial number of whom are children.[16] Given the economic crisis and factory closings, women chose a more stable and predictable livelihood. The government and NGO's, in their attempt to bring women into factory work, were also guided by a morality that the women did not necessarily share.

I also visited women sex workers in Chennai in Tamil Nadu, India. Because I could speak the language, I was able to converse with women as they tried to do peer education with other women sex workers about HIV/AIDS. Most of the women I met had been married through arranged marriages to men who had either left them or abused them. Most of the women had children from their marriages. They explained that they had ended up as sex workers because it was the only way for them to make enough money to maintain their families in a big city. Not allowed to return home to their village because they were married, with children, they supported themselves with sex work.

At five P.M., all the women quickly left the movie theater where they had been working all afternoon and went to the courthouse. They told me that it was important to service their clientele who worked in the courts in case they were arrested and needed their help. As we stood outside the courthouse, I asked how the men knew who they were. One woman responded by saying that in India women generally never look men in the eye, and that the only women who could were the sex workers. It is important to appreciate that within the social and economic constraints under which sex workers live, there is agency, however distorted, in terms of the decisions they make.

Vignette 4

In New Delhi, again during one of my visits as a distributor of funds, I had a day to myself. I decided to stay in my hotel room and watch television. As I switched channels, I came upon Phil Donahue talking to women about orgasms. I decided to watch, both because of the content and also because it was familiar to me as an American show. Many women, all white, all heterosexual, talked very explicitly about what gave them orgasmic pleasure. Many complained that often their men would not "go down on them." I thought about what it meant for these women to want to go on television and talk about sex. I was simultaneously repulsed by and admiring of their frankness. I thought about growing up and being secretively given a copy of *The Hite Report* by a friend of the family when I was eighteen. Talking about sex was such a taboo; it represented in many ways the fear of immigrant parents of losing their daughters to this new world. I remember suddenly coming out of my familiar comfort zone of American culture and realizing that I was in New Delhi.

Later in the day, I was talking to a female relative who mentioned that she and her husband had just watched the same show. I wondered what it meant to them, what impact it had, at least in the silence it might produce as they went to bed. I do not want to claim that sexual pleasure is not a part of people's lives in middle-class India, but that this kind of conversation about individual pleasure, especially women's, is not a part of public discourse. I then started to think about a grandmother and granddaughter, relatives of mine, both hooked on the American soap opera *The Bold and the Beautiful;* they discuss the extramarital affairs of the characters they watch, even though in their family, sex was spoken about only occasionally and then in reference to procreation. Do young Indian girls who grow up watching American television start thinking about romance, love, orgasm, and pleasure, where Indian middle-class society strictly prioritizes arranged marriage, caste, class, procreation, and property?

The open-market economy is one in which goods flow from country to country and the global media helps convince people of the ever-growing number of commodities they can decide to want. Transnational capitalism would very much like the middle-class consumers of India, around 300 million people, to keep buying more of what they produce. "According to the trade journal *Advertising Age*, which should know, in 1994 the U.S. spent

$147 billion for advertising—far more than on all higher education."[17] Clearly, the global media wants us all to consume more and more, because the process of accumulation requires an adequate demand for commodities. The promise of capital, secular salvation, is never quite fulfilled, because if consumers were ever completely satisfied, capitalism would self-destruct.[18] Women who earn wages and are in control of providing for their wants are part of the larger order. This larger order is the expansion of global capitalism that makes these same women feel they can only become whole by endlessly consuming goods.

The impact of global media on sexuality can be traced through the manner in which it constructs our social context. This is the case because sexuality and sexual behavior, including sexual desire—though seemingly such an individual matter—are shaped within the social context.[19] Does the opening up of a public discourse on sexuality mediated by Western media, however, allow for a space that can generate forms of transgressive feminist cultural politics? The discourse of rights—women's rights, gay and lesbian rights—is also becoming a part of the progressive political agenda in India. The construction of the individual and of self-determination is intrinsically tied to the notion of rights.

The same media that has India watching *Baywatch* almost as much as it watched the *Ramayana* also has shows that interview openly gay men, that feature young women talking about romantic love and arranged marriage, and that air Hindi songs with disco dancers who imitate Janet Jackson.[20] The evolution of the individual within social structures of capital allows for a notion of self that can bring about a transgressive politics. As we are all asked to conform to a global market culture, there is, I think, room for politics that can subvert the dominant culture.[21]

In the vignette about sex work, women directly sell their bodies as a commodity, which leads to a distorted sense of agency, but one in which women nevertheless make choices; the decision to use one's body as an object is made under conditions of restricted choice. Television discourses and representations of sex—where sexuality is used to set up a commodified culture—also help women construct a sense of an individual self with choices and desire constructed for this new social context. Within capitalism, media are used primarily to instill commodity consciousness, but this also can have transgressive moments. Media create a space in which conversation about orgasm and alternative sexualities and about choices with respect to sexual activity and partners can take place. The opening of discourses also makes it possible to break out of a social structure that has told women a differently repressive story of what their sexuality should be like.

Vignette 5

When I recently went to a new K-Mart in lower Manhattan, I noticed that many of the shoppers were poor people from the housing project nearby. The shops in the neighborhood had become increasingly expensive, catering to a richer clientele. At K-Mart, the women were buying nice cotton underwear very cheaply. They were given more choices in wanting what they want, and at very low prices. Looking at the labels on the underwear, I registered that these women could buy these products only because some women in Bangladesh had moved from their small towns and left their families to work in Dhaka at garment factories making cotton underwear.

This took me back to my last visit to Dhaka, where I met two women leaders of a union movement. Out of horrible working conditions and increasingly lower wages, the factory produced garments for export. The union organizer told me that her family did not even know that she was the president of a fast-growing union in Dhaka. She had come once to the United States to testify in Congress about the conditions of work in the garment factory. When I queried her about her visit, particularly her short stay in New York, she told me that one of her biggest frustrations was that she was not able to communicate with the homeless and poor people that she saw. She wanted to know more about their lives so she could understand the connections between hers and theirs.

The connection that struck me was the interdependent nature of the sense of individuation of these two groups of women on different sides of the globe, in Manhattan and Dhaka. The work that gave Bangladeshi women a sense of self because their human capacity was valued by the market, outside prior social norms, was the same labor that allowed poor U.S. women to exercise autonomy by having a greater number of goods they can decide they want.

Feminist concern over self-determination and the construction of the private are inherently linked to capitalist development and exploitation. Capitalism can embody the principle of autonomy and the pursuit of individual self-interest. The problem, however, is that it threatens self-determination by fostering hierarchies of personhood that encourage the violation of autonomy.[22] The belief in a return to the local does not address the liberatory moments of capitalist expansion, which must be acknowledged before this expansion can be adequately critiqued. Embedded economies do not allow women self-determination. It is important to disentangle the web of desire, power, pleasure, sex, and capitalism—carefully, instance by instance, letting each situation present its own complexities—to achieve an emancipatory understanding of sexuality, equality, and citizenship.

A feminist oppositional narrative to transnational capitalism must be developed that can fully grapple with the contradictory ways in which capital can be both exploitive and liberatory. The religious right's opposition to transnational capital often targets women as the vessels of Western values, of individuation and control. The salvation that the religious right promises does not offer people, particularly women, the opportunity to define themselves. It is important to wrestle with the self that capitalism produces and to challenge the unmet yearning for salvation that this secular religion, capitalism, promises. This narrative needs to encompass a system of values that can transcend the theology of the market but at the same time allow a self that can exercise the full play of its possibilities, with human dignity. This system of values has to understand the self as a constantly shifting set of relationships in order to reinvent the whole.

Part II
Prices of Sex

Around the world, the prices and methods of payment associated with how sexuality is constructed differ. In some settings, women are often murdered or forced into marriage; in other contexts, women's sexual delight is erased, motherhood is made compulsory, or both. Even when the prize is believed to be worth the price, hidden costs emerge. In all, women pay dearly simply for being women. Insightful analyses in this section equip women to begin to reconfigure these equations.

Pinar Ilkkaracan, a Turkish social psychologist and community organizer, in "Islam and Women's Sexuality: A Research Report from Turkey," looks at the interaction of Islam with specific economic and political conditions that shape gender and sexual behavior. She focuses on religious practices and customs regarding marriage, reproductive behavior, and adultery in eastern Turkey. Practices such as honor killing, bride price, polygamy, child marriage, and forced marriage, although in breach of official civil laws, are still prevalent in the region. She concludes that education is one of the most important tools women need to end practices that violate their human rights, and she seeks ways to make that education available more widely.

Patricia Beattie Jung, a U.S. theologian, describes another high price in "Sanctifying Women's Pleasure." She reviews several specific individual and cultural indicators of women's lack of sexual delight. She relates this problem to the church's emphasis on procreation, expressed in its continued prescription of coitus only and its failure to denounce the absence of women's delight. By such silence, she argues, the church sanctifies this way of constructing sexuality. Yet sharing pleasure and making love are closely connected. Consequently, only when the moral goodness of women's delight is explicitly confirmed and its nurture commended will the church be able to teach with consistency and credibility that partnered sex must be unitive in order to be good.

Wanda Deifelt, a Brazilian theologian and Lutheran pastor, in "Beyond Compulsory Motherhood" looks at how having children is obligatory in Brazil. She demonstrates how cultural, economic, and religious factors converge to reinforce this pressure. She highlights the role of compulsory motherhood in the sale of new reproductive technologies available to wealthy women. She describes *marianismo,* a cult of the Virgin Mary, as the female counterpart to machismo, naming them as two components of the gender scripts that undergird contemporary Brazilian society. While these scripts constrain women in many ways, under the surface of these traditions women exercise significant, though all too limited, moral agency.

Suwanna Satha-Anand, a philosopher from Thailand, in "Buddhism on Sexuality and Enlightenment" describes a Buddhist way of looking at the price of sex. Reproduction represents the ensnaring power and danger of pleasure, legitimate for laity but renounced by all serious truth seekers. Enlightened beings are beyond all sexual entanglements, as they would be beyond all other forms of worldly attachment. Nevertheless, such renunciation ought not to reinforce patriarchal structures in monastic, civil, and domestic life. Buddhist women need not pay the price of sexism for their salvation.

Five

Pinar Ilkkaracan

Islam and Women's Sexuality
A Research Report from Turkey

The control over women's sexuality through restriction, coercion, violence, or more complicated forms of political and social manipulation remains the most powerful tool of patriarchy in the majority of societies. Religion is often misused, both as an instrument of this control mechanism and as a cultural system, to legitimize the violation of women's human rights. However, concentrating on the role of religion in constructing women's sexuality without taking into consideration its interaction with the economic and political structures in a particular community can lead to erroneous conclusions.

Like many other religions, Islam does not have a static or monolithic tradition. Islam has interacted with the sociopolitical and economic conditions of a particular time and geographic location in order to ensure its survival and power. In the process, it has absorbed not only the practices and traditions of the two other monotheistic religions born in the same territory, namely Judaism and Christianity, but also the pre-Islamic practices and traditions of the geographic location in which it has striven to survive and gain power as a cultural and political system. Thus, it is very difficult to define what is intrinsic to Islam in organizing sexual behavior. The issue becomes even more complicated when we look at the interaction of such factors as class and race with Islam at a particular time and place, which has led to different religious interpretations and practices. All of these factors often produce different schools of Islamic thought, some of which can exist even within the same community.

Discourses on sexuality in Islam often fail to consider differences in practices in different Muslim communities as well as the spaces of negotiability created by social taboos and silences related to sexual behavior.[1] Nonetheless, even discourses based on an analysis of the Koran and the literature traditionally accepted as establishing the normative practices of Islam can lead to contradictory conclusions about the construction of women's sexuality. On the one hand, Islam has recognized both women and men as having sexual drives and rights to sexual fulfillment. Eroticism is presented as a good in itself, both a foretaste of heaven and on earth a divinely ordained necessity for reproduction. Women, like men, are believed to experience orgasms. On the other hand, particularly in terms of sexual drives, males and females are construed as opposites, men as rational and capable of self-control; women as emotional and lacking self-control. Female sexuality, if uncontrolled, is portrayed as leading to social chaos (fitna). Social order thus requires male control of women's bodies and sexuality.[2] However, the specific patriarchal mechanisms that are utilized to maintain this control differ according to geographical location, time, class, and race and depend on the economic and political realities of a given community.

The historical role of the interaction of Islam with specific socioeconomic and political systems in shaping women's sexuality in different Muslim communities is still a relatively unexplored issue. Although the 1990s witnessed a spurt of new research on women's history and gender organization in Muslim societies, the accumulated knowledge is still too rudimentary to throw light on such a complex and sensitive issue as women's sexuality. Even in recent decades, women's own accounts of the issue have remained rare. In most Muslim societies, there is a striking lack of empirical data on sexual behavior, especially women's.

In such a context, research on the official, religious, and customary laws and practices that determine the organization of gender and the context of women's sexuality in different Muslim societies could throw light on the ways religion is used to create and perpetuate the oppression and injustice women experience in these societies. It would also play an invaluable role in deconstructing the myth of a uniform Islam, which fundamentalists claim consists of "a divine and eternal truth." The Women and Law action-research program of the international network of Women Living under Muslim Laws (WLUML) has evolved as a response to this need. Under this program, many country projects are conducting comprehensive studies of laws and customary practices that shape women's lives, as well as women's strategies in diverse situations.[3]

This chapter, which is based on data collected by Women for Women's Human Rights in eastern Turkey within the framework of the international Women and Law action-research program, examines laws and practices related to important elements in shaping the context of women's sexuality: civil versus religious marriages, bride price, polygyny, women's consent to marriage, reproductive health, the possible consequences of extramarital relationships for women, and domestic violence. The analysis is based on interviews conducted with 599 women in eastern Turkey.[4]

A Unique Confluence of "Western" Secular Laws, Muslim Culture, and Regional Differences

Turkey, which is a predominantly Muslim country, is the heir of the Ottoman Empire in which the Koran formed the basis of family law. Turkey was founded as a republic in 1923 as a result of the victory of reformists over foreign occupying armies as well as over conservative forces at home. The founding of the republic was followed by the introduction of revolutionary changes for women. Turkey is unique in the Muslim world in the extent of its secular, progressive reforms of the family code affecting women's lives.[5] In 1926, the introduction of the Turkish Civil Code, which is based on the Swiss Civil Code, banned polygamy and granted women equal rights in matters of divorce, child custody, and inheritance. Yet, even several decades after these reforms, customary and religious laws and practices that often breach official laws are used as tools to control women's sexuality and to maintain the imbalance of power in sexual relations. This is especially the case for women living in eastern Turkey, which can at best be characterized as a semifeudal, traditional, agricultural economy. The situation of many women living in the region has worsened as a result of the armed conflict since 1984 between the Turkish security forces and the separatist Kurdistan Worker's Party (PKK).

Eastern Turkey has a multiethnic character. Besides Kurds and Turks, the largest ethnic groups, the region also includes Zaza, Azerbaijanis, Arabs, Christians who speak the Syriac language, and others.[6] As has been the case in the rest of Anatolia, over the centuries different religious schools of Islam have established themselves in the region. Although most of the population follows Sunni/Hanafi Islam, there are also followers of Sunni/ Shafi or different Shi'i traditions. The followers of the Alevi tradition claim devotion to Imam Ali, and so they are categorically defined as Shi'is, although Alevi philosophy and practices are quite different from those of the orthodox Shi'a.[7] Alevis in Turkey are estimated to constitute at least one-quarter of the total population of the country and have a distinctive religious culture that includes elements of Anatolian Sufi tradition and Turkoman shaman ideas.[8] The Anatolian Alevis have traditionally rejected gender segregation in both the religious and social spheres of public life and have survived in Anatolia despite being the target of intense political pressure and fundamentalist attack under the Ottoman Empire. At various times, Alevi practices—including ceremonies in which women and men perform religious rituals with elements of music and dance, the rejection of the veil and of seclusion for women, and the acceptance of alcoholic beverages in social gatherings—have been deemed un-Islamic by Sunni authorities. These claims have often been used as a pretext for political pressure ranging from persecution to massacre.

Turkey is one of the countries suffering from problems resulting from regional disparities in socioeconomic conditions. The unfavorable effects of these disparities are experienced more by women than men. Western Turkey consumes most available resources and is highly urbanized, while in the eastern section most of the population lives in rural areas.[9] Although primary school education has been mandatory in Turkey since 1927, in 1990 half of the women in eastern Turkey were illiterate, compared with 21.6 percent of the men. The illiteracy rates are much lower in western Turkey, at 19.7 and 7.4 percent for women and men respectively. As a consequence of the armed conflict, the number and quality of the educational institutions in the region is declining, limiting still further women's educational opportunities. Regional differences in women's participation in the labor force are also striking. In the west, the proportion of women working for pay is 40 percent, while in the east approximately 90 percent of women are still unpaid family workers.[10]

Semifeudal structures still constitute the main social framework in the region and for many women dictate the organization of both gender and sexual relations. Most of the Kurdish population in the region is dominated by tribal structures organized around big families with the characteristics of a clan; the feeling of group solidarity involves a large number of members, extending the family and including responsibilities toward the community.[11] The *aşiret* or tribal system is usually characterized by large areas of land held by a tribal leader, who is the landlord. The members of the *aşiret* usually do not own land but work the landlord's holdings.

In such an economy, the traditional Middle Eastern patrilineality and patriarchy that favor endogamy and cousin marriage still form the basis of practices related to sexuality and gender construction. This is of particular interest when we consider arguments that women's oppression in Muslim societies has nothing to do with Islam but can be traced to ancient times and the beginning of the patrilineal society in the Middle East, itself a product of the agricultural revolution. Valentin Moghadam asserts, for example, that "it was endogamy, the practice of marrying within the lineage, that set the shape for the oppression of women in patrilineal society, long before the rise of Islam. Endogamy kept property (land and animals) within the lineage and protected the economic and political interests of men."[12] Moghadam further argues that practices such as unequal inheritance rights, polygamy, and the extensive control of women by male members of the kin group, supported by the Maleki law, facilitates and reflects the maintenance of tribal communities. The existence of similar practices in eastern Turkey, where Sunni/Hanafi law has been dominant for centuries, indicate that other schools of Islamic law can also be interpreted as compatible with such practices.[13]

In eastern Turkey, the ongoing armed conflict has strengthened the male-dominated structure of the community not only through the increase in militaristic cooperation between the state and Kurdish tribal leaders, landlords, and sheikhs but also through the rise of militaristic values in the society. A similar development has taken place in Afghanistan, where tribal structures are still prevalent.

The eastern region has the highest fertility rate in the country. In 1992, the fertility rate in the region there was 4.4 compared with 2.0 in the western region and 2.7 in Turkey as a whole. Some of the reasons behind the desire for a high number of children in the region are the aspiration for a powerful tribe, family elders' expectations of a boy child, and the belief that Allah will always provide food for each person.[14] Approximately 11 percent of women living in the east have their first child between fifteen to nineteen years of age, compared to 8.3 percent in the west. The level of current use of contraception is only 42 percent in the east, whereas it exceeds 70 percent in the west and 60 percent in other regions of Turkey.[15] When asked about the total number of their children, mothers often mention only the number of sons, omitting their daughters, as girls do not count. The situation has worsened as women's bodies have become the sites of the conflict between the Turkish security forces and PKK. The Turkish state is interested in reducing the fertility rate in order to increase its economic and political domination of the region, whereas the PKK propagandizes against contraception of all kinds, which they define as "a tool of the state to eradicate the Kurdish folk."

In recent decades, the dominance of market mechanisms and the modernization efforts of the state, including large-scale investments such as the construction of massive dams and irrigation projects in southeastern Turkey, are expected to lead to the dissolution of feudal structures in the region. However, most of the technological training and development projects are planned for men. As a result, modernization projects reinforce the traditional distribution of labor based on gender hierarchy and women's passive role in civil society.[16]

Marriage, Religion, and Sexuality

Marriage is almost compulsory for women living in the region. Of the respondents who were over twenty-four years of age, 97 percent were or had been married, as had all of the women who were over thirty-four years of age. Only a small percentage (0.6 percent) were divorced, indicating the rarity of marital dissolution in the region.

According to civil law, only civil marriages are legally valid in Turkey. Under the Civil Code, religious marriages confer no legally binding rights, including those related to divorce, maintenance, or inheritance from the husband. A religious ceremony can be held only after the civil ceremony.[17] Otherwise, both the couple and the religious official conducting the marriage are deemed to have committed an offense punishable under the Criminal Code.[18] Despite these regulations, 20 percent of the respondents had only a religious marriage. This percentage is much higher than the average in Turkey (8.3 percent) and the average in western Turkey (2.2 percent).[19] Moreover, both the mean and median ages of participants (17.9 and 17) at the time of the religious ceremony were lower than the mean and median ages at the time of the civil marriage ceremony (20.4 and 19); the religious ceremony is very often held before the civil ceremony, even though the practice is forbidden by law. Most women (92.9 percent) who had only a religious marriage indicated that they wanted a civil marriage. The main reasons for being prevented from having a civil marriage contract were: the husband's marriage to another wife (31.1 percent), the husband's refusal (29.7 percent), or the woman's youth (being under the minimum age required for a civil marriage, fifteen for women; 9.6 percent).[20] In fact, holding a religious ceremony before the girl child reaches the legal minimum marriage age of fifteen is often a strategy applied by families to bypass the civil law. Of women who had only a religious marriage, 16 percent were married under the age of fifteen. In contrast to Hanafis and Shafis, almost all the Alevis and Shi'i/Caferis had a civil marriage, indicating that there are differences between religious schools of thought in the attitude toward civil marriage.

The issue of civil marriage continues to be an arena of struggle for women in many other Muslim countries. In Morocco, for example, women who criticized the denial of equal rights to women based on texts of Koran and a range of appendages attached in the Middle Ages collected a million signatures to have divorce and child-custody rules transferred from the Muslim Family Law to the Civil Code. Similarly, in Lebanon, where laws on women's personal status are governed by religious tribunals, a proposal calling for the adoption of a civil marriage law has been bitterly opposed by religious leaders of various denominations who are afraid that it would divert power from the one area over which they exercise total jurisdiction.

Bride Price: A Tool for Commodization of Women's Bodies

As it is practiced in eastern Turkey, the payment of a bride price—the sum given by the husband or husband's family to the bride's kinsmen for the realization of marriage—symbolizes men's control over a woman and over the transfer of her productive and reproductive capacities to her husband's kin group.[21] This tradition is widespread in the region and plays an important role in the attitude of men, who assume that through this payment they have gained all rights over their wives' sexuality and fertility. Sixty-one percent of women indicated that their husbands had to pay a bride price for them. In fact, this tradition of families selling women for marriage remains prevalent despite the fact that more that three-quarters of the women (78.9 percent) indicated that they were against the tradition. More than half of the women (56.3 percent) responded to an open-ended question about their reasons for opposing the bride price by saying, "because women/human beings are not a commodity to be sold." It is interesting to note that at least one-fifth (21.4 percent) of the respondents stated that the main reason they were against the bride price was that they considered the tradition to be "against Islam" or "a sin." On the other hand, none of the women who supported the bride price saw it as a religious practice. Thus, the bride price constitutes a clear example of a patriarchal custom practiced even if it is perceived to be incompatible with religious laws.

Polygyny and Forced or Arranged Marriages

In the Muslim world, the opinions of religious thinkers on polygamy and practices related to it differ widely. Some believe that Islam does not allow polygamy, basing their arguments on Koranic verses Surah an-Nisa, which forbids polygyny unless the husband treats his wives equally and does not differentiate in the slightest degree between them.[22] Nonetheless, polygyny has become an established part of traditional religious law and practice in many Muslim countries. Polygamy has been banned in Turkey since 1926. As a result, in polygynous marriages, only one wife can have a civil marriage; the others can have only religious marriages. This situation immediately creates inequality between the wives, as only one of them has access to legally binding rights under the Civil Code, such as rights related to divorce, maintenance, inheritance, or custody.

One out of ten respondents in eastern Turkey was living in a polygynous marriage. None of the women who had a Shi'i Caferi background was in a polygynous marriage, while the next lowest percentage of polygynous marriages was among Alevis (5.6 percent). More than half of the women in a polygynous marriage (65.3 percent) stated that they had serious problems with the other wives. Despite all the disadvantages of a polygynous marriage, almost half the women in such marriages stated either that they had arranged the marriage themselves or that they had married of their own free will, indicating an acceptance of polygyny by some women. This acceptance appears closely related to educational level. None of the respondents who had secondary or higher education was in a polygynous marriage, compared with 13.4 percent of those who had no schooling at all.

Under the Turkish Civil Code, the consent of both the woman and the man is a precondition for marriage, yet women living in the region often have no influence over the choice of their prospective partner and are frequently married against their will. In fact, even in cases in which women are consulted about the choice of a husband, they cannot exercise their right of consent to the full because of a high degree of social control over women's sexuality maintained by the taboo on premarital sex, the practice of endogamy, or the threat of violence against women who do not comply with the choice of the family.

Most of the marriages (61.4 percent) were arranged by the family, and only one in four marriages was arranged by the couple themselves. Although the percentage of married Alevi women who had arranged their marriages autonomously was well above the average, the majority of Alevi marriages were also arranged marriages. Even when the marriage is arranged by the couple, the agreement of their families is very often a precondition to it. Every twentieth marriage was a *berdel* case, a tradition in which a woman is offered as compensation to the family of her father's or brother's wife. These marriages are based on the exchange of brides that have "equal value," which means that if one marriage fails, the other has to fail too. In such marriages, the women are more or less hostages. Families are not likely to allow them to run away or divorce.[23]

The tradition of betrothing girls while they are still infants seems to be disappearing, although it continues to be practiced (0.9 percent). One woman was offered as a wife to a family as compensation for an offense committed against it by her male relatives, and another was forced to marry the younger brother of her deceased husband. About 5 percent of the women stated that they had asked their husbands to kidnap them or that they had eloped with their husbands of their own free will. This is a strategy applied by women when their families do not allow them to marry the partner of their choice or when he is not able to pay the bride money requested by her family. Although this might seem a strategy through which women can select their own partners, it can result in the women paying a high price for their action. Yalcin-Heckmann, in her research on women's strategies in the tribal cultures of eastern Turkey, concludes that women who have been "kidnapped by their husbands by their own will" are almost always considered "to have eloped" by their husband's family, which often leads to a loss of prestige and status for the woman and even to violence against her.[24]

More than half of the women (50.8 percent) were married without their consent and 45.7 percent were not even consulted about their partner or the marriage. Those who had not met the husband before the marriage constituted 51.6 percent of the participants.

More than half of the yet unmarried women (58 percent) believed that they would be able to decide on their partner themselves, indicating an increasing autonomy over the choice of partner. This view is also supported by the mothers. When asked who would decide on their daughters' prospective husband, 52.5 percent answered that their daughters would make the decision themselves. But the proportion who stated that their sons would choose their partner independently was much higher, 75.5 percent. Only 46.4 percent of women who believed that they would arrange their own marriage responded positively to the question of whether or not they could choose to have a boyfriend, indicating that this autonomy does not necessarily include the possibility of getting to know the partner before marriage. In fact, even in cases of marriage arranged by the couple themselves, they are often allowed to meet each other only after the ceremony has taken place. The level of education is an important determinant in the women's empowerment to choose prospective partners. The percentage of those who think that they have the right to choose their prospective partners increases to 89 percent among those who have completed secondary or higher education, compared with 40 percent of those who have had no schooling or a primary education.

Reproductive Rights

There are no legal restrictions on contraception in Turkey, and family planning is increasingly encouraged by the state. Family planning seems to be acceptable in many Muslim countries and societies, especially when economic conditions require it. Since 1983, abortion has been legal until the end of the tenth week of pregnancy.[25] However, in eastern Turkey, as in the rest of the country, contraception, like childbearing, is considered to be applicable only to married women, as sex or childbirth is a taboo issue for most unmarried women. As a result, many women have no chance of receiving any information about contraception before marriage.

The most common source of contraceptive information for married women was health institutions (44.7 percent), and the least common source was the family (4.9 percent), indicating the taboo nature of the issue within the family. The average number of living children per woman was 4.8, and every third woman had more than 6 children. Only half of the currently married women between fifteen and forty-nine years of age were using a contraceptive method at the time of the research. The reasons for not using any contraceptive methods included: having no knowledge of them (15 percent), the husband or the family not allowing her to do so even though she wanted to (12 percent), and lacking the financial means (5.7 percent). Every third woman who had ever used a contraceptive method complained about side effects and health concerns related to the method. Most complaints related to the pill included weight problems, tension, and stomach pain, whereas the most common problems related to the use of an IUD were irregular bleeding or spotting. Almost one in ten married women had tried to induce an abortion at least once in her life through methods such as using injections for certain diseases (one of whose side effects is supposedly a miscarriage), jumping down from a high place, inserting soap into the uterus, or carrying heavy objects. One woman tried to induce an abortion by inserting a knitting needle into her uterus. Six out of ten women stated that the method they had used to induce an abortion had seriously damaged their health.

Extramarital Relationships and Honor Crimes

At present, neither the Turkish Civil Code nor the Turkish Criminal Code differentiates between men and women on the issue of fornication. Proof of fornication entitles the injured party to file for divorce on the grounds of infidelity, which can be proved by any means (e.g., witnesses) and enables the injured party to claim damages.[26] However, extramarital relationships are an absolute social taboo for women living in eastern Turkey, whereas men's extramarital affairs are widely accepted and even socially legalized in many cases through the institution of polygyny. The majority of women interviewed (66.6 percent) believed that, contrary to the law, even if they wanted to, they could not divorce a husband who committed adultery. Although an increase in women's educational levels increases women's openness to the possibility of divorce, 31.5 percent of women who had secondary or higher education still believed that they could not divorce their husbands on the grounds of adultery. There was no difference in the perception of possible divorce between women living in urban and rural areas. It is interesting to note that the percentage of women who believed divorce to be possible in the case of the adultery of the husband was highest amongst Alevi women (50.3 percent), despite the strict prohibition of divorce in traditional Alevi practice.

In contrast to many men who can practice adultery without fear of divorce by their wives, even though such divorce is allowed by the Civil Code, the customary penalty in the region for a woman suspected of this offense is death. These so-called honor killings are one of the most dreadful examples of collective control of women's sexuality. *Honor killing* is a term used to describe the murder of a woman suspected of having transgressed the limits on sexual behavior as imposed by tradition, specifically, engaging in a premarital relationship with the opposite sex or in a suspected extramarital affair. The use of the word *honor* in relation to the crime of murder is reflective of a culture where men define their personal and family honor through the sexual behavior of their women kin. This custom is in sharp contradiction to the official law. Since June 1998, fornication, either by women or men, has not been defined as even a criminal offense in Turkey.[27] Thus, there are no official laws in Turkey restricting the right of a woman to engage in a relationship with any man or woman of her choice before, during, or after marriage.

Only 27.5 percent of the respondents believed that the possible reaction of their husbands toward an extramarital affair of theirs would be divorce. The majority (66.6 percent) thought that their husbands would kill them if they suspected them of an extramarital affair. This percentage was higher among those who had little or no education, those who had only a religious marriage, and those who lived in rural areas. Although the percentage of Alevi women who feared death as a consequence of an extramarital affair was much lower than the average, this tradition also seems to affect many Alevi women; 38.6 percent stated that their husbands would kill them in such a situation. Most of those who thought that a husband would do something other than divorce or kill them stated that he would beat her up severely.

The practice of honor killings is not based on the Koran. Although the Koran forbids adultery[28] and foresees heavy punishment (one hundred lashes) for both women and men guilty of adultery or fornication; it requires four witnesses to the act. [29] Otherwise, if a woman denies the accusation, then it is her word that must be accepted rather than that of her accusing husband. The Koran states that not only should the evidence of men who accuse women of being adulterous without producing at least four witnesses be rejected, but also that they should be punished by eighty lashes, as they are deemed to be "wicked transgressors."[30] However, 46.3 percent of women who feared being killed if they committed adultery stated that the only customary proof required for an honor killing was the husband's claim to have seen it with his own eyes; the women often added that they perceive this practice as the utmost injustice. They noted that even if the husband was lying, he would be believed by the community, as a man's word is generally accepted to be true. Only 18.6 percent stated that the husband had to have witnesses to the act, while 27.3 percent said that he needed to prove it in some other way.

Although no provision in the Turkish Criminal Code explicitly refers to "crimes of honor," the tradition of honor killing is supported by the law that considers an extramarital affair involving a husband or wife to be a "provocation" and reduces the sentence by one-eighth if such provocation is considered to have taken place.[31] In most cases, in order to escape sentences required for murder under the Turkish Criminal Code, the so-called family council does not hesitate to order a male child in the family to commit the murder. Such a youth would be expected to receive a lighter punishment, based on the law that a sentence is reduced by one-third if the crime is committed by someone who is considered by law to be a minor. In such situations, the members of the family council—male relatives of the woman who have actually decided and planned the murder—receive no punishment. The lack of legal recognition of honor crimes is a severe violation of women's basic human rights. The feudal structure and the absence of a local women's movement in the region are serious impediments in the fight against honor crimes.

Violence against Women and Marital Rape

More than half of all married women living in the region stated that they were subjected to physical, emotional, and verbal violence by their husbands (57.9 percent, 56.6 percent, and 76.7 percent, respectively). Those who were subjected to sexual violence (marital rape) constituted 51.9 percent of the participants. As the educational level of women and their husbands increases, the extent of domestic violence declines but by no means disappears. One-third of women who had a secondary or higher education were subjected to emotional and physical violence by their husbands, and one-quarter indicated that they had experienced marital rape. The extent of domestic violence experienced by women, including marital rape, not only negatively affects women's sexual health and their perception of sexuality but also reduces their chances of creating and applying strategies against the violation of their rights.

The Turkish Criminal Code does not contain special provisions relating to the use of violence against women in marriage. The husband is usually charged under the general provisions of the Criminal Code, which provides for imprisonment of up to thirty months for the maltreatment of a family member in a manner that contravenes the accepted understanding of affection or mercy.[32] In order to benefit from this law, the woman subjected to the violence must file a complaint. However, only 1.2 percent of those who had experienced domestic violence notified the police, and the proportion who had filed a complaint was even lower, 0.2 percent. The most common strategies used by women against violence by their husbands were to leave home temporarily (22.1 percent) and to ask for help from families, friends, or neighbors (14.7 percent). There are no shelters or institutions in the region to help victims of domestic violence. This contributes to the helplessness of women who suffer domestic violence.

An additional local obstacle to the filing of a complaint by women in the region is a distrust of the security forces as a result of the ongoing armed conflict. This distrust is due not only to the atmosphere of political and social suppression by the security forces, but also to violence by them. The number of respondents who had been subjected to physical or emotional violence by the security forces constituted 1.3 percent and 3.4 percent, respectively, of the total. Two percent indicated that they had been sexually harassed by members of the security forces. In fact, the situation is in line with observations by the World Health Organization (WHO) that the general breakdown in law and order which occurs during conflict and displacement results in an increase in all forms of violence, including domestic violence against women.[33]

Good Sex: Setting the Context

The internalization of gender roles by women in a particular culture is often directly related to the impact of specific mechanisms that control women's sexuality, which are often of a collective nature.[34] Religious and customary practices are often misused as instruments of these control mechanisms. However, a study of the role of religion in constructing the context of women's sexuality must include an analysis of the interaction of particular religious schools and customs with the socioeconomic conditions and politics in a particular geographic location at a particular time.

The research findings detailed here all reflect a number of control mechanisms on women's sexuality in eastern Turkey, economically the least developed region of the country, where semifeudal structures still dictate both the organization of gender and sexual relations for the majority of women. The social pressure on women to marry early, forced and arranged marriages, the tradition of bride money, the extended exchange of wives between families, and the extent of the threat of violence against women who transgress the limits on sexual behavior as imposed by traditions constitute some of the control mechanisms supported by customary and religious practices in the region. These findings show that compared to women belonging to other religious sects, the Alevi women have relatively more autonomy on most of these issues, in line with the Alevi tradition that rejects gender segregation and values gender equality. Research findings also indicate that education is often one of the most important tools for women in countering the violation of their human rights.

As in many other countries, most women in the region are not aware of their rights, and there are no services to which they have access to learn about them. The expansion of such services for women is one of the main preconditions for their creating strategies to defend their rights. Since 1997, Women for Women's Human Rights has been conducting women's human rights training programs in the region to respond to this need. The expansion of such programs and services is necessary in order to empower women to fight the violation of their basic human rights.

To raise public awareness of, and to create preventive strategies against, these practices, it is essential to identify and integrate them into the women's human rights agenda on the national and international levels. This is a crucial step in the fight against conservative and fundamentalist politics aimed at stifling the debate on the violation of women's human rights through practices deemed "Islamic." As Riffat Hassan asserts, the most important task for Muslims today lies in making peace, "provided they understand that peace is a dynamic state predicated on the idea of justice for all, and justice not only in the legal sense but also in the socio-economic, political and personal sense, i.e., justice between man and man and—what is perhaps even more important—justice between man and woman."[35]

Six

Patricia Beattie Jung

Sanctifying Women's Pleasure

Good sex bespeaks devotion to a rich complex of goods. While all these are important, I am concerned in this chapter to highlight the goodness of women's sexual delight. In brief, I argue the discernment of women's sexual pleasure as morally good must be communally nurtured and sustained. At least in North America, that most women enjoy sexual activity cannot be presumed. Indeed, reliable social scientific data from a variety of studies suggests that many do not. Silence within the church about the absence of such delight for many women is problematic. For the church to teach with credibility and consistency about the goodness of the unitive, or love-making, pair-bonding function of human sexuality requires that this silence be broken. Church teachings about the moral significance of sexual delight need further development. In sum, I establish that the nurture of mutual pleasure should be commended as a morally significant component of every good sexual relationship on the basis of a traditional Roman Catholic ground: the wisdom of the body.[1]

Many women in North America do not routinely enjoy sex. Amazingly, there is very little attention paid to the absence of pleasure in the sexual experience of so many women. This reflects a disregard for their delight. This unconcern has been socially constructed. People, at least in North America, have been scripted to treat this absence of joy as merely a personal problem. Yet the devaluation of women's pleasure has deep cultural roots. It is reinforced at certain decisive junctures by Christian, especially Roman Catholic, teaching on sexuality.

While there is certainly more affirmation of the value of sexual pleasure among heterosexual married people in contemporary Roman Catholic teaching, the church continues to prescribe only vaginal-penile intercourse. Christine E. Gudorf notes in her groundbreaking book *Body, Sex, and Pleasure* that according to the church every other sexual activity is either "foreplay" or perverse.[2] To be precise, the Roman Catholic Church teaches that only conjugal coitus can be good. Furthermore, even though the procreative purpose of the marital act no longer has primacy over its unitive end, official church teaching continues to emphasize as the only elements necessary for the completion of the marital act (1) penile penetration, (2) the insemination of the vagina, and since it is requisite for ejaculation, (3) male pleasure and orgasm. What John C. Ford and Gerald Kelly pointed out decades ago is as true today of church teachings as it was in the early 1960s: the wife's only essential role consists in her willingness to receive semen.[3] Though viewed as permissible, even desirable, the wife's sexual pleasure is not seen as essential to the marriage act. In sum, as the Roman Catholic Church prescribes it, sex can be morally good apart from a woman's delight. My point is simple: this teaching conflicts with what many women judge makes for good sex.

One probable assumption behind such teaching is the mistaken notion that most women take delight in coitus. Gudorf notes that 56 to 70 percent of women cannot reach orgasm as a result of penile-vaginal intercourse alone.[4] This means that for many women, the church's current affirmation of venereal pleasure is merely theoretical. What the exclusive prescription of coitus teaches is that a woman's pleasure is not essential to good sex. Her delight not only does not warrant devotion; it does not even deserve attention.

The many activities that are more likely to prove pleasurable for women—such as the direct stimulation of their genitals by hand and mouth and other forms of rubbing—do not get identified in official magisterial teachings except when they are proscribed as "polluting." Sadly, this is frequently all many Catholic men and women learn about these activities. To be fair, many Catholic theologians commonly teach "that when the husband has his orgasm during coitus, stimulation of the wife *may* continue until she has orgasm."[5] Similarly, wives might take delight in foreplay to coitus, even have an orgasm, though multiple orgasms on her part were traditionally viewed as morally suspect.[6] Female delight in such foreplay—and after play—were permitted, because they were interpreted as having a moral unity with the coital act they accompanied.

Such activities were to be clearly distinguished from the engagement in those same activities apart from coitus; such stimulation of the genitals to orgasm would clearly be perverse. According to this line of reasoning, such mutual "masturbatory" (as it is officially labeled) activity, even when shared by spouses, trivializes the procreative value of sexuality.[7] What few Catholic theologians recognize—and what is not evidenced at all in official Catholic teaching—is that coitus alone is not a source of pleasure for all, or even most, women. Yet conjugal activity cannot be bonding or love making apart from shared pleasures and mutual delight. Thus the exclusive prescription of coitus trivializes the unitive value of sexuality for women. Since the church now teaches that the procreative and unitive meanings associated with sexuality are inseparably linked, they must both be considered essential to good sex. By its own logic, the traditional Catholic sexual prescription of coitus alone needs to be abandoned, on the grounds that it fails to take the unitive end essential to well-ordered sexual activity seriously. Furthermore, when pleasure is taken seriously as an additional premoral good linked to sexual activity, then the failure to share it (in otherwise responsible ways) is, as Gudorf puts it "a violation of the Christian obligation to love the neighbor."[8]

As Marie M. Fortune notes in *Love Does No Harm: Sexual Ethics for the Rest of Us,* when a husband rolls over and falls asleep immediately following his "release" night after night, in the eyes of most Christian ethicists, Protestant and Catholic alike, he may not be the ideal lover—indeed he may be an insensitive lout—but his behavior is not perverse, criminal, objectively disordered, or immoral. The sharing of pleasure is not widely seen as requisite to good sex.[9] Under present Catholic catechetical teaching about the main offenses against marriage, nothing is said about the need to share pleasure or even to avoid causing pain during intercourse. Yet Gudorf notes that, "even apart from outright sexual violence, sex can be not only devoid of pleasure but actually painful, especially for women."[10] This is not just a problem on the honeymoon, or after childbirth, or for a few isolated individuals, as at least some theologians presumed.[11] In her book *Women's Bodies,*

Women's Wisdom, Christine Northrup reports that 25 percent of women say they have painful sexual intercourse virtually all the time, and another 33 percent report dyspareunia some of the time.[12] It does not take a great deal of moral imagination to recognize that sexual activity not aimed at mutual pleasure will not serve the marital bond, will certainly not be love making and, if repeated, might well prove destructive not only of the relationship but of the self-esteem of the partner whose delight is so devalued.[13]

Despite its recent emphasis on the importance of the unitive function of sexuality, the Roman Catholic Church continues to prescribe coitus as the only form of morally good sex. This should not prove surprising. How can we expect the celibate men who reiterate such teachings to know what pleases women, when many married men and women do not know that the stimulation afforded by penile-vaginal intercourse is not sufficient to bring most women to orgasm?[14] Indeed, even today, some medical professionals presume the frequency of coitus to be an accurate indicator of the quality of a heterosexual couple's sexual relationship.

While the effort in this chapter to reconstruct church teachings to include more appreciation of the sharing of pleasure can be applauded, Grace Janzten eloquently points out in her own chapter that there is a danger here. This effort to valorize women's sexual pleasure might be simply one more expression of Western decadence. When we value women's sexual delight, do we do so only at the expense of much needed attention to the other problems women face, and to the public policies that engender them? Does this focus feed rather than challenge the growing sense of the privatization of sexual and reproductive matters, so that in the end the pleasures enjoyed by some women will be purchased at the expense of the well-being, indeed even the survival, of others? Every focus keeps us from seeing what recedes into its background. But I think it is wrong to dismiss carte blanche all concern about the devaluation of pleasure, because as I will show later, shared delight is one way we are connected to, rather than distracted from, precisely these other concerns.

The Problem

As one might expect, there is a range of views among contemporary Christians about the premoral goodness of sexual pleasure. Even among conservative moral theologians, sexual pleasure has enjoyed an upgrading. Most concede that the instrumental value of pleasure was over-looked in the tradition.[15] They now judge sexual pleasure an acceptable con-sequence of coitus (and generally presume it to be an automatic one!) and counsel that it is not wicked—indeed it is proper—for spouses to enjoy, even seek, this pleasure because of its service to both the procreative and uni-tive ends of marriage.

Still, conservatives warn that this appreciation of pleasure should be se-riously qualified. Perhaps more than any other good, sexual pleasure has the capacity to enslave humans and lead them astray. Our sexual desires can clearly exceed what is necessary for the service of the unitive and pro-creative ends of marriage. This, they argue, has resulted in the tendency in the West to overestimate the goodness of pleasure, as exemplified in the philosophical doctrine of hedonism. But as Beverly Wildung Harrison and Carter Heyward point out, it is not necessary to endorse a monistic value theory in order to embrace sexual pleasure as central to human fulfillment or even essential to human well-being.[16]

Predictably, many liberal moral theologians are less suspicious of sexual delight and, while aware that any good may be corrupted, celebrate plea-sure more wholeheartedly. Still, as Harrison and Heyward point out, for lib-eral Christians, sexual pleasure remains only instrumentally good. While few liberals mandate that it serve a procreative good (except perhaps in de-bates about the validity of heterosexism), according to this way of thinking sexual pleasure is good only insofar as it serves the "'unitive' and 'commu-nicative' values" essential to sexual intimacy.[17]

Some contemporary theologians—conservative and liberal—presume that the cultural shackles stemming from the debasing and vilification of women's sexual pleasure have been adequately identified and addressed. Of this I am not at all convinced.[18] With Gudorf, I would argue that "one of the major tasks of Christian morality in the present age is to claim sexual pleasure as a good."[19] One reason for this disagreement among theological ethicists is that the devaluation of sexual pleasure applies almost exclusively to women.

The Devaluation of Pleasure for Women

For many women in North America, genital sexuality is simply not any fun. It is not sensuous, joyful, playful, or orgasmic. In their 1999 report entitled "Sexual Dysfunction in the United States: Prevalence and Predictors," published in the *Journal of the American Medical Association,* University of Chicago sociologist Edward O. Laumann and his colleagues explored the pattern of sexual dysfunction in the United States. They note that 32 percent of the women they interviewed reported a lack of interest in sex (whereas only 14 percent of the men interviewed made a similar claim); 26 percent of the women surveyed said they regularly did not have orgasms, and 23 percent said sex was not pleasurable (as compared with only 8 percent of the men).[20] Researchers and the general public alike found these results regarding women and sexual dysfunction "stunning," but what is important to understand is that this lack of sexual pleasure is not only socially generated and organized but continues to be religiously sanctified.

Sexual delight is not only biologically but also culturally grounded and sustained. Pepper Schwartz and Virginia Rutter note that "women often learn to have orgasms much later in life" than do men and that "a minority have trouble ever becoming orgasmic."[21] The extent of such anorgasmia, notes Mary D. Pellauer, may be great. She cites the 1990 *Kinsey Institute New Report on Sex* claim that 10 percent of all women suffer from "total anorgasmia."[22] In the 1994 National Opinion Research (NORC) survey, 24 percent of the women who responded (compared to 8 percent of the men) reported difficulty having an orgasm in the last twelve months. Perhaps more revealing is the consistency of this difference in sexual experience: 75 percent of men, but only 29 percent of women, reported always having an orgasm during sex with their partner.[23] In the NORC survey, 19 percent of the women responding noted that they had difficulty becoming aroused (whereas only 10 percent of the men reported erectile disorders); similarly, twice as many women as men (33 percent compared to 16 percent) reported that they had experienced a significant lack of interest in sex altogether.

Women in North America cannot take the experience of sexual pleasure (including orgasm) for granted. We have been schooled to believe, mistakenly, that such sexual dysfunction is not the proper concern of the church. It is a private, perhaps medical or mental health problem—a tragic, accidental reality affecting isolated individuals whose personal problem deserves our pity. It is my conviction that this incapacity on the part of so many women to enjoy sex is a moral problem, originating in part from and significantly reinforced by many religiously blessed cultural scripts. The absence of sexual joy in so many women's lives is in part a consequence of the way good sex has been constructed in Christian moral traditions. While there is some room for women's sexual delight along the fringes of this sacred canopy, it is not highlighted under the big tent.

While many presume that such may have been the case even as late as the middle of this century, many people believe the sexual revolution of the 1960s and 1970s in the West dismantled the last vestiges in our culture of such nineteenth-century, Victorian attitudes toward women's pleasure, complex and ambivalent though they may have been. But as a matter of fact, it did not. Instead, the call to deconstruct these cultural messages on the not so revolutionary grounds that sexuality is a purely private affair left individual women blind to and powerless before social messages about their sexuality that remained fully intact and quite powerful, even if underground.

Sadly, the sexual revolution was in many important respects no revolution at all. Indeed, as a result of the loss of a sense of the social and cultural nature of our sexuality, many contemporary women experience efforts to celebrate the moral significance of their delight as burdensome. Contemporary accounts portray female sexual pleasure as if it were a purely private or individual matter; this legitimizes performance anxiety and the American tendency to turn sex into work.[24] For a woman exhausted by the work associated with her double shift (on the job and at home), enjoying sex becomes "just one more damn thing to do." Her woeful failure at it is simply one more indicator of her individual inadequacy and her marital or relational maladjustment.

Though I recognize that the changes my argument invites might be stressful, it is not my intention to add to any woman's burden.[25] Such responses stem from the highly individualized connotations associated with words like "should," "duty," and "obligation" in our culture. Just as we lack a clear sense of the way the sinful privation of this good has been and is socially structured and religiously reinforced, we lack a clear sense of the social dimensions of this grace—of the way such sexual pleasure could be communally nurtured, sustained, and enhanced within divinely sanctioned scripts for women.

Some of the Reasons for the Problem

There are many reasons why women don't enjoy sex, and the connection between the absence of sexual pleasure in women's lives and these other social factors is not always recognized. Hence the dire need to reform these institutional patterns and cultural messages is not recognized either. Our culture puts a damper on female sexuality in many ways. For any given individual, the operative configuration of these factors may vary. The point is that while the so-called sexual revolution brought more women in North America access to reliable contraception, it did not construct a culture wherein female sexual delight was valued and the pursuit of such joy respected. Ironically, even though North America has a highly sexualized culture, women's pleasure has not been prioritized; its maintenance and enhancement is not generally understood to be a significant moral or religious good.

It is very difficult to untangle the organic and social elements in women's sexual experience. In her *Promiscuities: The Secret Struggle for Womanhood,* Naomi Wolf notes that for decades comparative anthropology has made it clear that the "capacity for orgasm in women is a learned response which a given culture can help or fail to help women develop."[26] So integrated are social and biological factors in women's experience of desire and pleasure that it is difficult to tease them apart. The point here is not to discount the importance of the physiology behind female sexual pleasure. The point is to establish that such joy, like its loss, is not only biologically but also culturally grounded and religiously sustained.

There are many indicators other than their direct expression in the various forms of individual female sexual dysfunction detailed here of our cultural ambivalence about sexual pleasure in general, and our negativity about women's delight in particular. Let me briefly identify four.

The Politics of Research

Viagra (which sold for about 10 dollars a pill in 1999) may prove to be the most profitable prescription drug ever legally produced. Estimates within the industry place its potential worth at between 600 million and 1 billion dollars. While not disparaging efforts to address the problem of male impotence, I do want to compare them to the response to female erectile, libidinal, and other sexual disorders. While no scientists dispute the evidence that many women are unhappy with their sex lives, they all agree that not much is known about women's sexual response. Why is there little study of the primary sexual complaints of women? Neither the pharmaceutical companies nor various governmental agencies are as interested in women's sexual response as they are in men's. This is so, I contend, because many people still believe the only form of really good sex is coital, and therefore the only sexual problem that is legitimate to address is male impotence.

Instead of blushing when confronted with the facts about women's (lack of) desire, imagine what kind of moral teaching would undergird its recognition as an important issue and conceive of its relief as of genuine moral concern. A useful clue as to why we might find such imaginative work difficult is provided by sociologist Michael Kimmel, who notes that male impotence is rarely understood simply as men not getting enough pleasure.[27] Male sexual potency is defined in such a way that its absence threatens the individual's very sense of masculinity. It renders him less of a man. While this view certainly has negative dimensions, such a gender construction does have the benefit of illuminating the fact that men suffer from sexual dysfunctions. In an interesting piece, "Women and Sex," the *New York Times* in 1998 reported that a male CEO of a Wall Street investment firm privately donated $1 million to subsidize the distribution of Viagra to poor men who might not otherwise have access to it. Again, my agenda here is not to discount such generosity, but to explore why nothing analogous has ever been offered to poor women in need of sexual therapy. We do not seem to care that many women (as well as men) suffer from sexual dysfunction.

Heterocentrism

Schwartz and Rutter note that many "public arguments against homosexuality are influenced by negative attitudes toward sex that is *only* an act of intimacy and pleasure."[28] In sum, the problem with "gay" sex for many people is that it is so obviously (for) fun! It embodies a correlation that challenges what many Catholic girls learn about their sexuality. Same-sex activity clearly reveals that sexual activity can and should be about mutual pleasure. Heterosexists argue that homosexual partnerships can never be really life giving or love making; they presume that "only" mutual pleasure can be served in the homosexual unions they condemn. Even if one were to conclude that gay and lesbian sex is disordered because it is without pro-creative potential, logic demands only that these relationships be judged as falling short of the normative ideal. What becomes apparent, however, in such heterosexist arguments, is that the pleasure shared in gay and lesbian relationships is not understood to be of any intrinsic value, nor is it inter-preted as of instrumental, person-uniting value. From this heterosexist per-spective, homosexual activity can only be judged morally repugnant.

What I think gay, lesbian, bisexual, and transgendered (hereafter GLBT) sex makes clear is that the pleasures of sexual activity are not always tied to the joys and responsibilities of baby making. Some of the facts to which such gay life-styles testify are (1) that genital activities can be potentially person uniting only when they are mutually pleasurable; (2) that both plea-sure and love (for self and another) can be had quite apart from potentially reproductive activity—that is, apart from vaginal-penile intercourse, and (3) that love-deepening sexual pleasure can be shared, though not necessarily equally maximized, under a variety of terms of endearment.

And what has this to do with the question of the goodness of women's sexual delight in general? (1) GLBT sex underscores the fact that unless sexual activity is pleasurable, it cannot express or foster love. (2) GLBT sex highlights the fact that pleasures can be found in sexual activities morpho-logically not open to the possibility of procreation. (3) Indeed, internalized homophobia and compulsory heterosexuality may contribute to sexual dys-function in some cases. The fact is that women's sexual pleasure—includ-ing heterosexual women's pleasure—has little or nothing to do with its reproductive potential.

Pleasure and Sex Education

The vitriolic response in the United States to the suggestion in 1994 by then Surgeon General M. Jocelyn Elders that the subject of masturba-tion be addressed in the sex education programs offered at U.S. public high schools also indicates that there remains in place a powerful social taboo against sexual pleasure. Since boys usually teach each other how to mas-turbate during their early adolescence, the inclusion of masturbation in a sex education curriculum would serve primarily the educational needs of adolescent girls. "In a 1993 review of 177 studies of gender differences in sexuality Mary Beth Oliver and Janet Shibley Hyde found that the largest gender difference was in the incidence of masturbation. . . . Not only did fewer women masturbate, but in general, those who did masturbate had begun at a later age than the males. Virtually all males . . . masturbate before age twenty (most began between the ages of thirteen and fifteen) but substantial numbers of women reported masturbating for the first time at age twenty-five, thirty or thirty-five."[29]

In U.S. culture, while masturbation is seen as immoral for all who practice it, it is judged particularly wrong for women. The fact is that "more men masturbate more frequently" than women because "nice girls don't touch themselves."[30] This impacts women's very capacity for pleasure because unlike men, women need to learn in particular what pleases them. While this might be learned in relationship with another, traditional church teachings would label and condemn even such partnered explorations as masturbatory.

It is reasonable to argue that self-pleasuring in some contexts—devoid of pornographic aids, obsessive compulsions, and the like—might be a morally good, well-ordered expression of self-love. But regardless of how one evaluates solitary sex, some form of sexual self-exploration is necessary in order for women to know what pleases them. Hence, masturbation—solitary or partnered—is frequently the first therapy suggested by those addressing female sexual dysfunctions. Sexual self-knowledge is requisite for clear communication about what might prove pleasurable, and hence potentially unitive as well.

Pleasure and the (Re)discovery of the Clitoris

Through her examination of the constant need to (re)discover the clitoris, Wolf provides additional evidence of the ambiguity surrounding women's delight in the West. She demonstrates that the only role in our cultural script for women's pleasure per se is serendipitous.[31] Though scientifically "identified" as early as 1559 by an Italian as "preeminently the seat of woman's delight," the clitoris was presumed at that time to be directly associated with and at times declared requisite to conception. As late as the eighteenth century, female titillation and orgasm were thought at least to help women conceive. Though interpreted as the source of lasciviousness in women, the clitoris was also thought to foster procreation.[32]

Note, however, that by the end of the eighteenth century the idea that

white middle- and upper-class women were angelic creatures with less desire and capacity for sexual pleasure than men took deep hold in the West.
From this point on begins what Wolf calls "the great forgetting," so that by
the nineteenth century, "theories began to deny that it (the sex drive) even
existed biologically in women" except as pathological, predominantly in poor
women of color and perhaps lesbians.[33] Normal women desired not sexual
pleasure but motherhood. Female delight was held suspect and thought
debilitating; it was associated with madness, crime, and, ironically, infertility. By the public standards of the Victorian era, normal sexual intercourse
for married white upper- and middle-class women consisted of her fully
clothed submission to acts of vaginal penetration in the proper position (male
on top!) that led directly and quickly to gratification for him and (so hoped
the ideologues) to motherhood for her.

We know from the careful work of revisionist historians that even white
upper-class people's private experience (happily!) did not always match this
public ideology, but this cultural message about normative female sexuality in the West remains noteworthy. "The passionate nature of women, taken
for granted for millennia, had become a mystery."[34] Not only had the female ideal become sexless; but suddenly people began to debate whether
(morally) good women (that is, white rich women) even had sexual feelings. If such passions existed at all, many argued, they were normally dor-
mant. "Convoluted efforts were made to explain away the sensitivity of the
clitoris," notes Wolf; this led to the incredible "assertion that women may
have orgasms, but they certainly cannot *feel* them!"[35]

So powerful are the vestiges of these scripts that it remains difficult to
disentangle the Victorian constructions of a good woman's sexuality from
what might be the experience of women were it constructed in accord with
more pleasure-affirming scripts. Therefore, some feminists, like Cahill, can
"observe" that "male sexual drives are more genitally focused and urgent
than those of most women. . . . For women . . . sexual drives assume less importance on the landscape of identity. Although sexual pleasure may be a
good and a goal, uncontrollability is rarely an issue."[36] All of us need to ask
critical questions about the roots or basis of what we "observe" and presume to be the true or authentic sexual experience of women, given the
way it is constructed in our culture.

Only when placed against this powerful cultural backdrop, Wolf argues, can we have some idea of what is at stake in this century's repeated pattern of discovering, celebrating, and promoting the female capacity and desire for sexual pleasure. As early as 1899, an English physician decried as false the Victorian script for good women. A U.S. medical sociologist as early as 1902 noted that many good women are not asexual. They simply do not particularly crave coitus. Even though the thrusting associated with coitus can result in the rhythmic pulling of the clitoral hood and consequently provides some stimulation of the clitoris, women desire instead "the love touch" (by which this turn-of-the-century scholar probably meant cunnilingus and/or digital stimulation of the clitoris). In its 1990 report, the Kinsey Institute confirmed that "between fifty percent and seventy-five percent of women who have orgasm by other types of stimulation do not have orgasm when the only form of stimulation is penile thrusting during intercourse."[37]

Why did scientists have to discover over (in 1910), and over (in 1918), and over (in 1926), and over again (in 1930) that for many females penile-vaginal penetration is either an altogether ineffective form of genital stimulation or that it is not the easiest or fastest route to climax, and that most women delight in extensive, slow clitoral stimulation by hand and mouth? Wolf claims that each and every time, "the prevailing culture convinced us that the identification and celebration of female desire was revolutionary."[38] Obviously, this is a successful way of co-opting whatever challenges this "discovery" might pose to deeply embedded messages about what makes for good sex. What is new and revolutionary can hardly be expected to have impacted the routine.

What is so culturally dangerous, so politically incendiary, about this knowledge of the connection between "the love touch" and women's delight? Why do we insist upon keeping it a secret from our daughters and sons? Why must what it reveals be repeatedly erased, left for the next generation to (re)discover for themselves, or cloaked in shame? As Pellauer put it: "What stirs in our orgasms that there should be so many obstacles around them?"[39]

Paths toward a Solution
Official Tradition: Not Always a Usable Past

Grace Jantzen has documented in this volume that one will not find in the Christian tradition much affirmation of the inherent value of sexual pleasure.[40] The human capacity for pleasure is not described as a gracious gift from God for which North American Catholic girls are taught to be grateful. Instead it is virginity, especially as a sign of being sexually unawakened— of *not* knowing the desires and attractions that draw us into one another's arms—that is to be treasured. The enjoyment of "venereal pleasures" (complete or incomplete) outside of marriage is officially taught to be sinful. Their pursuit by "bad girls" is shameful. Their desire by boys and men, while dangerous, is (1) to be expected and (2) to be restrained, or at least controlled, by "good girls."[41]

Despite the Christian affirmation of the goodness of creation, and the beauty of the body implicit in the doctrines of the Incarnation and the resurrection of the body (in all its sensuality), sexual pleasure even within marriage is not presumed to be intrinsically good. It needs the justifications provided by the openness to the possibility of procreation and by its unitive function. This is not merely of theoretical concern. As early as 1953 in *Sexual Behavior in the Human Female,* Kinsey and his colleagues reported that Christianity "definitely and consistently" negatively impacted women's capacity for experiencing pleasure. The more intense their devotion, the fewer orgasms they reported.[42]

Historically, female physiology was not well understood or taken seriously in the formation of the Catholic moral tradition. Arguments based on the so-called order of nature were often based on what we now recognize to be the misunderstandings of ancient and medieval science, and they were by and large androcentric. Male sexual experience dominated the screen and distorted the perception of what was human. Within the Christian tradition, sexuality was described "overwhelmingly from the perspectives of men" and with an attitude "overwhelmingly negative towards, as well as, ignorant of, women's sexuality," writes Susan A. Ross. "Take the issue of masturbation— almost always discussed in terms of male experience. Unlike the penis, the clitoris has one function only: exquisite female sexual pleasure. It is not at all connected with procreation."[43]

What we now recognize as androcentric claims were based on false generalizations that suppressed important differences between men and women and thereby contributed to the oppression of women. "Although orgasm and ejaculation are not synonymous for men, they are nearly equivalent. Most men who get excited and have an erection will experience orgasm with continued stimulation."[44] Because in male experience orgasm is virtually identical with ejaculation, it was argued that for all humans the capacity for sexual pleasure was closely tied to reproductive activity.

From this "representative" fact, a norm was derived. Initially, the purpose of sexual desire was said to be *exclusively* procreative; gradually over the centuries reproduction was seen as the *primary* purpose of sexuality. Now the Roman Catholic Church officially teaches that openness to the possibility of procreation in each and every sexual act is *essential* to morally good sex.

Such openness of course can be expressed only in vaginal-penile intercourse. Obviously, this privileges heterosexual activity. And as Wanda Deifelt argues so poignantly in this volume, when sexuality is constructed as necessarily for procreation, it is done so often at the expense of the health, and in some cases the very survival, of women and their children, as well as at the expense of the well-being of the rest of creation.

But my point in rehearsing this tradition at length is to make it clear that it is a sexual ethic served in many instances also at the expense of women's pleasure, which unlike men's cannot be presumed to accompany coitus. It privileges male sexual pleasure. For heterosexual men, vaginal-penile intercourse is almost always somewhat pleasurable (though not necessarily orgasmic). Of this Pellauer writes: "In almost all cases (before advanced age or specific dysfunctions such as retarded ejaculation), if a man is having sex, he is having an orgasm. Most men cannot imagine having sex regularly, let alone for years, without orgasms.... Men are able to take pleasure for granted in sex.... The progress from desire to pleasure to ecstasy is precisely what women cannot take for granted in our society."[45]

In contrast, women who seem to be sexually active are often in truth really passive and experience sex without pleasure, even without desire, for years. Yet the absence of pleasure for a woman during intimate sexual activities was rarely judged morally problematic from a Christian standpoint; indeed, it was never even considered, so foreign was it to the experience of most men.

Deconstructing the androcentric foundation on which many of the world's moral traditions have been based is clearly useful. There is indeed much cruelty hidden deep in them. Recognizing and naming what makes for bad sex is important work, but women must begin to (re)construct their theological and moral traditions to offer society new accounts of what makes for good sex.

The Recovery of Women's Bodily Experience: Toward a More Useful Moral Tradition

I do not intend the following account of women's experience of sexual pleasure to substitute an equally rigid, sexual orthodoxy and praxis (albeit new) for the old. But one way to reform the cultural messages sent about women's sexual delight in North America is to challenge the moral traditions that undergird them. Once these traditional underpinnings are reconstructed, this new theological canon might challenge, if not subvert, the harmful messages sent to women about their sexuality. Religious convictions have the capacity not only to oppress but to liberate. Since mine is the Roman Catholic tradition, its further development shall be my focus. As noted earlier, one characteristically Catholic approach to the justification of sexual norms is to explore their basis in the body.

This is a methodological move not without its liabilities.[46] Furthermore, while it would be counterintuitive to disassociate fact from value, wrestling moral wisdom from human physiological experience is no simple deduction. It is a complex inductive process from which only tentative insights into value might spring. Other people's bodies are not exactly like ours; even bodily experience varies. And it is always interpreted from a particular social location. So prudence requires that such glimpses be subject to communal and cross-cultural tests, resulting inevitably in the qualification, if not the rejection, of what is discerned. The end result will be at best a process of incremental reform.

The Wisdom of Women's Bodies

In "A Theology of Sexual Pleasure," William R. Stayton treats the human body as a sacred text revelatory of the divine will for human females, who like their male counterparts are designed to enjoy sexual pleasure. Consider his interpretation of the mind of God: "While still in utero, females vaginally lubricate and males have erections. This phenomenon occurs while males and females are asleep, every forty-eight minutes, until death unless interrupted by disease. . . . The Creator intends sexual pleasure for the human creature. . . . Females have an organ, the clitoris, which has no other function than sexual pleasure."[47]

Though Stayton is himself a Baptist, his emphasis on the moral wisdom of the body is reminiscent of a Roman Catholic methodological approach. The turn to human physiology as a source of wisdom for the development of an authentically human sexual ethic is a traditionally Catholic move. Adequate consideration of the person surely requires reflection on the human body, (along with the careful consideration of much else). What is revealed in this bodily text—the clitoris? The enjoyment of sexual pleasure is intrinsically good![48]

Self-Love

Let us return to Pellauer's stark way of putting the question: "What stirs in our orgasms, that there should be so many obstacles around them?" What the experience of sexual pleasure can stir up in women, Audre Lorde suggests, is our sense of self-worth.[49] In her 1984 essay "Uses of the Erotic: The Erotic as Power," Lorde argued that once we taste such delight, women will demand "what is in accord with joy in other areas" of our lives. Women will "begin to give up . . . being satisfied with suffering, and self-negation, and with the numbness" that the culture demands of us.[50]

If sexual pleasure is a source of self-respect for women, then erotic delight is one sort of energizing experience that both embodies and enables revolutionary challenges to many cultural assumptions about the place of women. Audre Lorde confirms that this is what is at stake in the suppression of women's sexual delight. "In order to perpetuate itself, every oppression must corrupt or distort those various sources of power within the culture of the oppressed that can provide energy for change. For women this has meant a suppression of the erotic."[51] Pellauer summarizes: "to touch and be touched in ways that produce sweet delight affirms, magnifies, intensifies and redoubles the deep value of our existence."[52] We are awakened to our own loveliness and worth!

Making the Connections: The Other's Delight As My Own

Women's sexual pleasure embodies and enables not only self-love but other-love as well.[53] Arousal draws us toward others and ignites their attraction to us—sexual desire helps to sustain relationships. Even the delights of solitary sex can enliven in us our sense of connection to life. Sexual pleasure inclines those who enjoy it not toward a state of selfish isolation but toward the world. Pellauer describes the experience the French call *jouissance* this way: my "flesh has the capacity to burst me open to existence" so that my "connections to the rest of the universe are felt . . . as pleasurable."[54] Our sexuality draws us into one another's arms—and consequently into an awareness of and concern about the needs of that other.

The experience of shared pleasure challenges the way self-other relations are constructed in our culture. Presently, relationships are frequently organized as a zero-sum game; they presume we are basically created to be competitive with, if not downright antagonistic toward, one another.[55] What the sharing of sexual pleasure illumines is that one person's delight need not be purchased at the expense of another's. Instead, mutual sexual delight discloses the possibilities of creaturely interdependence and reciprocal enhancement. As Gudorf puts it, good sex reveals "that the overarching interests of individuals march together."[56] Self-love and neighbor-love are ultimately congruent—we were made for communion. Should we reconstruct our relationships in light of such shared delight, we might well engender a true sexual revolution.

Toward Sanctifying Pleasurable Sex

At present in the United States, many women do not enjoy sex. This problem is morally significant. Reflection on the female body yields as a reasonable ethical tenet that female sexual pleasure is of both intrinsic and instrumental value. Venereal pleasure, like other forms, is a basic premoral good for men and women alike.

Several specific individual and cultural indicators suggest the absence of cultural support for and religious encouragement of such sexual delight among women in particular. Certain teachings of the Roman Catholic Church actually reinforce this loss of sexual joy. The church's overemphasis on procreation, as expressed in its continued prescription of coitus alone, its failure to denounce (indeed even to take note of) the absence of such pleasure, and its continued condemnation of even partnered "masturbatory" explorations between spouses sustains the neglect of this good. Christianity's silence about this problem sanctifies it. Since sharing pleasure and making love are intimately connected, only when the premoral goodness of women's delight is explicitly confirmed and its nurture commended as morally good will the Roman Catholic Church be able to teach with credibility and consistency that partnered sex to be good must be pleasurable.

Seven

Wanda Deifelt

Beyond Compulsory Motherhood

Years ago, I was working in a rural base community in the Amazon area in Brazil as part of my theological education. The community where I lived was very poor. There was no electricity, no running water (apart from the stream), no grocery store nearby. The roof of the house where I lived was made with straw, and there was no floor except the ground. This shack, along with half a dozen other houses, made up the village where I did my internship.

One day, a thirty-two-year-old woman called Maria came into the village from inland to have her baby. This was her eighth pregnancy, and she had already had three miscarriages. In another nearby village, there was a health clinic. The woman doctor was called as Maria was being tended to by one of our neighbors. Without her husband knowing, Maria had taken birth control pills, but because she suffered from malnutrition, the pills did not work. Because she was so weak, the neighbors thought that they should call a priest, a pastor, or somebody from the church to take over when the doctor could not do anymore. So I, a white Brazilian woman preparing to become an ordained Lutheran pastor, had my first encounter with labor and its perils.

After several hours agonizing in labor, Maria finally delivered a baby girl. But Maria was not recovering. She was bleeding too much. While the baby was screaming life, Maria, who had brought forth life, was dying. That seemed a contradiction, life and death so close to one another. I was watching Maria bleed to death. By chance, the doctor had the proper medication to stop the bleeding. As she kept trying to find a vein in Maria's thin arm, poking her several times without success, Maria's face turned paler and paler. Finally, the doctor found the vein. The medicine was taking effect, and we looked at each other, the doctor and I, not quite believing the miracle that was taking place. Not the miracle of a baby, but the miracle that Maria was alive. She had survived.

When Maria was almost recovered, the doctor told her that another pregnancy would be fatal. She also told her that there were ways to prevent another pregnancy; perhaps she could have a tubal ligation. Even if Maria did not have the financial means for that, the doctor assured her that the community health clinic could help. Maria listened carefully to what the doctor was saying and then, turning her head toward the wall to avoid looking into our eyes, said: "It is not up to me to decide. You have to ask my husband if he will allow it."

The doctor walked out of the room, called the husband aside, and explained what needed to be done. She said clearly that, if Maria were to become pregnant again, she would most certainly die. The husband replied: "What will my friends say if I don't have any more children? They will think that I am no longer a man. If she dies, I will find me another one, younger and even prettier."[1]

I don't know what happened to Maria; I never heard anything about her again. But since our encounter, I have been concerned with the issue of compulsory motherhood as part of my thinking about good sex. Through that experience I discovered, painfully, that women do not own their bodies— Maria's reality is shared to different degrees by many other women I have encountered, regardless of their class, race, or religion. What makes women submit to the wishes of others, when those wishes have such gravely negative consequences? What are the theological warrants for the understanding that women's self-worth is based on compulsory reproduction? And finally, what are the signs of a different comprehension that breaks away from the bondage of reproduction, in which women have the right to give birth to themselves, make decisions regarding their own bodies, and consider themselves human beings? Some answers to these questions come through tracking the feminist movement over the past years, and the ways in which women's embodiment has become a common theme in research on and by Latin American women.

Bringing Women's Bodies into the Discussion

In Latin America, issues of human reproduction, reproductive rights, and health have been somewhat overshadowed by the analysis of production. In fact, a more common theme throughout the last decade of research, especially in Brazil, has been the analysis of female subordination engendered by economic, ideological, and political disparity. We have gradually moved from simply documenting women's roles in family and society to a concern about how to use women's own contributions as a source of empowerment and a basis for social change.[2] However, taking as our starting point an understanding of women as ethical subjects (not merely objects), we must question whether women's lives can be summarized by either of these roles, production or reproduction. In thinking about human sexuality, what do pleasure, well-being, satisfaction, and physical enjoyment with oneself and a partner have to do with women?

Among scholars, there is consensus that the past twenty years "show a progressive focus on methods and problem formulation to advance the economic and social status of women in Latin American society."[3] Two aspects of this research have been particularly important. One is the interplay between social reproduction, production for the market, and biological reproduction. The other is the disparity in gains within the work force, segmented by gender and ethnicity.[4] It is quite clear that during the 1970s and 1980s, priority was given to the study of the economic role played by women. There are many studies pointing out women's productive role in the industrial, agricultural, and domestic spheres, as well as the relation between women's reproductive role and their double work day as caretakers of families and as workers outside the home. In the 1970s, the plea of the women's movement was for equal payment for equal jobs and for kindergartens and schools for working women's children, to be provided at the job or by the employer.[5]

Comparatively fewer but still very much present in the 1990s are studies of women's activities as leverage for social change; these deal with women's participation in grassroots movements and in politics. The great challenge has been the discussion of women's sexuality and the ethical implications of taking ownership of our own bodies. In order to analyze the status of women, this discussion began to consider women's self-understanding and the concept of women's bodies as a locus of political decisions. In Brazil, the discussion has been widely documented through the media as it has focused more and more on issues such as sexual harassment, abortion, public health for women, the creation of Delegacias da Mulher (women-staffed police stations) in every state capital and major city, and stricter laws regarding domestic violence.[6] In other words, if the earlier women's movement in Brazil and other neighboring countries emphasized women's access to the job market, in recent years the emphasis shifted to give higher priority to issues of women's embodiment.

One subject that has not yet been fully scrutinized, however, is compulsory motherhood, an issue that parallels the compulsory heterosexuality critiqued in Judith Plaskow's chapter in this volume. It is estimated that in Brazil, 1 woman out of 139 dies due to complications during labor or unassisted abortions. In Paraguay, the death rate is 1 in 64. A less bleak figure is presented by Cuba, where 1 woman of 1,286 dies of reproductive-related causes.[7] In spite of the advances of the sexual revolution, access to methods of birth control, and overall changes in Latin American cultures, sexuality (primarily women's sexuality) continues to be associated with reproduction. There are many reasons for this, but religion seems to play the strongest role. In order to evaluate women's sexuality in Latin America, it is necessary, first of all, to look at motherhood.

Machismo and Marianismo

In Latin America, motherhood continues to be the role most women look forward to and expect to play. Sexuality, by and large, is perceived as necessary for procreation. There is a clear distinction between the social roles played by women and men. The same is true for sexuality, where the double standard remains. Anthropologists have analyzed this dichotomy and presented two guiding norms established according to gender that dictate the acceptable forms of behavior for men and women: machismo and *marianismo*.[8] *Machismo* means that men not only control the public activities of government and economics, but also rule over women and children. It is the ideological justification that underpins the alleged superiority of men. It is seen as natural that men assume more public roles, because men are more fit for them. Men are supposed to be more active and aggressive also in the sexual arena, and it is considered natural for men to have multiple sexual affairs.

The counterpart of machismo is marianismo. Based on the religious devotion to Mary, who is virgin and mother, marianismo depicts women as morally superior to men, spiritually stronger and purer, semidivine. Women approach sainthood by enduring a lifetime of suffering, especially if this suffering is caused by marriage or childbearing. The role models offered by Mary are either virgin or mother; that she was simultaneously both places her on even higher ground.

By presenting this polarity between machismo and marianismo, I do not wish to reject the positive role model Mary has offered to Latin American women, particularly Roman Catholics. The study carried out by Ivone Gebara and Maria Clara Bingemer, Brazilian Roman Catholic theologians, emphasizes the liberating and life-affirming message delivered by Mary, as seen in the Magnificat (Luke 1:46–55). In addition, that the concrete representations of Mary, for example, in the Guadalupe (Mexico) and Aparecida (Brazil), assume the features of the local population (mestizo and mulatto characteristics, respectively) is interpreted as a valorization of the local culture.[9] Without criticizing the work of liberation or feminist theologians who present the positive aspects of the cult of Mary, I want to examine marianismo's cultural underpinnings and oppressive aspects, especially as they refer to women's sexuality.

The basic idea is that the identification of Mary either as virgin or mother limits women's ideas of embodiment and sexuality. Sexuality continues to be identified primarily with procreation, and the role model of virginity still prevails. In a recent study on sexuality in which 2,052 Brazilians representing gender, race, class, and religious diversity were interviewed, 43 percent agreed that women should be virgin when they marry; 38 percent disagreed. Regarding male virginity, 66 percent said that men should not be virgin when they marry; 18 percent said they should.[10] There is clearly a double standard when it comes to virginity: women are by and large expected to be virgin when they marry, while sexual experience for men before marriage is not only condoned but recommended. Interestingly, there is a contradiction between people's public statements regarding virginity and their own practice: 67 percent of those interviewed say that they had sexual intercourse before marriage. Even if people's actions depart from what they consider the norm, the religious ideal is not necessarily challenged.

This gap is particularly apparent in the case of moral problems that arise when women break away from the moral standards expected of them (either virgin or mother) and are either (1) no longer virgin, married, and not yet a mother, or (2) no longer virgin, not married, and a mother. In the first case, sexuality is not used with the intention of reproducing. In the second case, the moral impediment lies with the institution of marriage. These two apparently deviant categories challenge the norm and show how women, although bound morally to the standard of virginity and motherhood set by marianismo, may not comply with it. And yet, a woman who finds herself in either category will still try to comply with the norm imposed by marianismo.

No Longer Virgin, Not Yet a Mother

In Latin America, as in some other contexts, the assumption is that women feel fulfilled through motherhood. The example of Mary, who was able to conceive even without sexual intercourse, idealizes procreation even more. With the religious component added, women's maternal fulfillment becomes mandatory. Yet in many instances, women are not able to procreate. Since biblical times, the barren woman is synonymous with a sad, despised, and lonely figure. Only God's intervention can assure continuity and descendents. Of course, the question of male infertility is never raised in the biblical context. Still today, the suspicion of infertility always falls first on women, and only when unproved there does it fall on men. Worldwide, it is estimated that between 23 and 60 percent of women who undergo in vitro fertilization do so at least to some degree because of their male partners' infertility.[11]

Because motherhood is perceived as the culmination of women's existence, the inability to bear a child becomes the source of social and psychological stigmatization and judgment. Infertility means crisis, and a popular remedy is the use of new reproductive techniques. Such techniques, from artificial insemination to in vitro fertilization to reimplantation of an embryo in a woman's body (whether she was the donor of the egg or it was produced by a surrogate mother), become sources of hope for many. However, as some scholars have already pointed out, the side effects of such techniques are not always made sufficiently explicit beforehand. For instance, the presence of multiple fetuses, as a consequence either of hormonal stimulation or of transferring several embryos into a woman's uterus, forces parents to select which fetuses will be carried to full term.[12] Less well known are other possible consequences of the exposure to such techniques: risk of pregnancies outside the uterus (ectopic pregnancy), higher risk of miscarriage, ovarian cysts, abdominal bleeding, increased risk of uterine and breast cancer.[13]

One of the most appalling aspects of the reproductive industry is the way fertility clinics distort their success rates. Gena Corea and Susan Ince undertook a groundbreaking study, in the United States, of hospitals and clinics offering in vitro fertilization and discovered discrepancies in the way success was reported.[14] Some clinics did not measure success by the number of live births, but by the number of successful implantations (regardless of whether they resulted in birth) and even by the number of chemical pregnancies (the elevation of hormone level that might or might not result in pregnancy). Also, many clinics did not include in their statistics the number of women who dropped out of the program because they could not produce eggs or because their eggs could not be fertilized. Some clinics report the success rate "per transfer," which does not indicate the number of children per mother but the total number born. Many women taking fertility drugs become pregnant with multiple embryos and thus deliver twins, triplets, or quadruplets. To report the rate of birth per transfer increases the apparent success rate because it gives the impression that one child per mother is born.

In Latin America, the situation is not very different. In a recent study in Argentina, one of the continent's major research centers in assisted reproduction, scholars pointed out that most users of new reproductive techniques were not aware of the relatively low success rates. According to Gisela Farias, the success rate in that country is between 15 and 20 percent.[15] In Brazil, unofficial data point to a higher rate: as much as 35 percent. Still, it is hard to explain why a technology with such dismal success rates and such high risks has been so easily accepted. Besides, it is an expensive technology. "Although rates vary, a conservative figure that clients pay is about 4,000 to 7,000 dollars per IVF cycle. Many women return for two, five, and some for more than ten cycles."[16] In Latin America, with insufficient government regulation and supervision, fertility clinics have become sources of revenue and investment.

The search for new reproductive techniques looks different when we consider that pregnancy is still a life-risking endeavor. It is estimated that two hundred Brazilian women die in labor for every 100,000 live births and that 5,000 die every year due to complications during pregnancy, or during or after delivery.[17] Today, although abortion is unlawful, it is still widely practiced in clandestine clinics (1.4 million illegal abortions are performed every year in Brazil). Yet statistics show that more women still die from pregnancy than from abortion.[18] Given such statistics, it is also worth questioning why so many women feel their maternal urges can be fulfilled only by pregnancy, when there are so many children available for adoption. It seems that the biological aspect as experienced in pregnancy and labor plays a more important role than raising children.

The new reproductive techniques have enforced the motherhood myth, giving the false impression that technology is the only answer for those incapable of procreation. The myth has also contributed to the notion that motherhood is a private matter, to the extent that, for women with plentiful economic resources, motherhood requires producing an offspring of one's own and not adopting a rejected child. It is not caring for a child that is a priority, but the biological experience of conception, pregnancy, delivery, and nursing, thus reducing women to wombs and breasts. By enduring the physical pain and psychological stress imposed by the use of reproductive technology, women are closer to the sainthood of mothering. In reclaiming the image of Mary, it is her capacity for reproduction that is emphasized, along with all the suffering that women undergo to achieve this biological experience.

Not Married, Already a Mother

The pressure toward motherhood is not always openly stated but may be presented as an ideal and a romantic state of grace. The message, most times, is veiled through an idealization of motherhood and through the common understanding that motherhood is a self-fulfilling and rewarding experience that will give a woman respect and raise her self-esteem. Research among teenagers, for instance, shows that many young women have knowledge of birth control methods, but they refuse to make use of them because pregnancy (and motherhood) can give them a new social status.

In fact, statistics show a dramatic increase in the number of teenage pregnancies in Brazil, where of the 2,718,265 child deliveries performed in 1997 by the public health system (responsible for 80 percent of all deliveries in the country), 26.5 percent were performed on women between the ages of ten and nineteen.[19] Since 1993, the number of teenage mothers has increased 4 percent. There is a significant correlation between teenage pregnancy and level of education. Among the teens surveyed, 54 percent of the women without any formal education, had already become pregnant. The number decreases to 29 percent of the women who had at least three years of schooling, and to 4 percent of those who had between nine and eleven years of education.

In an article on the issue of teenage pregnancy, Octávia E. Martin Danziato highlights the motives that lead teenagers into enacting their sexuality and becoming pregnant.[20] She points out the difference between a pregnancy that is unwanted and one that is unexpected. According to her, most teenagers are not unwilling to become pregnant. Pregnancy is understood as an aspect of life that will happen eventually anyway. Motherhood is part of the cycle of life. In their own understanding, their sexual activity simply precipitates something that is almost inevitable. Motherhood gives a new status to the teenager, a different position in the web of social relations. Teenage mothers are able to enjoy in advance the benefits of ensuring their own continuity. This ongoing pattern is well received, especially among low-income families, where a high number of offspring is still understood as a better guarantee for survival. For many teenagers, pregnancy is the official entry into the adult world, and motherhood a position that will guarantee respectability and status.

There is a correlation between the desire for such assurance of continuity, less access to education, and low income. Research by the Instituto de Pesquisa Econômica e Aplicada shows that teenage pregnancy is more a social than a medical problem: there are ten times more deliveries among poor teenagers than among rich ones.[21] Of course, to such statistics needs to be added the information that abortion is also a common practice, but in private clinics. An abortion costs between 150 to 2,000 U.S. dollars; a low-income woman cannot afford one.[22]

Following Danziato's train of thought, however, teenage pregnancy cannot be understood simply as fate. Motherhood as a social construction represents, for young women otherwise unnoticed and unacknowledged, the possibility of respect and dignity. As they see it, teenagers are not valued, but teenage mothers are. Behind this stands, of course, a notion of family that is completely different from that of the middle class or upper class. Venezuelan anthropologist Alejandro Moreno points out that, among low-income families living in the slums, the child of a teenage mother will not be raised by that mother, but by the grandmother, who in many cases was a teenage mother herself; almost always, the male figure is absent.[23]

Feminist studies have pointed out another important link regarding reproduction: motherhood as a way to overcome the guilt of pleasure. Women in general in Latin America are considered to be more sinful than men and are accused of sexual misconduct more often than are men.[24] Teenage pregnancy is viewed as a consequence of sin, since sexual intercourse outside of wedlock is condemned (particularly among evangelicals). In the previously mentioned study on sexuality done in Brazil, 30 percent of the Pentecostals interviewed stated that the sole function of sex is procreation, in contrast with 22 percent of the Roman Catholics and 24 percent of the Protestants.[25]

It is believed among Christians in Latin America that childbearing redeems the sinful woman. A common interpretation of 1 Timothy 2:15 ("Yet woman will be saved through bearing children, if she continues in faith and love and holiness, with modesty") suggests that childbearing repairs the wrongdoing associated with a woman's promiscuity and sets her on a new path: from sinner, through childbearing, she becomes saint. That procreation is women's obligation as a form of redemption is well expressed in the words of T.B., age thirty-nine, who was interviewed as part of a study of Brazilian workers:

> For me, motherhood is holy. It is like a tree. Every woman is a tree that has to bear fruit. Every child the woman has is like a fruit. In paradise, each of us has a tree planted; every child is a fruit that this tree gives. When the woman is hungry, in paradise, she will be fed by these fruits. A woman without children is like a barren tree, and she will be like a bridge for us, who have children, to come into paradise. We will step over them to enter into paradise.[26]

Reclaiming Women's Sexuality

In Latin America, the responsibility for contraception continues to lie with women, but the incidents of mass sterilization and improper use of birth control show that women do not always know their own bodies. Women who use birth control methods also occupy an ambiguous position. On the one hand, there is a great sense of relief without the fear of procreation of unwanted children. On the other hand, this does not always free them for a better sexual relationship. The majority of women still see their sexuality as in service of their male partners.

In light of this view, how can women contribute with their wisdom toward a new understanding of their sexuality that can be identified as "good sex"? This wisdom is precisely the unstated dissatisfaction with a comprehension of sexuality as geared exclusively toward procreation. This wisdom is the affirmation of women's active role in seeking pleasure, satisfaction, and fulfillment in ways other than motherhood. This wisdom is based on the disagreement with the moral and religious teachings widely disseminated in church and society. In the research in Brazil on sexuality mentioned earlier, when asked about the function of sex, 58 percent of the women responded: pleasure. The same answer was given by 47 percent of the men. Of the men, 26 percent answered that the role of sex was both reproduction and pleasure, versus 19 percent of the women. But 20 percent of the women still affirmed that the sole function of sex was reproduction, the same answer given by 23 percent of the men. Sex as pleasure was the answer given by those who had higher incomes (59 percent), were younger (56 percent), and were more educated (61 percent). Sex only for reproduction was defended primarily by those who were older (25 percent), were less educated (27 percent), and had lower family incomes (25 percent).

However, sexual pleasure continues to be, by and large, women's expectation, and not necessarily a reality in their relationships. Orgasm is experienced by 61 percent of the men interviewed, but by only 31 percent of the women. Interestingly, most women do not seem dissatisfied with their partner for their not achieving orgasm: 61 percent of the women rate their sexual performance and that of their partners as very good, 24 percent as average, and only 10 percent as bad. For these women's sexual enjoyment, orgasm seems to be somewhat overrated. Either they do not necessarily need orgasm to feel sexual satisfaction, or they are so bound to their relationships (with their sexuality geared to their partners' pleasure and not their own) that they do not feel confident enough even to criticize them.

One aspect of the Brazilian study, however, shows clearly that women's wisdom on sexuality moves beyond compulsory motherhood. The analysis of the religious background of those interviewed revealed that, when divided by religious preference, in every group, more people identified pleasure as the purpose of sex than any other option (sex for procreation or sex for pleasure and reproduction): 53 percent of the Roman Catholics interviewed, 47 percent of the Pentecostals, 45 percent of the Protestants, 54 percent of the Spiritists, 52 percent of those with other religions, and 63 percent of those without religion.[27] The unanswered question is how women will work out the moral dichotomy between the official religious teachings and their own sexual practice or personal opinion. Are women willing to engage in open disagreement with the ideal of marianismo and the idealization of virginity and motherhood? Or do women prefer to continue to live without questioning further the theoretical and ideological framework of a sexuality geared for male pleasure and for reproduction?

What seems to be happening is a resistance to the theological teachings of compulsory motherhood that does not always show up through open confrontation, but rather by a disavowal of these teachings in practice, in women's way of living out their sexuality. The opposition to compulsory motherhood is clear in the large number of abortions in Brazil. It is estimated that 1.4 million abortions are performed every year, compared to a little over 3 million births. These numbers are a strong statement that women do not perceive that each act of sexual intercourse should be followed by a birth certificate, although this is not presented in the form of a written manifesto.

Women's attitudes indicate that they seek private solutions for reproductive dilemmas instead of bringing them out into the open and discussing the theological foundations for the public policies regarding reproductive health.

Another example of this choice lies in the large number of women who have undergone sterilization, primarily by tubal ligation. According to Instituto Brasileiro de Geografia e Estatística, among Brazilian women between ages fifteen and fifty-four using any type of contraception, 44.4 percent had been sterilized, 41 percent took birth control pills, 6.2 percent observed their fertile period, 2.5 percent interrupted sexual intercourse, 1.8 percent used a condom, 1.5 percent had an IUD, and 1.7 percent used other methods.[28] The high number of women sterilized shows the proactive approach women in Brazil have taken toward reproduction. The myth of compulsory motherhood is undone: to avoid the risk that comes with the use of contraceptives, these women choose the radical approach of sterilization. This, however, can only be perceived through a careful reading of statistics, since it may not be verbally stated. Women want to enjoy their sexual life without the fear of pregnancy, but they do not dare to say so openly.

The study of women's embodiment and sexuality shows the ambiguous situation in which women find themselves. On the one hand, only a few women openly protest against the pervading notions of machismo and marianismo; on the other hand, the great majority, in practice, dismiss these teachings and act according to a more liberating, self-fulfilling, and autonomous ethos. Silence might be a survival strategy, considering the power issues. Since women do not have enough collective power to denounce a sexuality geared only for male pleasure and reproduction, they speak agreement but turn around and act as they please. However, this can also be a dangerous strategy, insofar as it gives the false impression that machismo and marianismo continue to be hegemonic discourses, when in fact they do not really impinge much on many lives.

Two of these dangers have already been analyzed here: women expose their bodies to the new reproductive techniques in order to produce a child of their own, and teenage women, knowledgeable of contraceptive methods, become pregnant to achieve a degree of respectability in their local communities. Both exemplify the dangers of compulsory motherhood, in which women find value and self-esteem only through procreation. If motherhood is an option, not an obligation, it can be fulfilling and life enriching. But women's existence should not revolve solely around this biological function. Motherhood should not be perceived as a fate or a way of self-promotion through the existence of another being. If women are ethical entities, capable of autonomous decisions, then women are entitled to make conscious decisions regarding their own bodies, about sexuality as well as about reproduction. For this to happen, women's sexuality needs to move from the private to the public arena.

So far, the issue of compulsory motherhood has not been sufficiently dismantled in the theoretical realm, although it is tumbling down in private practice. The deconstruction of compulsory motherhood will only be complete when women are involved in the public discussion of the ethical principles that guide sexuality. This discussion now reflects the monopoly and hegemony of the religious discourse from which women are excluded. Only by recognizing women as ethical subjects and historical agents is it possible to construct an alternative religious wisdom more in tune with reality and the practices of the women themselves.

Glimpses of such religious wisdom can already be identified within feminist theology in Latin America, for example, in the reclaiming of Mary as a full person, capable of decision making and engaged in proclaiming justice. This is the Mary of the Magnificat (Luke 1:46–55). Here, Mary goes beyond being either virgin or mother. She announces a new social order in a prophetic voice. Similarly, feminist theologians have reclaimed role models presented by other women in the Bible.[29] Such role models represent alternatives to compulsory motherhood, since they rescue the erotic and pleasurable dimension of women's sexuality, one that does not need to be bound to reproduction. Protestant feminist theologians who perceive the authority of the Bible as an important argument to deal with the domestication of women's sexuality and to offer a theologically sound comprehension of embodiment have emphasized this biblical interpretation.[30]

From this biblical perspective, an important contribution to overcome compulsory motherhood is the text of Luke 11:27–28.[31] One interpretation of the story is that a woman out of the crowd raises her voice, speaks in public, and addresses a man. This act itself is a transgression. However, when she opens her mouth, the woman makes a very conservative comment: "Blessed is the womb that bore you, and the breasts that you sucked!" She reduces Mary, the mother of Jesus, to womb and breasts. To this Jesus responds with a completely new alternative for women's existence. He says: "Blessed rather are those who hear the word of God and keep it." Instead of maintaining motherhood as the only alternative for women's existence, he offers women the possibility of thinking and acting. He proposes discipleship. Motherhood is not denied, but it is far from being an obligation. Women's worth is not tied to reproduction, but to the capacity of being human persons, in their own right, and not through the existence of another. Women are affirmed as ethical beings capable of decision making and living life to its full potential.

Coming Back to Maria

It is possible to imagine different outcomes to Maria's story shared at the beginning of this chapter. If she followed the common trend, she would probably undergo a tubal ligation, even without her husband's consent. However, she would not perceive this as a personal option, a conscious ethical decision to be made and discussed with others around her, and so involving a larger group in the dilemmas of human sexuality and reproduction. Rather, she would refer the decision to the doctor who recommended the intervention due to health risks. Thus, the ethical subject would not have been Maria herself, but another woman, the doctor (educated and in Maria's eyes more knowledgeable), who is then responsible for the fate of others. Maria would have survived, but her life might not have improved in terms of quality. Since her husband's notion of self-esteem depended on procreation to testify to his maleness, it is not difficult to imagine that the relationship would not survive. In that case, Maria would feel like a victim and probably portray herself as such. She would be alive but without a husband—a situation that is still discredited in some rural areas in Brazil, although not so much in the cities.

But by not talking about sexuality and reproductive rights, by not openly disclaiming the notion of compulsory motherhood and showing its dangers for women's well-being, Maria would probably pass her own fate on to her children. The chances are that Maria's daughter, born in the midst of Maria's struggle to survive labor, would also become a teenage mother. Pregnancy would give her a stronger sense of self, a purpose in life in a situation where women's only reason for existence is the care of family. In addition, her own pregnancy could be perceived (subjectively) as a way to rectify her mother's unwillingness to bear children. It would not be surprising, given the configuration of the story, if Maria herself were to become the caretaker of her grandchild, perhaps to compensate for her own guilt. Maria's daughter would continue to repeat the plight of her mother, and so on, in an endless cycle.

This bleak scenario shows the great risk that women run when we keep decision making regarding our bodies and sexuality private. Maria had done so earlier when she took birth control pills without her husband's knowledge. She did not have enough arguments to convince him differently, but she wished for a sex life free from the burden of childbearing. However, circumstances did not allow her to carry on with her practice; she had to bring the discussion out into the open with a larger group, involving doctor, clergy, neighbors, and friends as well. In other words, the discussion of Maria's sexuality and reproductive life would become part of a wider agenda, involving a larger group, because it was a life and death situation. When asked about the possibility of a tubal ligation, she referred the decision about her own body to her husband. But the labor did not happen in Maria's house, but in the village. She did not deliver her child by herself; she was not alone. If we call upon the surrounding community, holding it accountable for Maria's life, we can imagine another ending to her story.

Suppose that once Maria delivered her baby, the women in the village became aware of the situation. Since the husband had said publicly that he would not allow a tubal ligation, the other husbands told this story at home to their wives. Some of the husbands agreed, but others did not. Most of the women did not agree at all that Maria should go home without having had a tubal ligation. The discussion was open, and it involved not only Maria and her husband, but the whole village. The woman to whose house she had come to deliver her child did not allow her to return inland because, she argued, Maria was too weak to care for herself and the baby after such a difficult labor. She suggested that she stay at her house for some weeks until she was fit to go back. She also suggested that her own husband go back to stay with Maria's husband for a time, to try to convince him to see his wife's situation differently. During this recovery time, Maria had a chance to talk to many people. One of the things she heard was that women's role on this earth is not only for reproduction. She also participated in a small group that discussed women in the Bible, and she rejoiced to hear that having sex without having children was not a sin.

The decision ultimately had to be hers. But it is necessary to bring the discussion into the public arena in order to enable the sharing of experiences of women's sexuality and reproduction, and to envision a time in which women are truly ethical subjects. Only then can we become accountable for one another. In this way, women will learn that their individual practices may deconstruct the myth of compulsory motherhood, but we also need ethical discussion to strengthen women in our capacity for decision making. It is a small, difficult step, but it is one we must take to improve the quality of women's lives.

Eight

Suwanna Satha-Anand

Buddhism on Sexuality and Enlightenment

Since Isaline Blew Horner's pioneering work on women in Buddhism was published in 1930, there have been numerous works on this theme. The key questions they addressed were (1) what were the roles and status of women in original Buddhism and (2) whether and how had Buddhism contributed to the elevation of women's status as a result of the Buddha's permission to establish the *bhikkhuni sangha*, or the female monk order.[1] However, it seems to me that a more fundamental question needs to be addressed so that the Buddhist attitude toward women or the position of women in general can be better understood. The fundamental issue concerns the relationship between sexuality and enlightenment. How does Buddhism place sexuality within its scheme of ideals? This could be essential to a meaningful interreligious discussion of good sex.

As I explore this question here, I intend to illustrate that the overcoming of attachment to sexuality is a prerequisite for attaining enlightenment. Enlightenment, as a state of joyful bliss, is the Buddhist ideal of transcending death by overcoming the cycles of birth and death, which are themselves the locus of sufferings. Toward the end of the chapter, the question of sexuality *after* enlightenment will be addressed, revealing the implications for women's religious wisdom on sexuality.

Sexuality and Enlightenment

Unlike Christianity, wherein revelation is the source of religious authority, Buddhism, as a nontheistic religion, bases its religious efficacy on the enlightenment of the Buddha. Three major events have direct bearing on the understanding of sexuality and enlightenment in Buddhism. First, there are the three unseemly sights—old age, sickness, and death—spotted by Prince Siddhattha. These encounters with the truth of existence led the young prince into pondering ways to overcome these inevitable facts of life. Second, there is Prince Siddhattha's leaving the life of a householder on the same night his consort gave birth to their first child. Third, there is the last temptation of Prince Siddhattha by the three seductive daughters of Mara under the bodhi tree. The Buddha-to-be remained unimpressed by their seductive manifestations and became enlightened moments later.

These three episodes in the life of the Buddha indicate that the Buddhist truth is an attempt to overcome the sufferings of life and death. This search necessitates leaving the life of a householder and, among other things, going beyond sexual attachment. In other words, attachment to sexuality needs to be overcome in order to reach the ultimate truth.

Within patriarchical Hinduism, the religiocultural milieu from which Buddhism emerged, one of the ultimate goals is to acquire immortality through a father's continuing life in his son. A whole system of theology and ritualistic prescriptions are created to perpetuate the person of the father in the son. Within this scheme, the most important role of a woman is as the wife who by becoming pregnant helps provide rebirth for her husband in his son, and who herself can ultimately go to heaven with her husband. In this sense, a woman's sexuality as expressed through reproduction is needed to perpetuate a man's rebirth. And in so doing, she fulfills her religious roles. As Professor Patrick Olivelle puts it, "Women, in this ritual theology, are not independent ritual actors. They can only hope to get to heaven as wives, hanging on to their husband's ritual coat-tails."[2]

In Hinduism, the most important aspect of a human being is his personhood, essentially embedded in social relationships, explained and justified by an elaborate theology. Women are recruited members of this grand narrative. In Buddhism, on the other hand, it seems that the most important meaning of a human being is one's self, which is defined by one's individual karma, accumulating and operating across lifetimes.[3] In this sense, women as well as men are their own religiomoral agents. In contrast to its role in patriarchical Hinduism, reproductive sex in Buddhism is not a condition for being religious; rather, it needs to be overcome so that liberation from cycles of rebirth can be achieved. Sex as essentially related to reproduction is not the main concern for women in Buddhism.

Sex as Entanglement

According to the Buddha, women have the potential to become enlightened.[4] This means that women are independent religiomoral agents, not instruments. Although with initial reluctance, the Buddha gave permission to women to receive full ordination.[5] However, it is clear from the very first *vinaya*, or rule for monks, that sex is strictly prohibited. It is a violation that would entail permanent expulsion from the *sangha* (a community of Buddhist monks).[6] These two conditions taken together would indicate that it is sex, not women, that is an obstacle to the Buddhist's ultimate goal. This point is crucial, for a lot of literature on women and Buddhism, without making this distinction, still asks whether certain passages in the Buddhist Tripitaka (Buddhist Scriptures) are misogynist or not.[7] If we understand that the enemy in Buddhism is attachment to sex, not to women, then we understand that when a passage with disparaging statements about "women" is encountered, the content simply indicates the sexual. If the Buddha had been talking to women instead of to men disciples, he might also have made not so flattering statements about "men." And in those places, "men" would connote the sexual as well. However, as most of the records in the Tripitaka are about men disciples, the many negative passages apparently about women tend to create an image of misogynist groups.

According to the Buddha, for women as well as for men, nothing can take hold of one's mind (or "obsess the heart") as much as the bodily appearance, voice, scent, taste, and touch of the opposite sex.[8] Given this power of sexual obsession, it is not surprising to find the Buddha giving instructions to his monks not "to frequent householders, as frequenting leads to seeing (women), seeing leads to relationship, relationship leads to familiarity, familiarity leads to attention, attention leads to non-commitment to religious pursuits."[9] The dangers of being involved in potential sexual encounters are well documented in many disparaging statements made by the Buddha about "women," such as this one:

> It would be better, foolish man, to put your male organ into the mouth of a terrible and poisonous snake than into a woman. . . . It would be better,

foolish man, to put it into a blazing, burning, red-hot charcoal pit than into a woman. Why? On account of *that*, foolish man, you might die, or suffer deadly agony, but would not cause you to pass, at the breaking up of the body after death, to a lower rebirth, a bad destiny, to ruin, to hell. But on account of *this,* foolish man, [you may].[10]

These strong words are for his male monk disciple who, after ordination, followed the wish of his parents to have an offspring to carry on the family name. As the sole male heir of a wealthy family, he impregnated his former wife.

Many of the most disparaging statements about women are found in the Jataka (tales about different births of the Buddha-to-be).[11] In one of the Jataka tales, women are compared with lions who eat flesh and blood, animals that take pleasure in hurting and killing for food.[12] At another place, women are condemned to death, as they do not act loyally.[13] However, these statements can be taken to indicate the dangers of sexual attachment to one's pursuit of Buddhist truth.

Of course, one can argue that the act of equating sex with women is itself misogynist. But I think that this argument holds water only if the highest spiritual attainment is open to men only. Because the Buddha confirms women's potential for enlightenment (and there is the bhikkhunis' testimony of actual attainment of the Buddhist truth), I hold that sexual attachment, not women, is the ultimate problem.

According to some feminists in the liberal West, sex needs to be liberated from reproduction before sexual pleasure, especially sexual pleasure for women, can be explored. In Buddhism, sexual pleasure is clearly recognized as indicating the "five sensual pleasures," namely, pleasures of form, taste, smell, voice, and touch. However, Buddhism certainly does not credit these pleasures of the senses with the highest value. Rather it might be accurate to say that, according to Buddhism, these pleasures are short-lived and transient and will lead only to suffering and unfulfilling consequences. In many places in the Tripitaka, the enjoyment of pleasures is discouraged on the ground that the body, which is the seat of these pleasures, is itself an "ornamented pot of filth."[14] The body is compared to an abscess, an anthill, a ball of foam (which is quickly rubbed away), a pot (which is created and necessarily destroyed sooner or later), a hospital (in which consciousness lies like an invalid), and a prison.[15] To counterbalance the human tendency to take pleasure in the body and develop strong attachment to self through the body, the Buddha often encourages his disciples to meditate on decomposing bodies in the cemetery.[16]

So far, it seems that according to Buddhism, nothing positive can be said about sex or sexuality. One needs to keep in mind that Buddhism encourages the life of a renouncer as the most direct way to achieve enlightenment. Along that path, the attraction of lay life is always there around the corner. Buddhism does not condemn sexual pleasure or desire for wealth for lay people.[17] The only restraint required of lay society concerning sex is abstinence from sexual misconduct; this is usually interpreted as not committing adultery. It might then be inferred that Buddhism does not condemn sexual pleasure for lay people, whether tied to reproduction or not. But for those who wish to pursue enlightenment as a direct goal, abstention from sex and the absence of sexual attachment are required. For a world renouncer, the Buddha's strategy seems to be a withdrawal from dictates of lay life. Some scholars argue that in Buddhism "liberation was thought to be fostered, not by just social forms, but by renunciation."[18] The only feasible relationship with the larger lay society is not one of radical reform, but one of withdrawal. Buddhism essentially focuses its effort on those who are intent on achieving the ultimate end.

As withdrawal is the fundamental strategy of the Buddha, an intensity of practice is devised for those who focus their lives on the ultimate end. Monks live by 227 *vinaya* rules, fully ordained nuns by 311. Lay people are minimally required to observe five precepts. As a world renouncer, the Buddha seems to leave the lay world pretty much alone. Statements about the roles of wives seem to reflect what is needed for a sustainable family, rather than for gender equality. Except for faithfulness, the five obligations of wives to husbands are different from those of husbands to wives.[19] According to Buddhism, the primary focus of religion is not the existing social institutions centering around the family; rather it is to leave the household life and pursue the life of renunciation. In one sense, Buddhism is neither revolutionary nor radical, as it leaves the lay world of greed and lust alone. In another sense, Buddhism avoids the complexities of lay life by leaving it behind and creating a new society that does not reproduce itself in the biological sense. Sex, as the first condition for birth and attachment to life, needs to be left behind.

Sexual Considerations within Renunciation

Once the Buddha confirms women's potential to achieve full enlightenment, and insists that sex and attachment to life need to be overcome
in order to achieve the ultimate end for women as well as for men, it is interesting to explore how he would manage the relationship between the female and male sangha as religious organizations. In order to investigate this
issue, one needs to understand three key factors: (1) the Buddha's initial
reluctance to allow female ordination; (2) the Buddha's final permission to
establish the bhikkhuni sangha; and (3) the possible reasons for establishing the eight heavy rules (*gurudhammas*) for bhikkhuni, which seem to establish the institutional subordination of nuns to the monks.

The sangha does not provide for itself; all material support is from donations from lay society. This primary condition makes it necessary for Buddhism, as an organization, to gain respect from the lay world. During the
first five years of the Buddha's mission, there were only monks, no nuns. It
should not be beyond the imagination to envision that Buddhism would have
received many criticisms from lay society as it recruited its male members,
who are sons, brothers and fathers. If women had been allowed ordination,
would it not have created a semblance of another "family" of renouncers?
How about the fact that many women are the backbone of the family in a
much more radical sense than male members? Moreover, perhaps the Buddha knew his disciples well. Even when women were only householders,
the monks had great difficulty in overcoming sexual attractions. What would
happen if many women lived a similar and closely situated life with them?
All these are of course speculative reasonings. The reasons of the Buddha
were not directly recorded.

The Buddha's final permission to allow full ordination for women can indicate many things. It can be a testimony to the Buddha's respect for
women's religious rights. This perspective would highly enhance the prestige of the Buddha in the eyes of modern-day feminists. On the other hand,
the conversation with Ananda that led to this decision clearly indicates that
apart from women's potential to become fully enlightened, the Buddha made
the decision on the ground that Mahapajapati, his own aunt, nursed him as
a child. He would look ungrateful if he said no. From this latter perspective, it seems that the Buddha had to make room for family considerations
within his own religious organization, whose establishment started from
"leaving the life of a householder."

This reluctant permission is made even more complicated by the fact that the Buddha laid down a set of eight heavy rules for potential nuns as prerequisites for ordination. Three of these rules are: (1) nuns, no matter how long they have been ordained, have to show proper respect to monks; (2) female ordinations need the presence of monks as well as nuns, but not vice versa; and (3) monks can teach nuns, but not vice versa.[20] In addition to these heavy rules, which indicate the institutional subordination of nuns to monks, there are other instances of privileging monks over nuns. For example, there are only four major offenses that entail permanent expulsion from the sangha for monks, whereas there are eight major offenses for nuns. If a nun touches a man, she faces permanent expulsion; the same offense does not require expulsion for monks. Of the 227 rules for monks, about 5 to 10 percent (ten to twenty rules) are sex-related prohibitions, whereas these make up about 10 to 15 percent (twenty to forty rules out of 311) for nuns.

From these considerations, we might conclude at this point that the institutional structure of gender relations in the householder world seems to repeat itself within the sangha organization. It seems that the Buddha was radical in terms of criticism of the caste system, but that he was not a reformist in terms of gender relations for the lay society. On the contrary, he seems to have adopted some form of subordination of one gender to another even in his society for renouncers.

Sexuality after Enlightenment

If sex is seen in Buddhism as entanglement that leads to attachment to life and by implication to cycles of rebirth, then what would sexuality mean for those who have been enlightened? This subject needs to be explored by way of four different but closely related observations. First, the Therigatha (verses that record the spiritual achievements of the first bhikkhunis) gives a clear illustration that once sexual desires are overcome, a new sense of relief and blissful freedom flourishes. Second, within the body of an enlightened being or *arahat,* the biology of sex still operates in a natural process, just as in the body of any other ordinary person. Third, the difference lies in the absence of psychological attachment to the biological function of sexual drives. Fourth, the Buddha honors bhikkhunis for their spiritual ability, even for one of them who was raped by a former lay admirer.

If we should choose one word to describe the ethos of the Therigatha, that one word would be *freedom*. The verses of seventy-three bhikkhunis reflect their liberation from household chores, attachment to youth and beauty, attachment to their former lovers or family members, and rebirths. One bhikkhuni, Muttatheri, mentions her liberation from three "bendings," namely, bending from cooking, bending from using the pestle, and bending from serving her husband.[21] A former courtesan, a woman of entertainment who was worth half a city, announces her retirement from form, her release from seduction, and her liberation from rebirths.[22] A former chief consort of King Bimbisara, whose youth and beauty are tempting to Mara (a Buddhist personification of evil), declares that she has uprooted her sexual passions and has been liberated from all sexual pleasures, which are but spears and lances that make people hostage to the human predicament.[23] In a most dramatic incident recorded in the Therigatha, Supatheri, upon encountering in the forest a young womanizer who tries to seduce her with charming words, plucks out one of her eyes and gives it to him "to admire." She declares that she has uprooted her passions, which are compared to such experiences as being dropped into a hole of burning fire or falling into poison. Upon seeing her plucked-out eye, his passions are gone and he begs for her forgiveness.[24]

It is interesting to note that in the Abhidhamma section of the Tripitaka, questions arise about whether an arahat, an enlightened being, still emits semen. This question was first posed in asking whether various manifestations of sexual passion still exist in an arahat. The answer is in the negative. Then it is explained that the emitting of semen in an arahat originates from food and drink intake, not "sexual intention."[25] An enlightened being's sexual functions are merely "biological," they are not indicative of desires. Therefore, "an arahat still emits semen, but he neither engages in sex nor gives rise to sexual indulgence."[26] Another indicator that sex for an arahat is just a biological function without any psychological attachment is the fact that an enlightened being, when asleep, cannot have wet dreams.[27] For an enlightened being, sexual passions have been uprooted even from the subconscious.

Another most fascinating aspect of sexuality after enlightenment is the fact that the Buddha specially honored two of his most prominent female arahats, Khema and Ubonvanna, as exemplary disciples, the former having excelled in wisdom, the latter in performing miracles. These two bhikkhunis are honored in comparison to the Buddha's two chief disciples, Sariputra and Moggalana.[28] One should also take note that while meditating in the forest, Ubonvanna after becoming enlightened was attacked and raped by a former lay admirer. After the incident, the Buddha laid down the rule that nuns must not take up residence during the rainy season in a place where there is no monk. In a later commentary on the incident, the Buddha responded to some monks' discussion of whether an arahat still enjoys sexual pleasures in the negative: "People who are no longer attached to sexual pleasures are like drops of water on a lotus leaf, are like a tiny seed impossibly standing on a pointed end of an iron rod. I would say that they are brahmins."[29]

This same Ubonvanna-theri who was raped, and whose rape incident was used as context for discussing whether an arahat still enjoys sexual pleasures, is the Ubonvanna honored by the Buddha as one of his exemplary disciples. It is clear from the Buddha's response that the sin will be on the shoulders of the rapist. The Buddha not only saw the incident as irrelevant to Ubonvanna-theri's merit, he greatly honored her with a special place among his female disciples.

Sexuality of a Buddha

One of the thorniest issues about the status of women in Buddhism is the statement, "Woman cannot become a Buddha." Neither can she become a Universal Monarch, Lord Sakka, Mara (Lord of Evil), or Lord Brahma.[30] There are different sets of requirements for these four categories of being "lord."[31] It should be noted that not all of these categories are morally sound, but they all seem to share a common element: being in the highest position in a domain of *dhamma* (Buddha), of political world (Universal Monarch), of heavens (Lord Sakka), of the world of evil (Mara), and of the world of brahma (Lord Brahma). In other words, these are positions not merely of personal achievement but of highest power in a realm. As an example, I will discuss the impossibility for woman to become lord in the realm of *dhamma*.

Scholars sympathetic to feminism have been trying to discredit the idea that woman cannot become lord by pointing out that these statements were added to the text from a later period, probably between the late third century and the first century B.C.E.[32] The underlying assumption seems to be that historical authenticity depends on temporal proximity to the time of the Buddha. This argument might be valid from the point of view of textual analysis, but a question still needs to be answered, namely, Are those statements justifiable within the philosophical framework of Buddhism itself?

Traditional scholars of Buddhism tend to defend the impossibility of woman becoming a buddha on the ground that among the eight prerequisite conditions, there is one that is not possible for women, namely, being a man.[33] Moreover, according to a theory of the thirty-two auspicious bodily signs of a great man, having a concealed penis (penis in sheath) is one of the thirty-two bodily signs.[34] Since woman does not have a penis, it is not possible for her to have a concealed one. Therefore, it is impossible for her to become a buddha.

In Mahayana Buddhism, there are different strategies to deal with this issue. Sexual transformation of a female *bodhisattva* into a male form and absence of gender differentiation in *sunyata,* or emptiness, are two of the most common ways to argue against the impossibility of woman becoming a buddha.[35] However, it is my contention that one should also deal with this statement on philosophical grounds.

Although the statement was brought into Buddhism at least two hundred years after the death of the Buddha, it has been an issue of debate ever since. If we take Buddhism to be a universal message for the cessation of suffering for humankind, where all beings, male and female, encounter suffering through cycles of birth and death, where all beings, male and female, are the recipients and agents of their own karma, then the requirement of being "male" in these positions does not seem to be justifiable on philosophical grounds.

Are not the three characteristics of existence—impermanence, suffering, and nonself—and the eightfold noble paths, after all, gender blind? If we take away the sex requirements in each of the four types of being lord and consider only what each has to do, there seems to be no reason to conclude a priori that women, as women, cannot perform those tasks. However, if we include under the term *Buddhism* all the ideational elements and debates accumulated across the two and a half millennia of its history, we have to admit that this belief has been accepted and respected under the rubric of Buddhism. We should perhaps also keep in mind that if we accept that in

Buddhism a woman in this life can become a man in the next and vice versa, many times around, then there would be two possible contradictory solutions. First, the issue of being male or female is not crucial, as the boundary lines can be easily crossed. If a woman wishes to become a buddha, she just makes a wish to become a male in her future rebirth(s), or she can perform instant sex transformation, as in the cases in some Mahayana *sutras*. Second, the issue may have become absolute, precisely because as a woman now in this lifetime or in the female form, the possibility of becoming a buddha is not there. In both cases, though, the androcentrism of existing socioreligious institutions remains intact.

The Ultimate Test

It seems that Buddhism, by prescribing an ascetic life of renunciation, views sexual attachment as one of the major hindrances toward enlightenment. Sex is one of the major sources of sensual pleasures, powerful "entangling forces" that keep the aspirants within the web of household life. As an ideal, Buddhism offers a deathless life right now, in which liberation from cycles of rebirth, hence from suffering, can be achieved. The recognition that sex involves powerful pleasures is explicitly stated. But powerful pleasures lead only to more suffering, because of the inherent power of sensual pleasure and also because of its reproductive potential.

On the other hand, women as human beings are their own moral and spiritual agents and have the capacity to reach enlightenment. In this sense, Buddhism is not misogynist. However, in creating a religious organization, the sangha, which needs lay support for existence, the Buddha seemed to have adopted a very accommodating attitude toward lay society, not on caste but on gender issues. Some scholars call this ambivalence of Buddhism "multivocality" as opposed to an "inconsistent ambivalence."[36] However, as a religious institution, it is difficult to deny that in the sangha there are elements of female subordination to the male.

Another interesting position on women is that the Buddha bestows great honor on his female disciples, giving credit to some five hundred enlightened bhikkhunis and citing thirteen for their expertise in various fields of practice. The Buddha also honors one rape victim as a chief and exemplary disciple. Yet Buddhism as a historical institution has insisted on saving the places of highest power for males only. This position, I contend, cannot be defended on philosophical grounds within the conceptual framework of Buddhism itself. But there is no denying that the belief that only a man can attain buddhahood has been accepted as a Buddhist tradition for centuries.

When we have these two conflicting and contending positions on women in a tradition, it is my contention that the ultimate test would be whether either, and if so which, of the two would lead to liberation. Both the philosophy and the institution need to be tested against the ultimate end of Buddhism itself. The Buddhist wisdom on sexuality then indicates the power, the limitations, the ensnaring effects of sex that ultimately lead to suffering. Women's religious wisdom on sexuality helps lay bare where the problem is, namely within the hearts and minds of the practitioners, not in women's bodies. In comparing the verses on enlightenment of the *theras* (senior monks) in the Theragatha with those of the *theris* (senior nuns) in the Therigatha, one prominent difference emerges. There are many more negative passages about the ensnaring power of women and their bodies for the monks than there are for the nuns.[37] In many cases, the nuns present images of their once beautiful but now decaying bodies as a locus for the testimony of the Buddhist truth of impermanence. There is a conspicuous absence of disparaging statements about the ensnaring power of men or their bodies.

For an enlightened being, sex is a natural biological process, not a seat for sensual attachment. Institutional subordination of female to male renouncers is an ad hoc cultural construct that serves sociohistorical purposes, not spiritual liberation. All these issues as clarified through women's wisdom on sexuality can thus be relevant and efficacious for both males and females.

Part III
Reconstruction of Sexualities

Creative strategies for reconstructing sexualities on the basis of the foregoing and other critiques require careful religious and social consideration. In the chapters in part 3, the authors offer imaginative and transgressive thinking in order to reframe the contexts in which so many women suffer. One common thread here is that those who are most deeply affected have the right to name the situation as they see it, not to have interpretations laid upon them. These strategies with reference to sexualities can be part of a larger justice-seeking agenda.

Judith Plaskow, a U.S. theologian, in "Authority, Resistance, and Transformation: Jewish Feminist Reflections on Good Sex" raises the question of how feminists ground and argue for particular criticisms and constructive reworkings of tradition in thinking about good sex. Using the Jewish insistence on heterosexual marriage as a concrete example of religious barriers to good sex, she argues that a feminist constructive stance must begin with resistance to and criticism of the oppressive aspects of tradition. Feminists must then offer an alternative vision rooted not in some positive "essence" of tradition, but in the concrete struggles of particular groups working toward greater inclusiveness.

Dorothy Ko, a U.S. historian born in Hong Kong, in "The Sex of Footbinding" demonstrates how much culture matters in the creation of sexual desire by exploring interpretations of footbinding in their own cultural contexts. In the ambiguous space opened by three discourses about footbinding—those of a U.S. radical feminist, a Confucian male, and an elite Chinese female—she confronts the power and limitations of an ideology of the autonomous self as the seat of individuation and sexual pleasure. Ultimately, she argues, it is up to the Other woman in the reconstructive process to decide what constitutes good sex, and to decide how to authorize herself, whether within or outside her cultural tradition.

Mary E. Hunt, a U.S. theologian, in "Just Good Sex: Feminist Catholicism and Human Rights" offers a constructive model for holding the tension between an emphasis on sexuality and the urgency of other social justice concerns. She proposes a renewed human rights discourse to link women's sexuality to a larger struggle for justice. From a feminist Catholic starting point she promotes what she calls "just good sex" to describe sex that is safe, pleasurable, community building, and conducive of justice. This reconstructive move offers many goods—personal and social, moral and economic, traditional and innovative—as women bring their religious wisdom to bear on sexuality.

Nine

Judith Plaskow

Authority, Resistance, and Transformation

Jewish Feminist Reflections on Good Sex

The effort to develop feminist accounts of good sex within the context of patriarchal religious traditions raises a host of methodological problems. The very formulation of the project recognizes the tensions between feminism as a social movement committed to the liberation of women from all forms of oppression, and the direction and intention of traditions that have contributed directly and indirectly to women's subordination and marginalization in religion and society. The Good Sex project begins from the reality that women have rarely participated in the formulation of sexual norms and values in the major world religions, and that religious sexual values have seldom been conducive to the health or well-being of women.[1] In bringing together a group of women connected to different traditions, the project seeks to create a space in which the participants can "think new thoughts," reflecting on sexuality from the perspective of the concerns and experiences of women in our cultures. But at the same time, it assumes that these new thoughts will somehow remain in relation to the religions being transformed and will possibly authenticate themselves through connection to neglected or dissident strands within those religions.[2] The project thus immediately becomes entangled in fundamental questions about how feminists argue for and make change, especially when the changes envisioned may radically challenge central elements of tradition.

Defining the Questions

My interest in this chapter is not so much in defining good sex from a Jewish feminist perspective as in thinking about how to think about the issue. As a Jewish feminist theologian, I find that the task of transforming Jewish sexual norms raises questions about authority that I must sort out before I can begin to think substantively about the characteristics of good sex. The Jewish feminist movement in the United States has flourished in the context of a decentralized, remarkably diverse Jewish community, in which there are many competing visions of the nature of Judaism and many opportunities to shape Jewish life in new directions. In a situation in which the great majority of U.S. Jews have rejected or are redefining elements of traditional Jewish belief and practice, the issue of authority is crucial and has implications well beyond the area of sexuality.[3] The question of how to ground and argue for criticisms or constructive reworkings of religious tradition is pressing for any theology or group that does not simply assume the validity of traditional sources of authority, such as Scripture, revelation, or centralized religious leadership.[4] Yet, because sexual control of women is such a key element in broader patriarchal control, the topic of sexuality raises the issue of authority with particular vividness and urgency. On what basis can feminists advocate particular visions of sexuality in ways that will prove intelligible and convincing to others?

The problem of authority arises for feminists as soon as we begin to challenge any aspect of the status and role of women. Once we acknowledge the possibility of deeply questioning any element of tradition, we seem to undermine the hope of religious certainty at a level that goes far beyond the specific issue at hand. However narrow the grounds for a particular criticism—and feminist criticisms of the treatment of women and religious sexual values are in fact deep and wide-ranging—rejecting any element of tradition throws all the rest into question. This is because, however much feminists still may value certain insights and perspectives we glean from our traditions, we no longer value them simply because they are there. Rather, we are confronted with having to self-consciously appropriate and reappropriate from the conflicted strands within each tradition those that make sense and bear fruit in our own lives, finding ways to explain our choices that make sense both to ourselves and to others. Logically, we cannot have it both ways. We cannot both deny the authority of religious tradition where it negates our feminist values and, at the same time, build on that authority where it seems to support those values.

A lot of recent scholarship on Jewish attitudes toward sexuality intensifies this issue of authority in that it highlights the tensions and disagreements within Jewish tradition, denying the reality of any unitary perspective.[5] Such a move is enormously helpful in deconstructing fundamentalist appeals to religious authority, in that it makes clear that all claims to authority involve selectivity, that Jewish tradition by no means speaks on sexuality with a self-evident, unambiguous voice. This scholarship is also useful to feminist reconstructions of religion, in that it surfaces minority or dissident viewpoints in the Jewish past that may counter dominant perspectives on issues of sexual values. At the same time, however, in dissolving the purported unity of Jewish tradition into a series of dissonant and ever-shifting strands, it increases the difficulty of arguing for the priority or authority of one strand over any other. Jewish tradition—like all religious traditions—is characterized by continual contesting of key issues, which issues are in turn continually redefined in different geographic locations and different historical contexts. Notions of authority are also continually reinterpreted in accordance with the outcome of such contests. Claiming the authority of a specific strand, then, is not a matter of identifying the essential and authentic voice of *the* Jewish tradition. Rather, it is part of a contest in our own time over which voices claiming to speak for tradition will prove compelling to a significant proportion of the Jewish people.

The complex and contradictory nature of Jewish teachings on sexuality, moreover, points to another problem in privileging neglected, positive themes within Jewish tradition. All too often in feminist discussion, highlighting the liberating elements of a tradition as its authoritative voice involves disregarding the strands that have been oppressive. The troublesome aspects of a tradition do not disappear, however, simply because we ignore them, but are left to shape consciousness and affect hearts and minds. Thus, appealing to the first creation story, in which male and female are made in God's image, and ignoring the second, in which woman is made from man, leaves intact the latter account to be used by others as a continuing justification for the subordination of women. Similarly, appealing to those elements in Judaism that honor the importance of married sex as a value in its own right apart from procreation, while neglecting the ways in which even married sex is restricted and controlled, allows the sexual control of women to continue unexamined as part of the fabric of Jewish marriage. But if one does acknowledge and attempt to grapple with the oppressive aspects of a tradition, the question inevitably arises as to the grounds on which its nonoppressive elements can be considered more fundamental.

A final problem relating to authority concerns the sources that are relevant in thinking about the subject of sexuality. Given that any reconstruction of tradition necessarily selects from the conflicting voices on a particular issue, still, what texts are even germane to a consideration of this topic? It is striking that, when issues of sexuality are discussed in religious contexts, a handful of texts are often cited and argued about over and over, as if they were the only sources relevant to shaping norms around sexual behavior. In the Jewish community, debates around homosexuality have often revolved around two verses in Leviticus and rabbinic commentary on them, while Christians add to the scanty resources in the Hebrew Bible a third verse in Romans. This approach ignores the host of other injunctions in the Bible and rabbinic tradition about forming ethical relationships, creating community, and ensuring social justice. It fails to view sexuality as just one dimension of human relationship, embedded in a constellation of familial, interpersonal, and communal connections that shape, support, or deform it. Instead, sexuality is seen as a peculiar problem for ethics, a discrete and troublesome domain requiring unique regulation. In addition to confronting problems around grounding sexual values, therefore, feminist accounts of sexuality also need to locate the issue in a larger social context. Building on the early feminist insight that the personal is the political, feminists need to insist that good sex on the interpersonal level is possible only in the context of just social, political, and economic relations.[6]

Thinking about Compulsory Heterosexuality

I would like to illustrate the ways in which some of these issues concerning authority come into play in relation to a particular dimension of sexuality, by reflecting on compulsory heterosexuality within the Jewish tradition as a barrier to good sex. I choose to focus on a central oppressive element in my tradition rather than on some emancipatory theme, because I believe that it is the negative aspects of tradition that most profoundly shape women's current sexual situation, and that most require attention and transformation. In my view, the starting point for feminists in thinking about good sex must be resistance. Feminists must begin by examining and dismantling the institutions that stand in the way of women even imagining fully our needs and desires.

The concept of "compulsory heterosexuality," which Adrienne Rich placed on the U.S. feminist agenda through her well-known essay on the topic, refers to the complex social and political processes through which people learn how and are made to be heterosexual.[7] The first and simplest way in which heterosexuality is made compulsory is that other modes of sexual expression are forbidden on pain of punishment or death. Such a prohibition on male/male anal intercourse appears in Leviticus 18:22 and 20:13 and forms the starting point for all Jewish discussion of homosexuality—as well as Jewish gay and lesbian resistance to traditional attitudes toward homosexuality. Although lesbianism is not mentioned explicitly in the Bible, the rabbis find a reference to it in Leviticus 18:3, "You shall not copy the practices of the land of Egypt . . . or the land of Canaan." They interpret the practices in question as a man marrying a man and a woman marrying a woman. Both the Palestinian and Babylonian Talmuds also contain brief discussions of whether women who "'rub' with each other" are considered to have committed an illicit sexual act and are therefore forbidden to marry a priest.[8] The rabbis' consensus that such acts are "mere licentiousness," that is, not real sex, and therefore not disqualifying, reveals another weapon in the arsenal of compulsory heterosexuality: rendering sex between women invisible by defining it as impossible.[9]

While contemporary Jewish debates about homosexuality generally revolve rather narrowly around these verses in Leviticus and the few rabbinic sources interpreting them, I find this material less useful for understanding heterosexuality as an institution than the pervasive assumption in biblical and rabbinic texts that heterosexual marriage is the norm for adult life. In getting at this larger context of Jewish attitudes toward marriage and family relations, Genesis 3:16—"Your desire shall be for your husband and he shall rule over you"—is far more revealing than Leviticus 18 and 20, because it names the connection between gender complementarity, compulsory heterosexuality, and the subordination of women. Gayle Rubin, in her classic essay "The Traffic in Women," argues that, in traditional societies, the social organization of sex is built on the links between "gender roles, obligatory

heterosexuality and the constraint of female sexuality."[10] Gender roles guarantee that the smallest viable social unit will consist of one man and one
woman whose desire must be directed toward each other, at the same time
that men have rights to exchange their female kin and control their wives
in marriage that women do not have either in themselves or in men.

Genesis 3:16–19, which describes God's punishments of Adam and Eve
for eating the fruit of the tree of knowledge, offers a remarkably condensed
and powerful statement of the connections laid out by Rubin. In increasing
Eve's pain in childbearing and punishing Adam with having to sweat and
toil to gain his bread, God assumes or ordains differentiated gender roles
and, at the same time, defines them asymmetrically. Eve's (heterosexual)
desire for her husband will keep her tied to childbearing, despite its pain-
fulness, and will allow him to "rule over" her. My point is not that compulsory heterosexuality as a Jewish institution is rooted in this story, but rather
that this myth of origins provides a lens for examining interrelationships
that are spelled out at length in Jewish narrative and law. In the Jewish case,
as in the traditional societies Rubin discusses, rigid gender roles support
the channeling of sex in marriage. A man who is not married (the texts
speak from a male perspective) is seen as less than whole, for only a man
and woman together constitute the image of God. The extensive laws regulating women's sexuality and placing it under the control of fathers or husbands ensure that women will be available for marriage to men who can be
fairly certain that their wife's sexuality belongs only to them.

In a context in which good sex is defined as sex that is under male control, the question of what constitutes good sex from women's perspectives
simply cannot be asked within the framework of the system. For the Bible
and for the rabbis, good sex is sex that supports and serves a patriarchal
social order. The so-called divinely ordained laws concerning marriage and
divorce, adultery, rape, and so on, allow for the regular and orderly transfer of women from the homes of fathers to the homes of husbands, or, if
need be, from one husband to another. Women's fears, desires, and prefer-
ences, their efforts to find meaning in or to resist this legislation, are
nonissues and "nondata" that are also nonsense in the context of the rabbinic world view.[11] As Rachel Adler points out in a powerful article about
women's role in the Jewish covenant community, the categories of a system of thought determine the questions it can ask, allowing it to pile up huge

amounts of information on certain questions while rendering others invisible. The problems that receive extensive attention in Jewish law are the "status problems of marriage, desertion, divorce and *chalitzah* [leverite marriage] which the tradition itself created and from whose consequences it now seeks to 'protect' women, since by its own rules they can never protect themselves."[12] Insofar as the rabbis do attempt to "protect" women—by trying to find ways to get a husband to divorce his wife if she so desires, for example—they indicate some awareness of the limits and injustices of the system they have created and, in this sense, offer some resources for criticism. But insofar as they are willing to address these injustices only within the framework of the system that gives rise to them, they close off any possibility of women entering as subjects and reframing the issues in genuinely new terms.

As Rubin's analysis suggests, however, control of women's sexuality is just one dimension of the institution of compulsory heterosexuality, which is also spelled out in *halakha* (Jewish law) in terms of property rights, work roles, and religious obligations and exemptions. In her book on the construction of gender in Roman-period Judaism, Miriam Peskowitz examines a Mishnaic passage that shows the rabbis in the act of extending a husband's power over the property his wife acquired before marriage, so that, while the wife may continue to own property, the husband controls it and is entitled to the profits that flow from it.[13] In their ensuing debate about the validity of this legal innovation, the rabbis involved presuppose that a man has authority over his wife. What they need to determine is the extent of that authority in the sphere of property ownership, much as in other contexts they will discuss a husband's power over his wife's sexuality. The conversation, Peskowitz argues, reveals that there are many nodes "in the construction of sexual difference," sexual control constituting only one area in which marriage allows a man to "rule over" his wife.[14]

The Jewish division of religious labor also presupposes and helps construct a social structure in which heterosexual marriage is the norm. The exemption of women from positive time-bound commandments—in particular, set times for daily prayer—assumes that they are involved in household obligations that are their first responsibility and priority. In caring for small children, observing the rules of *kashrut* (dietary laws), and preparing for holy days by cooking special foods and making their homes ready, women free men for their own prayer and Torah study and enable them to observe the dietary laws and the Sabbath and holidays fully. For their part, women need men to take the ritual roles in the home that they themselves are neither obligated nor educated to assume. In other words, the whole series of laws that exclude women from public religious life, laws that Jewish feminists have analyzed and criticized from the perspective of women's spiritual disempowerment, are also part of the system of compulsory heterosexuality. That system is not just about sex, but also about the organization of daily life around gender role differentiation and the power of men over women.

Because compulsory heterosexuality is interstructured with a whole network of sexual, social, economic, and religious relations in Jewish law, creating the preconditions for good sex cannot end with questioning the few biblical and rabbinic passages on same-sex relationships. The material on such relationships is scanty and specific, so that those advocating expanded rights for gays and lesbians have been able to challenge it from a number of directions. Are other forms of male sexual interaction, other than anal intercourse, forbidden by Leviticus?[15] Did the Torah or the rabbis have any concept of homosexuality as an orientation, or were they condemning homosexual acts performed by heterosexuals?[16] While such critical questions are important and useful in trying to gain acceptance for gays and lesbians within the framework of Jewish law, they never step outside that framework to confront the broader system of compulsory heterosexuality. That system controls and marginalizes all women, whether or not they are heterosexual, and whether or not they are married. It also makes illegitimate any sexual or life choice outside of heterosexual marriage, so that self-pleasuring, celibacy, singleness, cohabitation without marriage, et cetera, all constitute forms of resistance to compulsory heterosexuality.[17]

Once one begins to see the relationship between compulsory heterosexuality and sexism in its myriad forms, however, the questions about authority that I raised in the first part of this chapter return in all their power. How does one question this central aspect of Jewish tradition and still remain in relation to the tradition? Are there voices in traditional Jewish texts that dissent from or reveal fractures in this system, and on what basis can they be mobilized? Where do I, where does any contemporary feminist critic, stand in even raising these questions?

Starting Points

I would argue that the feminist critic must begin, not by allying herself with dissenting voices within her tradition, but by questioning the authority of tradition, resisting any framework that leaves no room for women's agency, and then proceeding to transform tradition by placing women at the center.[18] Feminism begins in resistance and vision, a resistance and vision that are not simply personal but are rooted in "communities of resistance and solidarity" that are challenging specific forms of oppression out of concrete experiences of alternative ways of being in the world.[19] Thus, the feminist and the lesbian, gay, and bisexual movements have allowed women to feel the power and potential of bonds between women; to experience an intimacy, sexual and otherwise, that often has been trivialized or undermined; and to claim our power as agents to participate fully in society and religious communities on terms that we define. This experience of the power of being, as Mary Daly described it early on, over against the institutions that have consigned women to nonbeing, does not of itself threaten these institutions or render them harmless, but it does provide starting points for imagining a different future and criticizing the forces that stand in its way.[20] To my mind, this experience, rather than any dissident strands within patriarchal religion, is the authoritative foundation of resistance and transformation. Given the conflicting voices within any normative text, the decision to claim such strands must come out of some experience of their greater power to support fullness of life for a larger group of people. Out of participation in a community of resistance and transformation, one then looks for and consciously claims the resistive elements in a particular tradition, in order to mobilize them toward a different future.[21]

What does this mean and not mean in relation to compulsory heterosexuality? Beyond the dimension of critique, which I see as central to a feminist appropriation of tradition, there are several ways in which feminists can find resources for resistance and transformation within our religious traditions. One is by deliberately allying ourselves with the self-critical strands in texts that have been understood as normative. In her early and influential reinterpretation of Genesis 2–3, Phyllis Trible pointed out that the explicit statement in Genesis 3:16 that a woman's "desire shall be for her husband, and he shall rule over [her]," occurs in the context of divine punishment for disobedience. Remarkably for a patriarchal society, the story does not depict women's subordination as natural and divinely ordained, but as a perversion of the created order that is a result of sin. Trible thus reads this story not as *pre*scribing male supremacy but as *de*scribing it, not as legitimating but as condemning it.[22] For her, the insight that male supremacy is a distortion of creation constitutes the true meaning of the biblical text, which thus stands over against patriarchy.

Given that the description of compulsory heterosexuality is part of the same passage, one could make a similar move, arguing that this aspect of social life too appears under the sign and judgment of sinfulness. But aside from the fact that such an approach would ignore Genesis 1, in which male and female together constitute the image of God, there are deeper problems with claiming to have found the true meaning of any biblical text. Just as every text was written in a specific historical, social, and religious context, so texts are interpreted in particular contexts that give rise to particular exegetical needs.

The current desire to find an underlying nonsexist or nonheterosexist vision in Scripture comes out of a political and religious situation in which various forms of fundamentalism are on the rise all over the globe and are attempting to tighten control over every area of women's lives. In the United States, the Christian Right has claimed the mantle of Christian authenticity, equating authenticity with control of sexuality and women, and the same dynamic is taking place within Judaism. As contemporary Judaism has become increasingly diverse and fragmented, issues of sexuality and women's roles have become the battleground for arguments about Jewish legitimacy. In a religious context in which the reactionary side of an increasingly heated debate claims divine authority for its position, it is tempting to argue that the essence or fundamental core of the tradition supports a progressive stance. But this is finally to get into an irresolvable shouting match in which each party claims God on its side. It also means that feminists accept in principle the authority of texts that are at many points antithetical to women's power and agency, and that can be used against the feminist cause as easily as for it.

Although the difference may be subtle, I see the claim to have discovered the authentic meaning of a tradition as different from self-consciously drawing on the dissident voices within it, while grounding oneself in a community that is actively working to create a Jewish future in which women are full Jews and full persons. For the purposes of resistance, it can be strategically useful to point to the contradictions or moments of self-criticism within normative texts, showing how opposing positions can be justified on the basis of the same sources. Yet it is not useful to debate about which position is finally more authentic. From the perspective of the texts, the question of authenticity has no meaning; the texts encompass genuine disagreements. The argument over texts is in reality an argument over competing social visions. Whose version of the future will hold sway? Who will have the right to determine the distribution of society's goods and resources, to say whether a given social or religious system meets basic human needs? Precisely because this is the real issue in question, however, it is important to highlight the dissident strands within a sacred text in order to crack open or challenge dominant religious and social perspectives and thus enlarge the space for change. From this point of view, it is useful to notice that women's subordination is conjoined with heterosexuality in the context of punishment for sin, not because this renders invalid two thousand years of sexist and heterosexist readings, but because it helps us to imagine an alternative future.

A second way to mobilize resources for resistance and change is to look at Jewish sources with an eye to the historical possibilities that they simultaneously conceal and reveal, so that one can make visible the existence of "forbidden" sexual practices or transgressive gender relations.[23] Thus, for example, the same rabbinic passages that can be read as denying the possibility of sexual activity between women can also be seen as acknowledging the existence of such activity, but regarding it as inconsequential. When the rabbis discussed the question of whether a woman who "rubs" with another woman is permitted to marry a priest, they may have been aware of the female homoeroticism amply attested in Roman sources but seen it as not worth punishing.[24] From this perspective, the relative silence of Jewish tradition regarding both female and male homoerotic behavior may be construed as a form of permission. To take this view is not to deny the importance of heterosexuality as an ideology and an institution, but it is to suggest that behavior that did not threaten heterosexual marriage may not have been regarded with much seriousness.[25] Reading Jewish texts in light of what we know of cultural attitudes and practices at the time they were written

begins to uncover the complex historical reality masked by an exclusive focus on official prohibitions. It also broadens the sense of historical possibilities on which feminists can draw in seeking to transform the tradition
in the present.

Still a third strategy of resistance and transformation that is especially
important in dealing with issues of sexuality involves broadening the context of teachings on sexuality by looking at them through the lens of attitudes toward social justice. Rabbi Lisa Edwards, in a sermon on the Torah
portions that contain Leviticus 18 and 20, argued as follows:

> We are your gay and lesbian children: "'You must not seek vengeance,
> nor bear a grudge against the children of your people' (Lev. 19:18); we
> are your lesbian mothers and gay fathers: 'Revere your mother and your
> father, each of you' (19:3) . . . ; we are the stranger: 'You must not oppress
> the stranger. You shall love the stranger as yourself for you were strang-
> ers in the land of Egypt' (19:34)."[26]

In reading the prohibitions against male/male sex in the context of surrounding injunctions about just social relations, Edwards risks getting drawn
into arguments about which is the more fundamental or essential dimension of the tradition. But by focusing on broader social justice themes, she
also makes the critical point that any choice of sources in a debate about
the meaning and intent of tradition always involves selecting from conflicting perspectives. Moreover, she places the biblical passages on homosexuality in the context of the gay and lesbian community of resistance, focusing
on the interconnections between sexual ideologies and social injustice,
rather than on private sexual behavior.

Resistance and Transformation

I began this chapter by raising issues of authority and tradition,
and the authority of tradition in thinking about good sex. To what extent
can we ground ourselves in the positive resources in our traditions in thinking about good sex? How do I justify the choices that I make as I lift up
certain strands within Jewish tradition and repudiate others? I have argued
that the authority for singling out the self-critical and dissident elements in
our textual traditions comes not from the traditions themselves, but rather
from the new possibilities envisioned and created by the particular commu-

nities of solidarity and resistance in which we participate. As I reflect on the Good Sex group itself as one such community, I am struck by the extent to which our initial work together provides us with methodological clues for approaching our common project. Brought together to think constructively about good sex from our perspectives as women, we found ourselves focusing again and again on the ideologies and institutions that stand in the way of good sex in our different cultures. We began, in other words, from a stance of resistance, realizing that the first task in creating a space for good sex is addressing the many injustices that make good sex unimaginable for many of the women in the world. We also, however, spoke of resources in our own experiences, in our cultures, and, occasionally, in our religious traditions that provide us with glimpses of a sexuality and sensuality that we would like to make more possible, both in our own lives and the lives of others. We repeatedly return to these glimpses to authorize ourselves as we seek to find our way between what is most women's sexual reality, and what we want it to be. Struggling with this gulf, both in our social institutions and our religious traditions, we look for energy and insight not only, and not primarily, in the positive strands of our religious traditions, but in our communities of resistance and transformation.

Ten

Dorothy Ko

The Sex of Footbinding

In China today, the occasional tiny-footed granny brushing past a curious tourist is a relic. By the 1920s, the practice of footbinding went out of fashion in the coastal cities, although in such remote interior areas as Yunnan, young girls did not cease to bind until the 1950s. In spite of, or perhaps because of, the death of footbinding as a social practice, its symbolic meaning hardens and grows in relevance with the passing of time. It is no exaggeration to say that footbinding is synonymous with patriarchal subjection and bodily mutilation, as well as the loss of autonomy and movement. The universal appeal of this symbolic identification, I would argue, derives from the power of an ideology of the autonomous individual that goes hand in hand with a view of the body as a container for the inner self. The purpose of this chapter is to show that this idealized autonomous self is that of the Enlightenment man, and that it is imperative to think beyond it if we are to appreciate the ecology of female pleasures and the possibilities of good sex in times and cultures other than our own.

In other words, our primary concern is not footbinding as a social practice but its representation. Only by examining footbinding as a subject of knowledge can we begin to see that there is no innocent reader, just as it is impossible to obtain objective knowledge about other women's bodies. This will become clear when we consider how different is the image of footbinding produced by three writers from disparate locations: a 1970s radical feminist, a thirteenth-century Confucian male scholar, and an eighteenth-century Chinese footbound woman. Whereas the first imagined a new cosmology in which good sex is homoerotic and liberating, the Chinese male and female shared the prevalent view of their culture that individual pleasure is but one of the goals of good sex, and that the best sex will lead to the conception of a fetus. These divergent notions of good sex bespeak fundamental cultural differences on the cosmological location of individual bodies and their social significance.

The Cultural Contingency of Sex

The notion of sex as an end for individual happiness or personal intimacy, often in opposition to or detached from procreation, is alien to many peoples outside the modern European tradition. Historian Charlotte Furth has warned that modern readers of traditional Chinese medical discourses would be surprised to "confront an unfamiliar, holistic view of the human body which integrates primary vitalities at work in sexual acts with the overall organic processes of birth, growth, and decay." Furthermore, the reader has to take account of "a social construction that does not privilege erotic pleasure alone over all other possible aspects of the 'sexual.'" The alien character of traditional Chinese concepts of body, power, and cosmology challenges the modern reader to expand her boundary of the sexual.[1]

The importance of culture to this redefinition is stressed by cultural critic Rey Chow: "The term 'sexual' should be interpreted to mean not merely physiology or genital sex," wrote Chow, "but those areas of psychic life that are excluded from the conscious mind as a result of the pressures of *culture* and that are available to us only in 'irrational,' apparently disconnected forms."[2] The culture that represses the sexual by dismembering the self is not only Chinese or Confucian but also American or capitalist, as Radhika Balakrishnan's chapter has shown. It is important to critique the latter along with the former, so that we do not end by condemning the barbarism of "Chinese culture" using the yardstick of bourgeois individualism disguised as the universal good. And to begin to understand the sexual as defined by various cultures, we must also anchor our quest for the sex of footbinding in specific historical times and spaces.

In expanding the rubric of the sexual beyond genital sex and personal pleasure, both Furth and Chow are clearing the ground for a new feminist reading as the basis for new forms of knowledge and activism. This reading has two components. First, the identification of the sexual with the repressed means that sex is often mystified to the point of becoming hidden or invisible. Demystification begins with a recognition of the power of language to make and reorder worlds. Second, the identification of the sexual with the irrational and fragmented means that demystification takes the form of restitching or reconstituting the whole from its parts, with holistic feminist logic. As Mary Hunt has observed, in Euro-American discourses, the only way to talk about the erotics of the foot is through the language of the fetish.[3] To view footbinding as dismemberment in fact perpetuates the mystification of sex, making it all the more difficult to envision the Chinese female body as a whole. We need to take a new look at the bound foot—not in isolation but as an integral part of self. This is what this chapter attempts to do.

It is useful at this point to articulate the differences between sex and sexuality in terms of footbinding. The sex of footbinding, in terms of bodily sensations, postures of intercourse, and the catharsis of pain, is empirically not knowable.[4] But what we can know, as I attempt to show, is the conflicting claims on female bodies and labor, the conflation of male sexual and social powers, and the fragility of female bodies and pleasures: in short, the sexuality of footbinding. To the extent that sexuality is rooted in cultural conceptions of the body and political constellations of power, it is never simply a personal matter. Hence, "culture" and "body" are categories we have to interrogate first if we are to understand good sex and sexuality as cultural constructs.

Mary Daly's Journey into the Other's Homeland

The sex of footbinding that concerns feminist philosopher Mary Daly is the sex of the Other. Twenty years and many debates after its first publication in 1978, Daly's *Gyn/Ecology* remains a powerful statement of a radical feminist agenda that no facile accusation of racism can dismiss.[5] Its power—and limitations, as we will see—lies in its understanding of sex by way of body and language but bypassing culture. Daly's heroes—called Hags, Amazons, Spinsters, Crones, Furies, Harpies, Lesbians, and Goddesses—are the self-professed Other who dare to name the enemy: patriarchy or phallocracy. As the "prevailing religion of the entire planet," patriarchy's love is necrophilia, and its ritual is goddess-murder by sado-ritual (39, 61). The logic of Fatherland is "doublethink/doublefeel/doubledream," which mystifies its misogyny and tricks women into complicity (368). To cut through the doublethink, Daly admonishes all women to slash with a double axe. "As A-mazing Amazons with our Labryses we cut them down and move deeper and deeper into the Otherworld, which—since we are Other—is our Homeland" (xvii).

The journey to Homeland is an intergalactic voyage comprised of three passages. In the first, the hag sees through the enemy's myth of procession, a linear and continual process of Father reproducing himself by erasing the creativity of the Mother/Goddess in the Greco and Christian traditions. In the second passage, the hag sees through the enemy's intent of goddess murder. It is here that Chinese footbinding figures as an example of Sado-Ritual, appearing between Indian suttee and African female genital mutilation, which is followed by European witch burning and contemporary U.S. gynecology (rooted in Nazi medicine) and psychotherapy. In the third passage, the hag journeys to the Otherworld to discover her true self; there she sits with a loom of her own, spinning cosmic tapestries of texts/textiles.

Ethnic differences are both elided and highlighted in Daly's poetics. In highlighting the power of archetypes, she gives the impression that hags are hags everywhere. Defined as the Other of patriarchs, women transcend cultural and temporal variations. Apart from an occasional "universal," Daly prefers "intergalactic" or "planetary" in describing this commonality of cosmic proportions (172). Against this cosmic scheme, the insertion of such ethnic markers as "Indian," "Chinese," "African," "European," and "American" before each case study of the sado-ritual syndrome creates the impression of a recurring pattern. But the parallel between African and U.S. customs is an illusion. The hag-as-Other-of-man is more at home in the Christian tradition, as evinced by the vast discrepancy in length, texture, and nuance of the three "ethnic" chapters compared to the Euro-American chapters. Conceived in 1975, at the height of postwar disillusionment with the West, *Gyn/Ecology* is a radical critique of the Christian and capitalist religions; herein lies its subversive power. In this regard it is remarkably similar to an otherwise different work, Julia Kristeva's *About Chinese Women*. First published in France in 1974, Kristeva's reading of footbinding as women's claim to the symbolic serves to criticize Western epistemologies by idealizing China.[6]

Without detracting from Daly's pioneering vision and lasting influence, it is necessary to acknowledge that the feminist utopian Homeland of the Hag is not cosmic or a realm of freedom beyond culture, but a product of Daly's own culture-bound notions of body, language, and selfhood. She sees and knows the ethnic Other in terms of her own culture. Central to Daly's critique of footbinding and other sado-rituals is the bifurcated body and mind, even as she proclaims the interconnectedness of the two. Hence, "the foot purification (mutilation) ensured that women would be brainwashed as well."[7] Body binding *necessarily* results in mind binding, not only for footbound women but also for the scholars whose detached, objective tone was said to normalize and legitimize the practice (144). Daly has taken an anti-intellectual stance in her radical attempt to repair the Cartesian mind-body split. There can be no mind without the body. Moreover, it is a body that can feel the pains of other bodies, but Daly does not explain how this can come about. One can only surmise that this communion of bodies across cultures occurs by sympathetic magic, a mystical process.

Daly's endorsement of Andrea Dworkin suggests that the only responsible knowledge—the only feminist way to talk about footbinding and other women's bodies—is by way of the body and senses.[8] Daly is heartened that Dworkin, who describes "the horrible physical reality" of foot maiming in *Woman Hating*, shocks the reader into activism by way of the physical body. Daly's and Dworkin's pathway to activism is bodily knowledge: "to know, to sense, become incensed."[9] The priority enjoyed by the physical body is unmistakable, despite Daly's insistence that holistic knowledge involves "mind/imagination/emotions" (151). The mind does not do much besides serve as an instrument of deceit in legitimizing atrocities. The body alone knows and acts. By harping on the body that pains and rages, the hag ends up privileging the body over the mind as the gateway to truth and freedom.[10]

If we recall that the sexual refers to "those areas of psychic life that are excluded from the conscious mind as a result of the pressures of culture and that are available to us only in 'irrational,' apparently disconnected forms," then Daly's phantom mind has taken on the characteristics of the sexual as the repressed and the cut up. The slippage, no doubt unintended, is revealing: in protesting the castrating impulse ("he cuts to pieces") of all men in all cultures, the hag cuts up her own being and exposes the fragmented feminist self in the United States in 1975. All the earnest pleas of "connection," "interconnectedness," and "sisterhood" fall short of restitching the parts into a whole because Daly does not question the terms of this incorporation (xvi). The utopian union of Self and Friend in Otherland/Homeland is necessary and desirable only in a culture whose image of selfhood is bounded, integral, and individuated (371). Similarly, the utopian union of erotic love and friendship between women is meaningful only in a Euro-American context, where the Cartesian split between mind (friendship) and flesh (eros) is a prevalent way of thinking (372–376). In embracing the body that feels and a language that moves, Daly reinscribed the terms of this bifurcation. In the end, *Gyn/Ecology* is not about India, China, or Africa but rather about Daly's body-bound yearning for transcendence in a mystical merging with the Other's body.

What purpose, then, does the inclusion of the ethnic Other serve? Why bother to bring in suttee, footbinding, and genital mutilation? As it turns out, the ethnic Other is essential to Daly's fantastic idealized self of "Mind/Spirit/E-Motion," or the self of knowing/acting/self-centering in the utopian woman-identified environment called Gyn/Ecology (xv, 315). For only in visiting the ethnic Other but erasing culture—the very nature of an intergalactic journey—can the hag forget her own physical body by giving it to the Chinese. Hence the admission: "Only Hags . . . can kick off spiritbindings. This is possible, for mind/spirit has a resiliency that feet, once destroyed, can never have again" (42). In theory, Chinese, Indian, and African women can become Hags, but Daly's mode of representing and identifying with them through their physical bodies and pain has foreclosed that possibility. So the identification of "hag: body" we have just seen is reversed when ethnic locations are brought into the formula. We have instead a set of dualisms, with "hags: West: spirit-mind" on the one hand and "victims: non-West: body" on the other.

Clearly, it is not the resilience of Chinese women's spirit but the resilience of Chinese tradition that stunned and impressed Daly; she mentioned that the ordeal lasted a thousand years four times in the first ten pages of her narrative on footbinding (135, 137, 141, 145). It is thus not surprising that despite a profusion of bodies and pain in ethnic Otherland, their bodies are phantoms and their sexuality hopelessly mystified. Squeezing, biting, and sniffing the deformed stumps for a thousand years, Chinese men could be nothing but oversexed perverts, whereas the women were undersexed and incapable of pleasures, their only desire being the desire to survive (145). In Daly's eyes, the sex of footbinding is bad sex, an unmitigated disaster with no saving grace.

Postsocialist Postscript: The Sex of the Bourgeois Individual

It is the ultimate irony that twenty years later, the most interesting part of Daly's discourse on footbinding is her insights into its cultural logic. Relying only on male-authored and faulty source materials, she cut through the mystification with her double axe and saw that footbinding can be explained as a fetish that functioned by way of the transcendence of culture (shoes as "cultural contrivance," quoting Ernest Becker) over the animal foot (147). As the Other, Daly offers remarkable insights that many Chinese critics missed. Admiring her passion and astuteness, I do not want to claim that I know more, as an "authentic native."[11] My contention is simply that *Gyn/Ecology* makes for a problematic agenda for a global feminist movement. Fortunately, we can all relax because, as Daly so astutely pointed out, footbinding is dead; the Chinese nationalists and communists had championed its end since the 1920s not because they were radical feminists but because they needed to mobilize female labor for nation building (142).

Unable to think beyond her body yet unable to think through it, Daly remains hostage to her culture. The sexualized female subject that she celebrates and struggles to realize is one who enjoys bodily integrity, control over reproductive options, and freedom of sexual expression. This is the female version of the classic Enlightenment man, who is individuated, in control, and given to sexual gratification. Sexual pleasure and reproductive choice have come to signify the individuality we valorize. I am not suggesting that this sexualized individual should cease to be our feminist goal, but that it is merely one of many possible ways to conceive of female sexuality and desire. As Grace Jantzen argues in her chapter, we should beware of the trap of "compulsory pleasure." So accustomed are we to thinking of sex as a personal act, if not an individual right, that we need to backtrack by uncoupling the sexual from the personal, which would allow us to explore constructions of morality, agency, and value that do not rest on bourgeois individualism.

Ironically, many Chinese in the 1990s are embracing bourgeois individualism as an alternative to the hollow models of sacrificial socialist heroes. Several Chinese women scholars are raising questions about this unquestioned acceptance of the myth of the rational, autonomous individual. As feminist critic Tonglin Lu put it: "Will women ever succeed in creating a space for themselves through the search for an individual identity? Since the notion of individual identities is predicated on male subjecthood, isn't the search necessarily doomed?"[12] These are not academic questions; the quest for an individual self has so suffused the postsocialist zeitgeist that it surfaces in every media and in cultures high and low. Allow me to quote feminist scholar Zhong Xueping at length:

> Within the context of Chinese culture today, the search [for the true meaning of being a woman] . . . represents a desire for a recognition of individual values and individual expressions by both men and women. The insistence on a non-gendered real self is what is problematic. Instead of being perceived as a cultural issue, which is related to the notion of ideology, constructions of subjectivity, and possibility for resistance, searching for a real self is represented as an existential issue with some ultimate truth to it.[13]

The desires of these self-searching women in China today are thus fraught with ambiguities. "What is problematic is that when they want to do away with conventional models for women, such as subservient wife and good mother, Marxist-Leninist granny, and androgynized professionals, they are left with the notion of a free individual, which many theorists have criticized as both patriarchal and ahistorical." The problem of a postsocialist sisterhood comprised of women questing for an ungendered self is curiously similar to that of Mary Daly's intergalactic sisterhood. Zhong Xueping suggests that "the bond among women to quest for such a self, then, becomes a paradox. When women come together not only to challenge social norms but also to search for an ultimate self, their desire for such a self-identity is very often interpolated back into the patriarchy, where they may become more ready to accept their natural roles to be a real woman. And the existence of a sisterhood based on such a desire becomes too contingent to claim its ground."[14] We will ponder the activist implications of this bind at the end of this chapter. Meanwhile, we return to the theme of good sex by tracing its vital importance to the reproduction not only of the Chinese family, but also of the Confucian gender system.

The Confucian "Natural" Body

Confucianism is a name manufactured by Jesuit missionaries in the seventeenth century. Not only does it impart an artificial coherence to pluralist systems of thought, it also creates the illusion that Confucianism is a religion comparable to Christianity that can be understood in terms of theology and liturgy.[15] While we cannot here ponder the question, What is a religion? suffice it to note that in the Ming (1368–1644) and Qing (1644–1911) dynasties, both elite and popular cultures were so suffused with Confucian, Taoist, Buddhist, and other folk practices that it is futile to make clear-cut distinctions. When I use "Confucian culture" or "Confucian gender system" in this chapter, they describe two intertwined elements: a culture-power nexus that valorized the written word, and a family-centered ethics that derived its authority from a state-sanctioned Confucian canon.

Mary Daly is misinformed in stating that "no one was to blame for the evil of maiming women, since the reality of evil and maiming was not acknowledged. There were only 'beauty' and 'the extremes of pleasure.' Among the Chinese, footbinding was universally legitimated."[16] Acceptance might have been the case in practice, but in rhetoric quite the contrary is true. Before the late eighteenth century, the predominant mode of writing about footbinding in Chinese took the form of radical critique, indeed of ruthless condemnation.[17] Even more curious, the logic of this anti-footbinding polemics by Confucian male scholars is remarkably similar to that of Daly: footbinding is inhuman and barbaric because it maims the natural body and renders it useless.

The earliest extant writing on footbinding as a social practice was an indignant passage in the collected works of Che Ruoshui, a scholar-official from the Southern Song dynasty (1127–1279). Completed in 1274, this work was written at a time when domestic gentry women began to imitate entertainers by adopting footbinding:

The binding of women's feet, one does not know when this practice began. A little girl not yet four or five [by Chinese reckoning, which assumes
everyone is one year old at birth] is innocent and guiltless, but infinite
suffering was being inflicted upon her. One does not know what good does
it do to have the pair of feet bound into such a small size. When Dai Liang
of the Later Han dynasty [25–220] married out his daughter, she was
dressed in a silk upper garment and plain skirt, holding a bamboo box
and wearing wooden clogs. That means one cannot blame footbinding on
the ancients. Or, some say that it started with Consort Yang of the Tang
dynasty [650–904]. But no citations can be found about this neither.[18]

Che's identification with the "innocent and guiltless" young girl and sym-
pathy for her "infinite suffering" might have struck some as hypocritical,
but I see his anger as heartfelt, because Che's assumptions and modes of
knowing are entirely consistent with those of a Confucian elite man educated in the classics. In fact, so seminal are his concerns with utility ("what
good does it do") and quest for knowledge by way of philology that this passage became a model for a Confucian critique of footbinding in subsequent
dynasties. Che Ruoshui cited the example of Dai Liang, an ancient from *History of the Later Han Dynasty*, to prove that footbinding was not practiced in
the Later Han period. This search for origins in the classics is the typical
mode of knowing for male Confucian scholar-officials. Philology reinforced
the authority of the classical canon and the male scholar's prerogative as
its sole transmitter and interpreter.

It is hard to exaggerate the extent to which language and scholarship—
and by extension politicocultural power—are androcentric in the Confucian
world. According to the neo-Confucian political philosophy enshrined as orthodoxy in the Song dynasty, males from all classes were, at least in theory,
eligible to become scholar-officials if they passed the civil service examination, from which women were barred. In other words, men alone were privy
to reading the classics, poetry, and histories; they were authors, commen-
tators, and teachers. When the examination was made the sole gateway to
officialdom in the Song dynasty, cultural power became synonymous with
political power. Male hegemony thus constituted a hermetically sealed universe, a "culture-power nexus." Elite women did become educated, but there
was no channel that could translate their cultural knowledge into political

power. Che's pity for the suffering footbound girls, however heartfelt, is thus an identification with the inferior and powerless Other, a subaltern who otherwise could not be heard. If the footbound woman is Daly's ethnic Other, she is the Confucian gentleman's gendered Other. In either case, she is the object being spoken for.

What good does it do to bind the feet of women? Che's question invites us to ponder the larger question about the usefulness of female bodies in the male-centered Confucian world. There are two answers, one explicit and the other repressed and unspeakable. The explicit answer is that the female body is an instrument of finality (*xiao*) indispensable to a male-to-male transmission of bodies and ritual authority in the patrilineal family.[19] In Confucian canonical and didactic texts, this function of the female body as a womb is acknowledged, albeit only with averted eyes. The female body that did appear in texts is the body of decorum; her sexuality is elided, repressed, or denied. A good mother performs her duty not in the act of giving birth but in tending to the food and wine. A good widow is commendable not in battling her desires but in demurely spinning into the depths of the night.

The female body was more visible in a genre of medical texts offering advice on begetting children. Indeed, male physicians recognized and legitimized the importance of female pleasures to the goal of procreation. Charlotte Furth has written: "In this genre of writing, which became increasingly popular in the Ming and Qing, eros was valorized in a context which also encompassed successful conception, healthy gestation and childbirth, and even aspects of pediatrics."[20] Both male and female bodies were to be instruments of the Confucian family. This medical definition of good sex as sex that led to conception of a fetus promoted self-mastery and moderation. By luring the family men into self-dissipation, footbinding is at best marginal and at worst detrimental to this overarching concern. For this reason, footbinding was repeatedly condemned by Confucian scholars.

The second and unspeakable answer to the question of the usefulness of female bodies is that they exist for male erotic pleasure. Living in the age of its initial spread, scholar Che Ruoshui might have truly found footbinding repulsive. Yet there is no question that a gradual transformation in male erotic taste took place between the thirteenth and eighteenth centuries, as the bound foot became an object of male erotic fantasies. The decorum of the Confucian male-centered discourse, however, precluded male desires from being articulated except by way of such tactics of indirection as analogy, and only in selected genres: poetry, memoirs, and fictional male desires for the bound foot in particular and for female bodies in general had to be mystified if females were to continue to subscribe to the ideology of good sex as sex for procreation.[21] All the sexually explicit descriptions of unwrapping the binders or licking the bare foot were products of the nineteenth and twentieth centuries, when the very foundation of the patriarchal family came under attack.

Until then, the unspeakable male sexual fantasies were often expressed in terms of male desires for social power. As Tonglin Lu pointed out in her comparative readings of *Les Liaisons dangereuses* and a seventeenth-century Chinese erotic novel, in the French novel, "sexual power is identified with power of speech. . . . By contrast, in the Chinese erotic novel, *The Golden Lotus*, sexual power is much more closely associated with social position . . . an exclusive propriety of men."[22] This insight provides a partial explanation for the spread and normalization of footbinding: men's quest for social power. The bound foot was useful as a marker of elite status—not of the woman but of her man. This transfer of value from the woman's body to the social position of her men (and then conferred back to the woman as her social honor) is the principal operative mode in Confucian culture, evident also in the chastity cult. The economy of exchange is one of body for power, or to be exact, female body (either cut up, as in footbinding, or intact, as in the chastity cult) for social position or elite status as public expression of male power.

Yet it is here that a contradiction in the desires of the Confucian man is exposed. Earlier, we saw that the sanctioned answer to the question of a female body's usefulness is filial piety, expressed in terms of social motherhood. Filial piety also demanded, however, the preservation of a naturally integral body—the progeny of one's parents. Logically speaking, a Confucian man who desired a female to mother his son could not also desire her maimed foot. Many arguments against footbinding were in fact made on this ground; they are reminiscent of the Confucian attack on the Buddhist practice of cremation. There are, of course, no natural bodies in the Chinese cultural world as in ours. We cannot see or hear the body except by way of culture. Bodies are amorphous; in themselves, they do not say much. The first order of business for dominant ideologies is to engineer and police the boundaries that make gender, class, and ethnic distinctions visible but seemingly natural. Footbinding made it easier to tell females from males, but it did so by calling attention to the contrivance of culture, the fluidity of gender, and the conflicting allure of purity and danger embedded in female sexuality.

Contrary to modern assumptions, keepers of the Confucian tradition did not consider footbinding a Confucian practice; no mention of it can be found in the didactic literature for women. In diverting the female body, intended as an instrument of finality, to other nonproductive use, footbinding can even be said to be anti-Confucian. The incessant attacks on the practice, however, did serve a useful purpose in enabling the discursive formation of a natural body. It is in condemnation of footbinding that we find the most graphic descriptions of the natural body as integral, even geometric, and purposeful.[23] The relationship between footbinding and Confucian culture is thus fraught with ambiguities. From the one-sided discourse of footbinding, we begin to see how Confucian culture repressed the sexual. Furthermore, this repression exposed the contradictory male desires for woman to be both saint and tramp. Female sexuality is thus hopelessly mystified in the androcentric discourse.

Bifurcated Female Sexuality: The Saint and the Tramp

The conflicting Confucian claims on the female body found an unsatisfactory resolution in a bifurcation between "domesticity: wife" and "brothel: concubine-cum-prostitute." This bifurcation of female sexuality is expressed in terms of the bifurcation of the legal-social status of the individual woman into good/mean *(liang/jian)*. Goodness and meanness carry clear moral implications, but a socially mean woman is not automatically considered morally dubious. The policing of this stratified female sexuality took the form of periodic raids of brothels, temples, bookshops, and opera venues. These antipornography campaigns staged by imperial county magistrates and modern officials were never successful, because bad sex is in fact the supplement of good sex, completing the claims of the latter while exposing its inadequacies.

The dynamics of bifurcated female sexuality are so entrenched that it recently created a stir in modern Taiwan. The prosperous island may not look like a Confucian society, but after decades of education in Confucian morality, the population remains steeped in the habits of Confucian mores.

Rey Chow relates the remarks of a feminist, Xü Xiaodan, as she campaigned for a seat as lawmaker. Xü promised her supporters: "I will enter the Congress in the image of a dissolute woman; I will love the people with the soul of a female saint." In this posture, Chow sees the possibility of a radical feminist activism: "Women's sexuality, hitherto strictly organized according to the difference between the female saint and the dissolute woman, returns to a freedom that is not an arbitrary freedom to act as one wishes, but rather a freedom from the mutual reinforcement between education and morality, which are welded together by stratifying female sexuality."[24] In other words, this freedom is not modeled after that of the Enlightenment male subject but is instead a refusal of the roles prescribed by Confucian ideology.

To Chow, a truly radical feminist analysis and activism is built on a subject position like Xü's, one that encompasses the "bad" and the "good" woman. Only thus can we be sensitive to the inequality not only between the elite class and the masses, but also between the speaking subject and the spoken-for object.[25] From this perspective, good sex is the sex of a holistic woman, at once tramp and saint, who is beyond reproach.

The Good Woman Speaks: Texts, Not Textiles

If Confucian ethics demands that male desire be narrated with indirection, how much more treacherous it is to talk about female desires! The relegation of woman to the subject position of the spoken for is the clearest manifestation of the power of Confucian patriarchal culture. In such a predetermined discursive field, how does one retrieve female pleasures and desires? I offer no brilliant answer but merely a tactical reminder that we have to be mindful of this male-centered nature of literature and literary production in the Confucian-culture world when reading male representations of female desires. We have to be even more careful when reading female representations of their own desires (always in a language not their own). Because of the hegemonic nature of the Confucian discourse, there is no pure or authentic female voice outside it.

Mary Daly's Labrys is a useful tool as long as we wield it not two ways but four ways: what has to be cut through is not merely the doubletalk of male deception (the myth of the natural body) but also feminist self-deception (the myth of an ungendered autonomous self). A footbound woman's relationship with patriarchal culture—or an unfootbound woman's, for that matter—is at once identification and opposition. A woman could be identifying *and* resisting in being a tramp; she could be identifying *and* resisting in being a saint. Female desires are neither pure nor impure; intimations of "false consciousness" are counterproductive. Our concern is not intention but the economy of exchange or power inequalities in each case: Who benefits? Who pays the price? Who is speaking? Who is spoken for?

With this four-way axe, I wish to read a poem by an eighteenth-century poet, Hu Shilan. Hu, a gentry woman from the northeastern province of Zhili, fell upon hard times in midlife and started to work as an itinerant teacher. In a poem, she tried to recuperate the value of gentility in a nostalgic gesture:

> Remember those bygone days in the depth of my inner chambers,
> Perfumed pouch brushed against flesh tender as jade.
> My little maid held me as I stood by the flowery shades,
> Lest my arched shoes slip on mosses so green.
> Little did I know that in mid-life I would have to roam around,
> Braving the scorching sun and furious storms.[26]

The garden of her family mansion, the maid, jadelike flesh, and arched shoes all serve as props in the recreation of a leisurely childhood before class degradation. Through the symbol of footbinding, Hu expresses her desire for female seclusion as a class phenomenon. This is the most explicit Chinese statement that lends support to Thorstein Veblen's famous formulation that footbinding was a form of conspicuous consumption.[27] What do we make of this view of footbinding as the mark of gentility?

It is clear that Hu Shilan saw dependency or freedom in terms very different from ours. Seclusion in her inner chambers did not signify imprisonment but contrarily the freedom afforded by her elite status. Similarly, Hu's physical dependency on her maid was a performance that reversed the truth: the maid was the one dependent on her for economic sustenance. All the social power of elite men was conferred on their women as long as the latter fulfilled their filial duties as mothers and wives. No wonder that elite women were defenders of the Confucian status-class system and the patriarchal family.

Yet the elite woman's identification with her male counterpart is not complete. Hu Shilan's opposition to the official discourse is most evident in the latter half of her life as described in the second half of the poem. In resorting to the poetic convention of complaining about the hardship of life on the road, she remained loyal to the taste of her class. But her chosen profession—a teacher of females in the classics—allowed for new gender configurations. Traveling from female quarters to female quarters, professional teachers like her opened the way for a female-to-female tradition of learning that at once opposed and identified with the Confucian male discourse. It is significant that Hu's poems appear in an anthology compiled by another educated elite woman, Wanyan Yunzhu. It is also significant that the anthology was entitled *Correct Beginnings*, an allusion to the Confucian classic *Book of Songs*.[28] Both Hu and Wanyan claimed their cultural and moral authority by adhering to (some would say appropriating) the Confucian creed; they claimed their right to speak and write by rediscovering learned women in the classics.

In the end, Hu Shilan reinscribed herself as an elite woman by way of her learning and lyricism. Not only did she speak for her maid, she also continued to claim the power of representation, and the power of making a living through writing instead of manual labor or handiwork. Mary Daly's goal of a union of text and textile (*texere* in Latin means both) remains utopian in the mid-Qing cultural landscape Hu Shilan occupied and helped create.[29] No matter how poor and beleaguered, in her learning and sensibilities she remained an elite woman. The power of the word, once acquired from her elite kinsmen, became cultural capital for life, just as her bound feet remained a mark of her genteel upbringing. In using her literacy, she was at once identifying with and resisting the terms of male dominance in the Confucian world that worked by bifurcating text and textile, just as it bifurcated female sexuality. Although she was too modest to state it, Hu probably agreed with her men that good sex is sex that begets children.

Beyond Individualism and the Politics of Identification

To summarize the journey we have taken: we first dislodged sex from the personal and returned it to culture; then we considered how culture represses the sexual by mystifying it; we argued that this mystification can be undone to some extent if we read realistically instead of romantically; with a clear eye on how culture bound we all are, we searched for traces of the workings of body and power in specific historical and textual locations.

Now we may finally ponder the meaning of good sex and return sex to the personal in the process. Sex can be good to the woman concerned, her men, her family, women's networks, society, nation, and spiritual communities. *Goodness* is a productive term in its very ambiguity. Good sex—in excess, moderation, or abstinence—can be pleasurable or painful, wasteful or productive, self-effacing or self-affirming. The gaze finally returns to the woman. She chooses, acts, expresses, and creates, albeit not entirely as she pleases.

One footbound woman has spoken, but her voice is ambivalent. She did not speak the language of sado-ritual Mary Daly imagined, nor did she speak the language of defiant resistance we often wish a female speaking subject would. The ambivalence of Hu Shilan's voice echoed her ambivalent social location. As a literate woman and teacher of females, she was at once within and outside the male-centered Confucian learned tradition. She surprised us; the clarity of her tone conceals the complicated negotiations she had effected. Instead of offering easy, a priori answers, Hu Shilan invited us into her world. She implored us not to judge by our standards, values, and commitments but to listen to her regrets, pride, and remembrance. We have entered a new space between self and Other, where our bodies are not bound by the culture of bourgeois individualism. This space is not a garden in which multicultural flowers bloom equally bright; cultural relativism is wrought of rigidly demarcated self-Other boundaries that are in fact restrictive and parochial despite its global pretensions.

For us to visualize and realize this space as the basis of a new global community or solidarity, we need to revise the politics of identification that has constructed our perception of the Other: in order to complete our own selfhood and agency and in order to act, we have searched for the unfree Other who serves as the antithesis of everything we are and aspire to be. The footbound woman is useful to us because we need her to complete our own cherished sense of self. Herein lies the symbolic poignancy and continued relevance of footbinding, long after it has ceased to be a living social practice. In defining with whom we identify and whom we oppose, it is easy to fall into the habit of mirroring, reversing, or standing the enemy on its head. To counter gender stereotypes, postsocialist Chinese women yearn for an ungendered self; to fight the fragmentation and isolation of bourgeois individualism, many feminists strive for a transcendental global commonality.

This kind of politics of identification, based as it was on dualistic oppositions, made sense in the context of anticolonial nationalistic struggles in the first half of the twentieth century. In his study of the British colonization of Egypt, Timothy Mitchell has observed that "in the metaphysics of capitalist modernity, the world is experienced in terms of an ontological distinction between physical reality and its representation." He calls this power to manufacture a split between reality and representation a "colonizing power," one that is still at work after the sun set on the empire.[30] It is important to view this mechanism not simply as a malice of the West but as a fundamental dynamic of the operation of power in the modern world. Only thus can we begin to move beyond the episteme of dualisms.

We need to reimagine ourselves without knowing what forms and colors our new selves will assume. So what if we do not look at all like a bourgeois male subject, or if we begin to resemble the unfree Other? Beyond the dualities of self and Other, subjection and resistance, or body and mind lies a new way of seeing and knowing.

Eleven

Mary E. Hunt

Just Good Sex

Feminist Catholicism and Human Rights

Christianity, in particular Catholicism, has a well-earned reputation among progressives for being antibody, antiwoman, and antisex through centuries of dogmas, doctrines, and dealings that admit of few other interpretations. Virtually all nonfeminist Christian sexual ethical work has been done without reference to the widespread problem of male battering of women, the assumption that women are moral agents, and the claim that same-sex relationships, including sexual expression, can be morally good.[1]

These newly recognized factors that emerge from feminist theopolitical work set a fresh context for problematizing women's sexuality from a Catholic starting point. By theopolitical, I mean concern for meaning and value that incorporates both religious insight and claims about the divine, as well as a concrete praxis for social change. I propose to look at sexuality assuming that these factors are in place rather than setting about once again to prove them. I will explore what a Catholic feminist perspective might be on sex that is safe, pleasurable, community building, and conducive of justice, what I call "just good sex." I place it in the larger conversation about human rights that is indeed being rethought to reflect current concerns. This is a feminist theopolitical contribution to a global, interreligious conversation in which women's bodies, women ourselves, and women's sexuality are valued.

I intend *sexuality*, in its broadest sense, to encompass the range of ways

158

in which embodied beings, namely, people, interact in physical—sometimes, though not always, genital—fashion, as a means of self-expression and communication. Unless restricted by a modifier, I always intend *sexuality* to refer equally to everyone, without privileging heterosexuality in any way. This is clearly a different way of framing the term than traditional Catholic teaching in which *sexuality* refers only to heterosexuality, usually married and procreative. I suggest this basic move is necessary to level the ethical playing field as a precondition for respectful conversation.

My concern with these matters stems from my struggles as a white, U.S., lesbian feminist from the Catholic tradition to bring about social and especially sexual justice for women. As a Western woman with educational privilege, I take seriously my responsibility to transform a religious tradition that has colonized continents, as well as to counter the Vatican (both as church and as city-state) in its efforts to influence public policy against women's well-being. I restrict most of my analysis to the U.S. context to underscore how such problems are rooted firmly in the belly of the colonizing beast.

I make no pretense of speaking for all women in my situation, nor do I assume that my analysis applies across the board. In fact, being a woman, indeed a lesbian, is a small step away from the rest of the white, Western, monied hegemonic power I share. But such essentialism leads to divisions, where solidarity and resistance, as Judith Plaskow has observed in this volume, are needed. I prefer to locate myself in terms of a long-range commitment to and struggle for all women's well-being in a tradition that has codified a male-privileged anthropology. The consequences of this patriarchal view are played out in laws restricting access to birth control and abortion, as well as in customs that permit discrimination against lesbian, gay, bisexual, and transgendered people. These are some of the issues this volume lays the groundwork for changing.

For some, the very notions of feminism and Catholicism seem antithetical. However, Catholicism, contrary to the wishes of the kyriarchal church, has many expressions, including the women-church movement of which I am a part.[2] Women-church adherents prioritize social and sexual justice as basic expressions of faith. We find more in common with those who struggle for justice from other religious perspectives than with many Catholics whose priorities are antithetical to ours. I acknowledge the inherent ambiguity in such efforts, as well as the reasoned choices of some feminists to leave behind their patriarchal religions. But for me, a commitment to the value of sacrament and solidarity and a recognition that patriarchal Catholic actions cause concrete harm are reason enough to live with the tension.

Starting with biblical injunctions urging wives to be subject to their husbands, and progressing through patristic views of women's nature ("woman is the devil's gateway," writes Tertullian), the trajectory was set early in Christianity's history for what has become a sexual ethical tradition built on prohibitions. Of course, such a tradition takes many twists and turns, but the lasting impression remains negative in that it also restricts women's access to leadership and ministry.

The prohibitions take the form of bans on certain behaviors that, when understood from women's perspectives that have been lacking until now in the analysis, produce radically different conclusions. Worse, they result in the erasure of women's basic rights to health, choice, and well-being. For example, the ban on so-called artificial contraceptives (*Humanae Vitae*) has been seen as a law against the use of certain effective, economical, and, in some places, still unavailable forms of birth control. This results in dangerous conditions for many women. Its equally pernicious impact is a denial of moral agency to women of child-bearing age, in this case women's ability to make choices about their procreative possibilities. In a wider sense, the ban hinders women's ability to fulfill their moral responsibilities as they determine them. Read from Catholic women's experiences, it is precisely this religious law that prevents them from fulfilling their moral obligations to the common good.

Motherhood has been extolled endlessly in papal documents as the ultimate reason for women's being and sexuality. Yet when lesbian women decide to have children, there is a quick and reflexive condemnation from Rome. Obviously, by the logic of the Vatican's position, if one mother is great, why aren't two mothers greater? The reductive patriarchal anthropology of female-male complementarity (read: discrimination against women) comes into play. But a consequence of critical feminist theological work is that Catholicism can no longer have it both ways. Rethinking from women's religious experiences, however late, will expose these contradictions. While feminists have begun to deconstruct and reconfigure some Catholic sources, the prevailing impression among them in the United States, and perhaps elsewhere, is that "Catholic equals fundamentalist equals sex negative equals useless" when it comes to creating a society in which responsible, consensual sexuality is a human right.

One understandable feminist reaction to Catholic rigidity is simple rejection of Catholic or even Christian teachings, followed by the exploration or adoption of other religious options. But another possibility, the one I choose for this essay, is looking critically at and trying to change official Catholic policy by which governments enforce laws that are harmful to women. For example, abortion remains illegal in virtually every country in Latin America in large measure because of Catholic teachings. The impact on women is detrimental unto deadly. Such oppression demands response from responsible Catholics as part of a larger commitment to that tradition's fundamental teachings of love and justice.

My feminist theopolitical method is both critically deconstructive and imaginatively constructive. It is critically deconstructive in line with the three decades of scholarship by hundreds of women who, from various starting points and in various situations, have rejected patriarchal theology. It is imaginatively constructive because the lack of a tradition that takes women's sexuality seriously *on women's terms* demands that one be built or that Catholic sources simply be left aside. Theologian Laura Donaldson claims that feminists in religion must begin to "construct an elsewhere of vision that will lead us into a truly liberating future."[3] It is imaginative because none of us has ever lived in a just context, one in which equality is the norm. We can only imagine it, not as fluffy indulgence in fantasy, but as a strategic way of moving beyond current constraints.

I focus my critique and construction in three parts: (1) women's sexuality is dangerously domesticated in a context that is increasingly global, pluralistic, and violent; (2) women's sexuality is misconstrued in private/individualistic terms—its consequences are social and communal; (3) just good sex is a basic human right.

Women's Sexuality Is Dangerously Domesticated

In a context that is increasingly global, pluralistic, and violent, women's sexuality is dangerously domesticated.

Christian images and symbols of women's sexuality have a distinctly domestic flavor, as if what is at stake were something usually at home, un-connected with anything larger. Of course, it is the case, especially in the early centuries of the tradition, that women's activities were described pri-marily as household related, for lack of any other loci for them. However, it is remarkable to note how static this conception has remained to the present.

Contemporary Catholic documents offer an odd assortment of examples, beginning with Vatican II, in which women are described in terms of their stay-at-home motherhood: "This domestic role of hers must be safely pre-served, though the legitimate social progress of women should not be underrated on that account" (*Gaudium et Spes,* par. 52). How such contra-dictions are to be fulfilled remains a mystery. Likewise, even when women are lauded or said to possess full rights, the documents usually contain a qualifier that makes clear that such is not really meant after all. For example, the bishops write: "It is appropriate that they [women] should be able to assume their full proper role *in accordance with their own nature.* Every-one should acknowledge and favor the *proper* and necessary participation of women in cultural life" (par. 61, italics mine). Such phrases become quite clear in their misogynist meaning when coupled with the exclusion of women from the Catholic priesthood and from most significant decision making and therefore widespread influence. They are clearer still in the ab-sence of any such claims about the nature of males, who are assumed to be normatively human.

Women involved in the Second Vatican Council, whose stories are only beginning to surface, describe phenomenal if unsuccessful efforts to explain the basic facts of women's lives to those who had the power to vote, namely, male clerics. For example, Patty Crowley, Catholic mother of many, details the papal rejection of her committee's counsel on the issue of birth control.[4] Likewise, women auditors at Vatican II, whom most Catholics did not know existed, were involved in many conversations around the edges of the meet-ing. It can no longer be said simply that women were not present. Rather, it must be admitted that women's experiences were simply passed over in a show of kyriarchal force.

Surely women, especially the nuns who were the majority of the audi-tors, would not have construed sexuality so narrowly, confining its impact to the husband and family. While they may not have had as much sexual experience as some of the other women, the nuns in their reports indicate that they would have analyzed women's sexuality quite differently than the stereotypes in the documents: in economic terms, noting the deep financial impact of unplanned-for children; in emotional terms, reflecting the real stresses of having limited if any effective control over fertility; and in social terms, explaining the disproportionate responsibilities women carry for child rearing in a patriarchal society.[5] The most minimal internalization of these experiences would have rendered the localized, ethereal language of the documents moot. But it was not to be. Because Catholic women were not considered moral agents, they were not allowed as full participants in the council that shaped Catholicism in the second half of the twentieth century.

The same dynamic can be found in U.S. Catholic bishops' statements, most vividly displayed in the attempt during the 1980s to write a pastoral letter on women, which was eventually voted down by the bishops themselves. In successive drafts over nine years, and with increasing Roman intervention, women went from advisors whose insights were sought in partnership, to research subjects whose lives were scrutinized, and finally, to objects whose options were circumscribed. Why?

As in the case of Vatican II, the linchpin issue was not women's economic, emotional, or social well-being, but women's sexuality. Again the advisors were mostly nuns, and again the impact of their message was simply too hot to handle. In addition to offering realistic if unremarkable testimony on women's sexuality, the women advisors (some of whom resigned in frustration) and other women theologians and activists demanded a change in method. Instead of being auxiliary to the bishops who were writing the letter that carried the working title "Partners in the Mystery of Redemption," the women, logically enough, expected to be partners. Anything less was inadequate, both because it did not reflect the goal, and, of greater significance, because it prohibited women from fulfilling their responsibilities as adult members of the tradition.

The result of this process imposed by churchmen is the continued limitation of women's sexuality to the most local sphere. In a context that is increasingly global and interreligious, and where male battering of women is a serious and growing problem, such a condition has proved intolerable for Catholic feminists, who are now engaged in its reshaping. A look at globalization, pluralism, and violence clarifies why.

Globalization

Globalization is the "expansive evolution of systems such as economies, governments, media, culture and communications toward international integration and coordination."[6] In practice, globalization has many familiar aspects: air travel, Internet access, and a market that privileges some and robs many. In reality, globalization amounts to more decisions being made for increasingly larger sectors of the world by increasingly fewer people. There is no reason to think that sexuality is exempt from this phenomenon. Rather, there is reason to suspect that sexuality is a globalized commodity in "the religion of the market," with women's sexuality sold cheaply and controlled from without.[7]

Globalization is turning out to be one more form of colonialism. The forced displacement of populations, the migration of labor following capital, and the rank ordering of people according to skin color and ethnic background are reminiscent of earlier forms of colonialism in which Christianity played such a sinister role. Moreover, it means collapsing important *different* ways of thinking into models and structures that privilege certain assumptions and values while ignoring others.

Globalization calls for new ways of thinking about how people are religious. Terms made popular during the heyday of liberation theologies, for example, "local theologies" and even "base communities," become rather quaint when technology makes it possible for people to be closer, both literally and ideologically, to those who share their economic, educational, and theological privilege than to those with whom they share the grocery store, the sidewalk, and the school. The very internationalization of theology in a globalized economy can be an exercise in increasingly sophisticated injustice, if it simply replicates the hegemonic discourse of Christendom. Such is the stark specter of Catholic sexual teaching as it spreads electronically throughout the world. Its proponents have already joined forces with other conservative authoritarian groups (for example, certain Protestant evangelicals and Islamic fundamentalists) to influence international policies that oppress women.

Religious Pluralism

Growing religious pluralism is a second major factor in the changing context of the United States and increasingly in other parts of the world.

Diana Eck, professor of Comparative Religion and Indian Studies and director of the Pluralism Project at Harvard University, describes one aspect of the situation: "Today, the Islamic world is no longer somewhere else, in some other part of the world; instead, Chicago, with its fifty mosques and nearly half a million Muslims, is part of the Islamic world."[8] From a three-religion culture (Protestant, Catholic, and Jewish, though of course Native Americans had their own tradition, and other small groups were permitted) in the early part of this century, "America today is part of the Islamic, the Hindu and the Confucian world. It is precisely the interpenetration of ancient civilizations and cultures that is the hallmark of the late twentieth century."[9]

For Catholic theopolitical work, this is not something that can be denied or ignored. The Vatican's unsuccessful attempt to block consensus at the U.N. Meeting on Population and Development in Cairo in 1994 established its international reputation as a religious group and government that attempts to foist its narrowly construed views of women on programs and policies that have an impact well beyond its scope. Later, at the Fourth World Conference on Women in Beijing, in 1995, with a conservative Catholic attorney, a woman, heading its delegation, the Vatican tried again unsuccessfully to impose its theological view on public policy.

A coalition of progressive women from a variety of religious traditions, with Catholics for Free Choice (CFFC) providing strong support, countered these efforts at both meetings. The interreligious discussion and strategizing necessary to hold the line proved that women's sexuality, far from being a domestic issue, is a global health and human rights concern that some religions, notably Catholicism, seek to thwart. Of course, there are varying views of human rights, given that some cultures put more emphasis on individual and others on social identities. But the rights of women, whether as individuals or as a group, are thwarted nonetheless.

It used to be conventional wisdom that to know one religion was to know all religions. Now it seems that to know one religion, as Diana Eck and others have observed, is to know no religion at all. A pluralistic religious context requires that what it means to be religious cannot be reduced to one approach without the serious risk of homogenizing what are finally very different experiences. Analogously, no one group, not even CFFC, can do the job. The best approach is through progressive coalitions in an increasingly globalized, religiously pluralistic situation.

Male Battering of Women

Male battering of women looms as the third shaping factor in this new context. The literature is extensive and the consequences devastating.[10] But what remains to be explored is the relationship between the limitation of women's sexuality, that is, the narrow construction of it in heterorelational and reproductive terms, and violence at home. For example, Catholic sexual teachings have been used to counsel women to remain in abusive marriages rather than to divorce. Remarriage after divorce is prohibited by the church without an annulment, effectively consigning some women to one bad choice or another.

Catholic moral theology of sexuality limits licit sexual expression to heterosexual intercourse open to procreation between married partners. There is precious little nuance in the teachings about the violence, coercion, or other oppressive experiences that accrue as long as these conditions apply. While I would not argue that Catholic teachings *cause* men to batter women, I would conclude that the absence of many explicit teachings to the contrary can be seen as contributing to conditions that favor male abuse of power and lead to battering.[11]

The teachings are problematic in themselves for heterosexual people who are unmarried or not interested in procreating. But they have an even broader reach. The same moral teachings, for example, sanction no lesbian sexual activity, however loving, tender, and fulfilling, including that which might be coupled with insemination and therefore procreative in a technical sense. Gay male sex is simply written off as wrong, without regard to context. Happily, in pastoral practice there is some leeway in these matters, some clergy having had sense enough to realize the folly of such pronouncements, and experience enough to have seen the sometimes tragic results. After years of observing such teachings as oppressive to women and lesbian, gay, bisexual, and transgendered people, I now classify them as a form of violence, a kind of spiritual domestic violence in one's religious home.

These three factors—globalization, growing religious pluralism, and the male battering of women, coupled with the rise of sexually transmitted diseases, especially HIV/AIDS—configure a new context that renders ridiculous localized or domesticated notions of women's sexuality. Too much is at stake to be satisfied with such a partial view, and too much damage is done by those who espouse such views to ignore them.

Women's Sexuality Is Misconstrued

A related problem is the construction of women's sexuality in private/individualistic terms when the consequences are also social and communal. Catholic theology is not alone in this mistake, but it functions as an important bellwether.

The problem can be traced to the denial of women's moral agency, in this case, the refusal to allow women to name and shape issues as they experience them. For example, the well-known Catholic position against abortion in virtually all instances is predicated on the absolute independence of the fetus from the woman without whose body it would not exist. Such contradictions lack the moral complexity that women experience and articulate.

This complex ethical relation of mother and fetus requires careful attention. But pregnant women name it on their own terms even if church officials, virtually all male, do not listen. Analogously, many white women have a hard time understanding that "blackwoman" is the integral experience of African American women, as articulated by Joan Martin, that is, that they do not, indeed cannot, choose between being a woman and being black.[12] More to the point, most white women do not realize that the very absence of a referent to race in their regard, a sign of hegemonic discourse, means that "woman" implies "whitewoman." Given the economic and political weight of whiteness, and the extent of U.S. cultural domination in the media and in business, this false universal obscures far more than it reveals. But none of this nuanced dynamic carries over into Catholic discourse. No one asks, What pregnant woman? or A girl pregnant at what age? That pregnant women's experiences will differ from those of the decision makers, and that such differences are relevant, seems entirely beyond concern.

When nonfeminist Catholics insist that a pregnant woman and a fetus are inseparable, and that one must be privileged over the other in an increasingly individualistic approach to the social problem of unintended or unwanted pregnancies, the results are disastrous. A woman's decisions concerning reproduction are complicated, richly layered, and textured—with pain and relief, dilemma and decision, self and family, emotions and economics, population concerns and personal desires. But these complications play a small role in the formation of kyriarchal Catholic sexual ethics. Feminists can do a better job.

One impact of privatizing sexuality in Catholic circles has been for many women to reject teachings such as those against masturbation, the use of effective contraceptives, abortion, and lesbian sexual activity. Their experiences, especially those that run contrary to official teachings, were not included. For some, the sacrament of penance or confession was, and for many women still is, the place where such matters were discussed. Ironically, many women heard from their more progressive priests that under certain circumstances prohibited activities could be licit, for example, use of birth control after multiple pregnancies. But the hush-hush approach continued, with women sworn to secrecy to protect the priest from ecclesial censure. Duplicity abounded—and abounds.

Still another way in which public, communal discussion, much less consensus, is blocked on these matters is the effective means Catholic institutions have for punishing those who offer other opinions, especially in the popular forum. A classic case is an advertisement that was placed in the *New York Times* by a group of ninety-eight "Concerned Catholics" during the 1984 presidential race in the United States. The Democratic vice presidential candidate, Geraldine Ferraro, was a pro-choice Catholic whose views were condemned publicly from the pulpit by Cardinal John O'Connor of New York City.[13] The ad was a statement about the diversity of opinion that exists among committed Catholics concerning abortion.

The signers of the ad included twenty-five nuns, several brothers and priests, activists, and theologians who signaled their commitment to public discussion without censure for Catholics on the matter of abortion. Rome was horrified. Virtually all of the signers paid high prices for their actions. Many lost jobs or were not promoted. Some had speaking engagements canceled and were banned from working in certain dioceses. The nuns were singled out for special punishment, since they were regarded as "public members" of the Catholic community. In fact, they were easier to target because it could be done through the hierarchy of their religious orders. For all, reactions caused harm and created fear.

The bottom line is that sexuality—in this instance, abortion—was supposed to be kept a private matter, despite its widespread use by Catholics. The issue was not so much abortion per se, but talking about it and demonstrating that, rather than private, it is a social, economic, and political issue. Debate, while normal among academics who disagree for a living, is simply perceived to be too threatening to a controlled system like Roman Catholicism.

Lesbian, gay, bisexual, and transgendered Catholics are familiar with this tactic. Content to stay quiet and closeted, or better, also to remain celibate, Catholic "lesbigaytrans" people experience a minimum of public pressure. Once the facts are on the table, however, it is a different story. For lesbian women, this is made worse by nearly complete erasure of the particularity of lesbian experience, both in distinction to gay male (read: normative) experience and, in a peculiar way, from heterosexual women's "transgressive" sex of many sorts.

However, women's extensive and intense discussions have rendered these differences significant and bonding rather than insignificant and divisive. More remains to be said and is being said by feminist scholars and activists who respect the capacity of women to name their own experiences and evaluate them on their own terms. The challenge is to find ways to make this part of religiously founded justice-seeking lives that are recognized as Catholic in good standing. Imaginative construction is required to make this happen, because the current context renders it a dream.

Just Good Sex Is a Basic Human Right

I begin this work by searching for a framework in which to understand what good sex might look like from a Catholic feminist perspective. The search itself is vexed, given my reluctance to adopt an overarching program that matches my white, Western biases at the expense of other important considerations. Rather than abandon the pursuit, I respectfully offer a solution, for consideration by colleagues who share some of my concerns, albeit from different religious and national starting points.

One paradigm that seems sufficiently broad to encompass women's sexuality in a global, pluralistic, and dangerous situation for which only the public communal approach will be sufficient is that of human rights. The fiftieth anniversary of the U.N. Universal Declaration of Human Rights has taken as its motto, "All human rights for all," with the clear implication that we are far from the mark. Contemporary human rights discussions are not exempt from the problems of hegemonic discourse, but at least they are recognized as loci for concern about a set of issues that affects the common good, not just individuals in it.

Human rights is a hotly debated concept in a postmodern context in which absolutes are all but gone, individualism is valued, and religious and moral claims are suspect. Such rights have been interpreted in post-Enlightenment terms of entitlements that accrue to individuals rather than reciprocal responsibilities in a just society. Moreover, they have been anthropocentric in that they apply only to humans and not to animals and the earth.[14] But it seems worth exploring the possibility that, as the concept of women's sexuality takes on new dimensions according to women's experience, the rubric of human rights can be imagined as one possible route for assuring that the gains are socialized, accessible to everyone, and related to the well-being of all creation.

The term *rights* remains ambiguous, given the highly context-specific nature of the current discussion. What I mean by the term is the social, and at the same time personal, expectation that certain matters of common human life will be guaranteed, one of them being the right to just good sex.[15] Difficult as it is to imagine how diverse countries will handle this without subjecting others or being subjected to normative claims, I nonetheless consider the effort to extend the concept worthwhile if it will at least lead toward greater safety.

Catholic teachings on human rights, for example, in *Gaudium et Spes* (par. 26), recognize the "increasingly universal complexion" of the common good and acknowledge that this "consequently involves rights and duties with respect to the whole human race." While Catholicism has no special claim to human rights, it does have a long tradition of attention to the matter, albeit with limited feminist input.[16] Rosemary Radford Ruether, a Catholic feminist theologian, makes a feminist case for universal human rights.[17] Aware of the problems of homogenization in this approach, Dr. Ruether bases her useful argument on a strand of natural law (a Catholic staple) that sees the cosmos as "a unified ontological whole whose nature implies ethical norms of right relationship."[18]

While well aware of the dangers of such an approach, I propose that just good sex could become another human right, like the right to be a person before the law, to not be enslaved, to have a nationality, and to assemble peaceably. I propose it as a rubric for discussion, a starting point for strategizing, a possibility for local definition and implementation, and not an absolute to be applied across the board. Just good sex as I intend it is sex that is safe, pleasurable, community building, and conducive to justice. This sort of definition, with its religious flavor, flows from what Catholic ethicist Daniel C. Maguire calls "the renewable moral energy of religion."[19]

Catholic women in large numbers are for the first time in a position to shape our religion in important and effective ways, the legacy of many women's struggles. I reject any prescribing in this regard, but I am equally leery of the total relativism that can result in danger and damage. Hence, I offer the formula "just good sex" as a framework for creative collaboration in the hard work of social change.

I suggest that we begin to think about just good sex as a human right expressed in many ways, just as the concern with Basic Human Needs is being discussed variously in different contexts. I imagine the United Nations discussing it, national legislative bodies voting on it, and one day women and men living as if it were a given. Meanwhile, the imaginative and constructive work must begin.

I add the notion of justice, or in my shorthand, "just," to "good sex" to signal my starting point in a religious tradition in which justice is central and to reinforce my goal of bringing about social change. The context as I describe it requires such a signal, lest the concern with "good sex" be taken as frivolous, solipsistic, or worse, that those who make the case for body-spirit connections start and end their work in sexual pleasure in the most narrow sense.

I urge that safety be a primary concern in a situation in which men abuse women. *Safe* in this sense means free not only from abuse, but also from sexually transmitted diseases, especially HIV/AIDS. It is also *safe* in the wider sense of uncoerced. Sex is safe when enjoyed knowing one has a place to live and a job. It is safe with regard to procreative choice and safe with respect to the gender of a partner, safe in the freedom to be sexual alone. The right to sexual safety is something a good society will seek to guarantee.

I describe just good sex as pleasurable, with Patricia Beattie Jung in this volume, in all of the conventional ways that people enjoy responsible sex: erotically fulfilling and physically satisfying. But I would add some other plea-sures as well, thus avoiding the trap of narrowing the focus to sexual plea-sure to the exclusion of other goods, as Grace Jantzen has warned against in this book. I would include the pleasure of knowing that children are fed, the pleasure of creating meaningful work, the pleasure of providing health care to all, the pleasure of living in a nuclear-free world, the pleasure of ending violence, the pleasure of stopping racism. Surely these linkages can only deepen sexual pleasure as commonly appreciated, whereas the severing of them from sex steals energy from struggles for social justice. As Audre Lorde observed: "The erotic is . . . an internal sense of satisfaction to which, once we have experienced it, we know we can aspire. For having experienced the fullness of this depth of feeling and recognizing its power, in honor and self-respect we can require no less of ourselves."[20]

Just good sex in this articulation is community building as a specific antidote to the couples trap or other privatizing moves. I do not mean to insist on multiple relationships, though I would not rule such out categorically if the persons involved are all consenting and happy about it (two conditions I have rarely seen sustained in such situations). Rather, I mean that love strikes me as gracious—more a matter of luck than of skill, more given than earned. Perhaps the intuition that it was meant to be procreative is not entirely wrong, only partial in that just good sex is really part of creating a new network of relationships that emerge from all love relationships. In this sense, the community is not only human but also earthly and even celestial.

This gives way to a fourth dimension, just good sex as conducive to justice itself. By this move, I reject the trap that says sex is sex and justice is justice. Here I join Dorothy Ko's urging in this volume that sex be looked at in public, communal ways, not simply private, individual ways. What I mean by justice is the feminist notion of "power-in-relation" that moves us toward "right relationship, with self, others, creation, God."[21] Insofar as sexual relationships are just, they reflect and enhance power sharing. Male battering of women, heterosexism, homo-hatred, and oppressive reproductive health policies all contravene justice. Likewise, fierce and tender friendships, the celebration of love in its various forms, and accessible choices about procreation can make sex another "renewable moral energy" source.

Roots of these elements can be found in Catholic theology, but frankly I am less interested in identifying them than in actualizing them. If the kyriarchal church adopts them as policy, that is fine. But more to the point is that they emerge from Catholic feminist theological insights, commitments, and struggles that are in themselves an extension of the tradition and a new source of Catholic teachings. They are then properly the fruit of some women's religious wisdom and a modest contribution to the global, interreligious conversation.

Conclusion

Future teams like ours have their work cut out for them. In this volume, we offer the fruits of one cross-cultural conversation, hopeful that many more will happen on specific issues such as reproductive health, the meaning of pleasure, lesbian experiences, the role of motherhood in our respective cultures, and the like. We see ours as but one methodological approach. We hope that it will encourage others to develop additional models.

Our aim was not to reach any specific conclusion, rather to learn how to talk with one another about issues that we experience and prioritize differently. Nonetheless, we noticed that for all of us sexuality is more than the private practice of individuals. It is behavior that arises within a complex set of power dynamics. In every instance, sex is intimately interwoven with the economic, social, and political possibilities of the actors. What is good about it varies widely. If there was any consensus among us, it was our commitment to transformation.

We found that human bodies, especially women's bodies, are the sites of endless contest. Whether in cultures that prize individuality or in cultures that encourage community first, the body as locus of power, pleasure, and justice is variously understood. We did not seek to homogenize such differences, rather to recognize them and the difference they make in global public policy decisions.

Our group had a strong consensus on the need to bring the insights of "good sex" into the religious education of our children in tradition-specific as well as more generalized ways. It is time to empower girls with the results of our research and invite them to ask and answer their own questions of meaning and value when it comes to sexuality. We can imagine intergenerational conversations, with women and girls learning from one another. We hope that this book will lay the groundwork for such exchange.

We are left with important questions for future discussion and action: (1) How can we bring these insights regarding women's views of good sex into the public policy mainstream? (2) How can we influence our various religious traditions to incorporate these women-generated views of sexuality into their teachings and practices? (3) How can we help to raise future generations of women, and of course men, who will hold these views as normative? The work of making good sex part of the global fabric of life has just begun, and it is a pleasurable beginning. But it is a beginning for which this volume may serve simply as a springboard. The next steps toward "better sex" await.

Notes

One Good Sex

I gratefully acknowledge the financial support of the John Rylands Trust for this and all my research. I am also grateful to the members of the Good Sex group, especially Radhika Balakrishnan and Wanda Deifelt, for their perceptive and challenging comments, many of which have been reproduced in this paper.

1. For a fuller exposition of this Platonic view, see Grace M. Jantzen, *Power, Gender, and Christian Mysticism* (Cambridge: Cambridge University Press, 1995), chapter 2.
2. See Peter Brown, *The Body and Society: Men, Women, and Sexual Renunciation in Early Christianity* (New York: Columbia University Press, 1988).
3. Augustine, *Confessions*: III.1.
4. This needs to be qualified, however, by the recognition that it was also held that sexual pleasure was necessary not only for men but for women too, if conception was to occur. See Brown, *The Body and Society*.
5. Barbara Newman, *Sister of Wisdom: St. Hildegard's Theology of the Feminine* (Berkeley: University of California Press, 1987), 111. The specific reference here is to Hildegard of Bingen in the twelfth century; but she echoes centuries of Christian thought on the subject.
6. The phrase is Tertullian's. It should be noted, however, that some writers, including Hildegard, held that female pleasure also was necessary for conception, a view that became prominent in early modernity, only to be lost again in the nineteenth century. See Thomas Laqueur, *Making Sex: Body and Gender from the Greeks to Freud* (Cambridge: Harvard University Press, 1990).
7. Again, this was not uniform. John Boswell has argued that in the early centuries of Christendom a much more relaxed view of same-sex love between men was prevalent: see his *Christianity, Social Tolerance, and Homosexuality* (Chicago:

University of Chicago Press, 1980). See also Mark Jordan, *The Invention of Sodomy in Christian Theology* (Chicago: University of Chicago Press, 1997), and Bernadette J. Brooten, *Love Between Women: Early Christian Responses to Female Homoeroticism* (Chicago: University of Chicago Press, 1996).

8. Thomas Aquinas, *Summa Theologia*: II/II q.154, a 11, a 12.
9. See Lawrence Stone, *The Family, Sex, and Marriage in England, 1500–1800* (London: Weidenfeld and Nicolson, 1977).
10. Ibid.
11. For an anthology showing the development of the private/public split in relation to the family, see Jean Bethke Elshtain, ed. *The Family in Political Thought* (Amherst: University of Massachusetts Press, 1982).
12. See Anne McClintock, *Imperial Leather: Race, Gender, and Sexuality in the Colonial Context* (New York: Routledge, 1995).
13. Wanda Deifelt, personal communication.
14. See Richard Dyer, *White* (London: Routledge, 1997).
15. Anthony Giddens, *The Transformation of Intimacy* (Cambridge: Polity, 1992).
16. Bryan Turner, "The Body in Western Society" in *Religion and the Body,* ed. Sarah Coakley (Cambridge, U.K.: Cambridge University Press, 1997), 30.
17. See also Turner, "The Body in Western Society," 31.
18. See Glenna Matthews, *"Just a Housewife": The Rise and Fall of Domesticity in America* (New York: Oxford University Press, 1987).
19. Michel Foucault, *The History of Sexuality*, trans. Robert Hurley (Harmondsworth, Middlesex: Penguin, 1976).

Two   The Muslim Religious Right ("Fundamentalists") and Sexuality

1. Afshamah Najmabadi, "Hazards of Modernity and Morality," in *Women, Islam, and the State,* ed. Deniz Kandiyoti (London: Macmillian, 1991), 63 (my insertion).
2. Farida Shaheed, "Controlled or Autonomous: Identity and the Experience of the Network Women Living under Muslim Laws," *Signs: Journal of Women in Culture and Society* 19/4 (1994): 997–1019.
3. The *hadith* consists of the sayings of the prophet Mohammed or anecdotes concerning his life recounted by those who were his contemporaries and passed on to others in a traceable line of transmission.
4. Formally systematized bodies of Muslim laws, combining jurisprudence, law, and theology.
5. See, among others, Leila Ahmed, *Women and Gender in Islam: Historical Roots of a Modern Debate* (New Haven, Conn.: Yale University Press, 1992), and Fatima Mernissi, *Women and Islam: An Historical and Theological Enquiry* (Oxford: Basil Blackwell, 1991), and *Beyond the Veil: Male-Female Dynamics in a Modern Muslim Society (New York: Schenkman, 1975).*
6. See Margot Badran and Miriam Cooke, *Opening the Gates: A Century of Arab Women's Writing* (Bloomington: Indiana University Press, 1990); Jean Boyd, "The Contribution of Nana Asma'u Fodio to the Jihadist Movement of Shehu Dan Fodio from 1820 to 1865," (M. Phil. diss., Polytechnic of North London, 1982); and Nikki Keddie and Beth Baron, eds., *Women in Middle Eastern History: Shift-*

ing Boundaries in Sex and Gender (New Haven, Conn.: Yale University Press, 1991.)

7. On Nigeria, see the work of Mary F. Smith, *Baba of Karo: A Woman of the Muslim Hausa* (London: Faber, 1954; New Haven, Conn.: Yale University Press, 1981), and that of Renee Pittin, "Marriage and Alternative Strategies: Career Patterns of Hausa Women in Katsina City," (Ph.D. thesis, University of London, 1979).

8. See, among others, Hanna Papanek and Gail Minault, eds., *Separate Worlds: Studies of Purdah in South Asia* (Delhi: Chanakya, 1982).

9. By *seclusion,* I refer specifically to the restriction of women's freedom of movement to domestic space, not to the whole panoply of dress codes, sexual segregation, and avoidance/deference behavior that is frequently collectively referred to as purdah. See Ayesha M. Imam, "Women and Religion—Islam," Workshop on African Women and Tradition, Culture, and Religion, *Newsletter of the African Centre for Democracy and Human Rights Studies* (Banjul, Gambia, 1994).

10. Compare Shelley Feldman and Florence McCarthy, "Purdah and Changing Patterns of Social Control among Rural Women in Bangladesh," *Journal of Marriage and the Family* 45/4 (1983): 949–959, and Imam, "Women and Religion—Islam."

11. For this and opposing views, see Abdelwahab Boudhiba, *La Sexualité en Islam* (Paris: Presses Universitaires de France, 1975); Mernissi, *Beyond the Veil*; Azzizah Al-Hibri, ed., *Women and Islam* (Oxford: Pergamon, 1982); and Fatna Aeit Sabbah, *Woman in the Muslim Unconscious* (New York: Pergamon, 1991).

12. Richard Antoun, "On the Modesty of Women in Arab Muslim Villages: A Study in the Accommodation of Traditions," *American Anthropologist* 70/4 (1968): 671–698.

13. Jane Schneider, "Of Vigilance and Virgins: Honor, Shame, and Access to Resources in Mediterranean Societies," *Ethnology* 10/1 (1971): 1–24.

14. Imam, "Women and Religion—Islam."

15. The amputation of the clitoris—in some areas including also the amputation of the vaginal lips (labia) and/or the sewing up of what remains—is often erroneously referred to as female circumcision. Circumcision in males excises only the foreskin of the penis, rather than the whole organ. The amputation of the prepuce of the clitoris, commonly referred to as *sunna* circumcision, is the equivalent. It has been noted to occur, but the frequency with which attempted *sunna* circumcision actually results in whole or partial clitoral amputation is still a question to be researched.

16. See Nawaal El Sadaawi, *The Hidden Face of Eve: Women in the Arab World* (London: Zed, 1980), and Nahid Toubia and Abdullahi An-Na'im, "Legal Dimensions of the Health of Women in Arab and Muslim Countries," concept paper for "Legal Dimensions of Women's Health," Population Council Meeting, West Asia and North Africa Region, 1993.

17. See Esther Dorkenoo and S. Ellsworthy, *Female Genital Mutilation: Proposals for Change* (London: Minority Rights Group International Report, 1992), and Mairo Mandara, "Prevalence of Female Genital Mutilation in Zaria: A Critical Appraisal," paper presented at the International Reproductive Rights Research and Action Group—Nigeria Workshop, Benin City, May 1–6, 1995.

18. The removal of a "too large" hymen, done usually seven days after birth. See Mandara, "Prevalence of Female Genital Mutilation."

19. On the 1940s and 1950s, see Smith, *Baba of Karo.*

20. Imam, "Women and Religion—Islam."

21. Juliet Mitchell, "On the Differences Between Men and Women," *New Society* (1980): 234–235.

22. See Jeffery Weeks, *Sexuality and Its Discontents. Meanings, Myths, and Modern Sexualities* (London: Routledge and Kegan Paul, 1985), and his *Sexuality* (Chichester: Ellis Horwood/Tavistock, 1986); Rosalind Coward, "On the Universality of the Oedipus Complex: Debates on Sexual Division in Psychoanalysis and Anthropology," *Critique of Anthropology* 15/4 (1980): 5–28, and her *Patriarchal Precedents, Sexuality, and Social Relations* (London: Routledge and Kegan Paul, 1983); Steve Burniston, Frank Mort, and Christine Weedon, "Psychoanalysis and the Cultural Acquisition of Sexuality and Subjectivity in Centre of Cultural Studies," *Women Take Issue,* Women's Studies Group, Center for Contemporary Cultural Studies (London: Hutchinson, 1978), 109–133; and Juliet Mitchell and Jacqueline Rose, eds., *Feminine Sexuality. Jaques Lacan and the école freudienne* (London: Macmillan, 1982.)

23. See Coward, *Patriarchal Precedents*; Amina Mama, "Race and Subjectivity" (Ph.D. thesis, University of London, 1987); and Ayesha Imam, "Subjectivity and Sexuality," (Division of Anthropology, Brighton: School of African and Asian Studies, University of Sussex, 1988).

24. Michel Foucault, "Disciplinary Power and Subjection," in *Power,* ed. Steven Lukes (Oxford: Basil Blackwell, 1986), 233.

25. See Antonio Gramsci, *Selections from the Prison Notebooks,* ed. Quintin Hoare and Nowell Smith (London: Lawrence and Wishart, 1971); Ernesto Laclau, *Politics and Ideology in Marxist Theory* (London: Verso, 1979); and Stuart Hall, "The Toad in the Garden: Thatcherism among the Theorists," in *Marxism and the Interpretation of Culture,* ed. Cary Nelson and Lawrence Grosberg (Urbana: University of Illinois Press, 1988), 35–57.

26. For more of such theorizing on the construction of subjectivity and sexuality, see Coward, *Patriarchal Precedents;* Amina Mama, "Race and Subjectivity"; and Imam, "Subjectivity and Sexuality" and "'If You Won't Do These Things for Me, I Won't Do Seclusion for You': Local and Regional Constructions of Seclusion Ideologies and Practices in Kano, Northern Nigeria" (Ph.D. thesis, University of Sussex at Brighton, 1994).

27. See "Fundamentalism in Africa: Religion and Politics," special issue of *Review of African Political Economy* 52 (November 1991); Gita Sahgal and Nira Yuval-Davis, eds., *Refusing Holy Orders: Women and Fundamentalism in Britain* (London: Virago, 1992); Women Living under Muslim Laws, "Special Bulletin on Fundamentalism and Secularism in South Asia," 1992; and Nira Yuval-Davis, "The Bearers of the Collective: Women and Religious Fundamentalism in Israel," *Feminist Review* 4 (1980).

28. Marieme Helie-Lucas, "The Preferential Symbol for Islamic Identity: Women in Muslim Personal Laws," *Identity Politics and Women: Cultural Reassertions and*

Feminisms in International Perspective, ed. Valentine Moghadam (Boulder, Colo.: Westview, 1994), 391–407.

29. Ibid.

30. See, for instance, Karima Benoune, "SOS Algeria: Women's Human Rights under Siege," in *Faith and Freedom: Women's Human Rights in the Muslim World,* ed. Mahnaz Afkhami (London: Taurus, 1995), 161–174; and Women Living under Muslim Laws [WLUML], *Dossier d'information sur la situation en Algérie. Résistance des femmes et solidarité internationale* (Compilation of information on the situation in Algeria: Women's resistance and solidarity around the world) (Grabels, 1995).

31. Yuval-Davis, "The Bearers of the Collective."

32. See Renee Pittin, "Women, Work, and Ideology in Nigeria," *Review of African Political Economy* 52 (1991): 38–52; and Ayesha M. Imam, "Women and Fundamentalism" and "The Development of Women's Seclusion in Hausaland, Northern Nigeria," *Women Living under Muslim Laws Dossier* (1991) 11/12/13: 13–15, and 9/10: 4–18.

33. See Al–Fanar, "Developments in the Struggle Against the Murder of Women against the Background of So-called Family Honour," *Women Against Fundamentalism Journal* 6 (1995): 37–41.

34. Some consider *mut'a* to enable women to exercise more rights and autonomy and expression of sexuality than do standard marriage forms . See Shahla Haeri, *The Law of Desire: Temporary Marriage in Iran* (London: Tauris, 1989). Others argue that it is women with social disabilities who are forced to accept such unions, and who would prefer standard marriages. See Ziba Mir-Hossaini, "Strategies of Selection: Differing Notions of Marriage in Iran and Morocco," *Muslim Women's Choices: Religious Belief and Social Reality,* ed. Camilla Fawzi El-Solh and Judy Mabro (Providence, R.I.: Berg, 1994), 55–72. I suggest that *mut'a* could be either autonomy giving or less advantageous depending on the general social, economic, and political conditions of women as a group and as individuals. Where women have high status and autonomy, then *mut'a* is a choice that may be advantageous; where they have low status and autonomy, it may be less so.

35. See "Fundamentalism in Africa: Religion and Politics," special issue, *Review of African Political Economy* 52 (November 1991).

36. See Imam, "'If You Won't Do These Things'."

Three   Guilty Pleasures

1. David Biale, *Eros and the Jews: From Biblical Israel to Contemporary America* (Berkeley: University of California Press, 1997), 104.

2. Genesis Rabbah 9.9.

3. Michael Satlow, *Tasting the Dish: Rabbinic Rhetorics of Sexuality,* Brown Judaic Studies 303 (Atlanta, Ga.: Scholars Press, 1995), 173–183.

4. The concept of *yetzer hara* makes clear the rabbinic ambivalence toward sexual desire, which was viewed at best as a necessary evil. See Biale, *Eros and the Jews,* 43–47, for a full explanation of the concept of *yetzer hara.*

5. Satlow (*Tasting the Dish,* 246–261) says the prohibition was not against spilling

seed, but against the temptation and disruption it would have caused. Autoeroticism was strictly prohibited, even to the point of forbidding the touching of the penis during urination

6. Female homoerotic behavior is not included because it is not considered sex and therefore does not disrupt the order of things.

7. B. Niddah 16b, quoted in Satlow, *Tasting the Dish*, 299.

8. On the subject of onah, see Biale, *Eros and the Jews*, 54; Satlow, *Tasting the Dish*, 265.

9. Satlow, *Tasting the Dish*, 320.

10. See Rebecca Alpert, *Like Bread on the Seder Plate: Jewish Lesbians and the Transformation of Tradition* (New York: Columbia University Press, 1997), 29–34.

11. Satlow, *Tasting the Dish*, 264.

12. Norman Lamm, *A Hedge of Roses: Some Jewish Insights into Sex and Marriage* (London: Clarendon Foundation, 1968).

13. See works such as Robert Gordis, *Sex and the Family in Judaism* (New York: Burning Book, 1967); Judith Plaskow, *Standing Again at Sinai: Judaism from a Feminist Perspective* (San Francisco: Harper and Row, 1990); and Eugene Borowitz, *Choosing a Sex Ethic: A Jewish Inquiry* (New York: Schocken, 1969).

14. Daniel Boyarin, *Unheroic Conduct: The Rise of Heterosexuality and the Invention of the Jewish Man* (Berkeley: University of California Press, 1997), 162–168.

15. See Arthur Waskow, *Down-to-Earth Judaism: Food, Money, Sex, and the Rest of Life* (New York: Morrow, 1997).

16. See Biale, *Eros and the Jews*, 225; and Boyarin, *Unheroic Conduct*, 180.

17. Jane Litwoman, "Some Thoughts on Bisexuality," *Lesbian Contradictions*, winter 1990.

18. See Norman Lamm, "Judaism and the Modern Jewish Attitude to Homosexuality,"*Encyclopedia Judaica Yearbook* (1974).

19. Quoted in Biale, *Eros and the Jews*, 104.

20. Marcia Falk, *The Song of Songs: A New Translation and Interpretation* (San Francisco: Harper, 1990), 145–147.

21. Quoted in Ephraim E. Urbach, *The Sages: Their Concepts and Beliefs*, trans. Israel Abrahams (Jerusalem: Magnes, 1975), 357.

22. The closet was also regulated by laws that could punish gay people with loss of jobs, family, and housing, and even with death. This is still true in certain settings and detracts from rather than enhances the pleasure of gay sex because it renders it immoral and illegal rather than simply illicit, in the terms we are using here.

23. Biale, *Eros and the Jews*.

24. Michel Foucault, *The History of Sexuality*, vol.1 (New York: Pantheon, 1978).

25. See Howard Eilberg-Schwartz, *The Savage in Judaism: Excursis in an Anthropology of Israelite Religion and Ancient Judaism* (Bloomington: Indiana University Press, 1990).

Four Capitalism and Sexuality

I would like to thank the participants of this project, particularly Mary Hunt, Patricia Jung, Grace Jantzen, and Judith Plaskow, for comments and edits. I would also like to thank Uma Narayan, David Gillcrist, and Vijay Balakrishnan for their editorial work and support during this project.

1. David Loy, "The Religion of the Market," *Journal of the American Academy of Religion* 65/2 (summer 1997): 275.
2. David Levine, *Self-Seeking and the Pursuit of Justice* (Aldershot: Ashgate, 1997), 66.
3. See Ayesha Imam's chapter in this volume.
4. For an example of this "radical critique," see Edward Goldsmith, "The Last Word," in *The Case Against the Global Economy and for a Turn toward the Local,* ed. Jerry Mander and Edward Goldsmith (San Francisco: Sierra Club, 1996). Here Goldsmith makes a case against the process of globalization and development because it removes control from the family and community.
5. David Shapiro, *Autonomy and Rigid Character* (New York: Basic Books, 1981), 26, quoted in David Levine, ed., *Wealth and Freedom* (Cambridge: Cambridge University Press, 1995), 25.
6. Levine, *Wealth and Freedom,* 40.
7. Lisa Lowe and David Lloyd, eds., introduction to *The Politics of Culture in the Shadow of Capital* (Durham, N.C.: Duke University Press, 1997), 21.
8. Lourdes Beneria, "Gender and the Construction of Global Markets" (forthcoming).
9. The burden here arises with the increasing market for dowries and the dependence on the cash economy, as well as the breakup of the landlord systems.
10. Aiwa Ong, "The Gender and Labor Politics of Postmodernity," in *The Politics of Culture in the Shadow of Capital,* ed. Lisa Lowe and David Lloyd (Durham, N.C.: Duke University Press, 1997), 70.
11. Ibid., 74.
12. Georg Simmel, *The Philosophy of Money,* ed. David Frisby, trans. Tom Bottomore and David Frisby (New York: Routledge, 1990), 298.
13. It is important to mention in this context that the agricultural economy that most of the women participated in had eroded, and so they had to seek money to support themselves and their families. I also found that, unlike female sex workers in many other places in Asia that I visited, Thai women who were sex workers were allowed to return home and get married.
14. Beneria, "Gender,"13.
15. Peter Dickens, *The Global Shift* (New York: Guilford, 1998), 314.
16. Ryan Bishop and Lillian S. Robinson, *Night Market: Sexual Culture and the Thai Miracle* (New York: Routledge, 1998), 102.
17. Loy, "The Religion of the Market," 287.
18. Ibid., 275.
19. Mary McIntosh, "Liberalism and the Contradictions of Oppression," in *Feminism and Sexuality: A Reader,* ed. Stevi Jackson and Sue Scott (New York: Columbia University Press, 1996), 333.

20. The *Ramayana* is one of the most famous Hindu epics.
21. My use of the term *transgressive politics* is informed by Deborah Cameron and Elizabeth Frazer, "On the Question of Pornography and Sexual Violence: Moving beyond Cause and Effect," in *Feminism and Sexuality: A Reader*, ed. Stevi Jackson and Sue Scott (New York: Columbia University Press, 1996), 321–333.
22. Levine, *Self-Seeking*, 66.

Five   Islam and Women's Sexuality

1. For a more detailed critique of dominant discourses of 'Islamic sexuality' in contradiction to existing practices in different Muslim communities, see Ayesha Imam's chapter in this volume.
2. See, for example, Fatima Mernissi, *Beyond the Veil: Male-Female Dynamics in a Modern Muslim Society* (New York: Schenkman, 1975); Fatna A. Sabbah, *Woman in the Muslim Unconscious* (New York: Pergamon, 1984); Nawal El Saadawi, *The Hidden Face of Eve: Women in the Arab World* (London: Zed, 1980); Charles Lindholm, *The Islamic Middle East: An Historical Anthropology* (Oxford: Blackwell, 1996); Bruce Dunne, "Power and Sexuality in the Middle East," *Middle East Report* 28/206 (1998): 8–11.
3. The research is unique in terms of the wide geographic range it covers, as well as in terms of the diversity of the issues it handles: women in the family, women as citizens, and women's bodily rights.
4. A weighted, multistage, stratified cluster sampling approach was used in the selection of the survey sample. The sample was designed so that a variety of characteristics would be analyzed for the region as a whole, urban and rural areas (each as a separate domain), and eastern and southeastern Anatolian regions (each as a separate region). The urban frame of the sample consists of settlements with populations of more than twenty thousand, and the rural frame consists of settlements with populations of less than twenty thousand.

   Different types of questionnaires were used for (1) women living in monogamous marriages, (2) women living in polygynous marriages, and (3) women who were still unmarried. The questionnaires were completed by the interviewers through face-to-face interviews. The interviewers, all from the region, had undergone lengthy, intensive training in all of the issues covered by the questionnaire as well as in interviewing and sampling techniques. The age of the participants ranged from fourteen to seventy-five; the average age was 32.1.
5. The reform of the Civil Code based on the Swiss Civil Code was a major success of the reformists against the conservative forces defending the religious family code in 1926.
6. At the time of the Islamic conquests, the term *Kurd* had meant nomad. By the mid-nineteenth century, *Kurd* was also used to mean tribespeople who spoke the Kurdish language. At present, insiders' and outsiders' views concur on the definition of *Kurds* as those who speak Kurdish as their mother tongue.
7. Melikoff goes further to assert that it is a mistake to consider Alevis as Shi'i, as Alevism does not have its origins in the Shi'a tradition. See Irene Melikoff, *Hadji Bektach, un mythe et ses avatars* (Boston: Brill, 1998).

8. Riza Zelyut, *Oz Kaynaklarina Gore Alevilik* (Alevism according to its original sources) (Istanbul: Yon Yayincilik, 1992).

9. Approximately three-fourths of the population in the western part of Turkey live in urban areas, compared with 46 percent in the eastern part.

10. State Institute of Statistics, *Il ve Bolge Istatistikleri 1994* (Provincial and regional statistics 1994) (Ankara: State Institute of Statistics, Prime Ministry, Republic of Turkey, 1996).

11. For more information on the Kurdish tribal culture, see David McDowall, *A Modern History of the Kurds* (London: Tauris, 1997); and Artun Ünsal, *Kan Davasi* (original title: *La Vendetta*), (Istanbul: Yapi Kredi Yayinlari, 1995).

12. Valentin M. Moghadam, *Modernizing Women: Gender and Social Change in the Middle East* (Boulder, Colo.: Lynne Rienner, 1993), 107.

13. In the early days of Islam, there were hundreds of schools of Islamic jurisprudence. By the eleventh century, the Sunni schools had diminished to four, named after their supposed founders: Hanafi, Shafi, Maliki, and Hanbali. The central school in the Middle East is Hanafi or Shafi, and the Malikites prevail in North Africa.

14. GAP–Southeastern Anatolian Project, *Yirmibirinci Yüzyilda Kadin ve GAP* (Women and the Southeastern Anatolian Project in the twenty-first century) (Ankara: Prime Ministry, Republic of Turkey, Directorate of Southeastern Anatolian Project, 1997).

15. Ministry of Health, Hacettepe University Institute of Population Studies, and Macro International, *Turkish Demographic and Health Survey 1993* (Ankara: Ministry of Health, Hacettepe University, and Macro International, 1994).

16. See also Yakin Ertürk, "Doğu Anadolu'da Modernleşme ve Kirsal Kadin" (Modernization and rural women in eastern Anatolia), in *1980'ler Türkiye'sinde Kadin Bakiş Açisindan Kadinlar* (Women from the perspective of women in Turkey in the 1980s), ed. Şirin Tekeli (Istanbul: Iletişim Yayinlari, 1993), 199–210.

17. Article 110 of the Turkish Civil Code.

18. Article 237 of the Criminal Code.

19. State Institute of Statistics, *Il ve Bolge Istatistikleri 1994*.

20. According to Article 88 of the Turkish Civil Code, the minimum age for a civil marriage, which is the only legal marriage ceremony in Turkey, is seventeen for men and fifteen for women. However, the minimum age for all legal procedures except marriage is eighteen.

21. Bride price is prevalent in societies where the contribution of women to production is high, but women's autonomy over marriage is restricted.

22. Surah 4, verse 3: "And if ye fear that ye will not deal fairly by the orphans, marry of the women, who seem good to you, two or three or four; and if you fear that you cannot do justice (to so many) then one (only) or (the captives) that your right hands possess. Thus it is more likely that ye will not do injustice." Mohammed M. Pickthall, *The Meaning of the Glorious Koran: An Explanatory Translation* (New York: Meridian, 1997).

23. Extended exchange of wives is not a Muslim or Middle Eastern tradition. The practice exists also in other parts of the world, for example, in China. See M.

Wijers and L. Lap-Chew, *Trafficking in Women, Forced Labour and Slavery-like Practices in Marriage, Domestic Labour, and Prostitution* (Utrecht, Netherlands: Foundation Against Trafficking in Women–STV, 1997).

24. Lale Yalcin-Heckmann, "Aşiretli Kadin: Gocer ve Yari-gocer Toplumlarda Cinsiyet Rolleri ve Kadin Stratejileri" (Women in tribes: Sex roles and women's strategies in migrant and semimigrant communities), in *1980'ler Türkiye'sinde Kadin Bakiş Açisindan Kadinlar* (Women from the perspective of women in Turkey in the 1980s), ed. Şirin Tekeli (Istanbul: Iletişim Yayinlari, 1993).

25. See, for example, Homa Hoodfar, "Bargaining with Fundamentalism: Women and the Politics of Population Control in Iran," *Reproductive Health Matters* 4/8 (1996): 30–39.

26. Articles 129 and 143 of the Civil Code.

27. Until 1996, the Turkish Criminal Code defined fornication as a criminal offense and differentiated between men and women in the definition of fornication. Articles defining fornication for women and men were annulled by the Turkish Constitutional Court on the grounds that differences in the definition of fornication for the wife and the husband violated Article 10 of the Turkish Constitution, which states that men and women must be equal before the law.

28. Surah 17, verse 32.

29. Surah 24, verse 2.

30. Surah 24, verse 4.

31. Article 462 of the Turkish Criminal Code.

32. Ibid., Article 478.

33. World Health Organization, *Violence Against Women* (Geneva: World Health Organization, 1997).

34. Deniz Kandiyoti, "Emancipated but Unliberated? Reflections on the Turkish Case," *Feminist Studies* 13 (summer 1987): 317–338.

35. Riffat Hassan, "The Role and Responsibilities of Women in the Legal and Ritual Tradition of Islam ('Shari'ah')" in *Riffat Hassan: Selected Articles* (Montpelier, Vt.: Women Living under Muslim Laws), 23.

Six   Sanctifying Women's Pleasure

I would like to thank Frank Catania, Philip Chmielewski, S.J., Bill French, Bill George, Shannon Jung, Dan Maguire, Susan Ross, Mike Schuck, Cristie Traina, and, of course, all the participants in the Good Sex Project, especially Rebecca Alpert and Wanda Deifelt. Though I alone am responsible for its shortcomings, this chapter is stronger as a result of their encouragement, their close reading of earlier drafts, and their steadfast collegiality.

1. This concern to highlight the value of sexual pleasure in general, and women's sexual pleasure in particular, in the framework of Roman Catholic moral theology stands in a long tradition. The shift away from an Augustinian ethic of sexual shame began long ago. In the thirteenth century, Thomas Aquinas argued that there was no venial sin attached to the pleasure produced by marital coitus. Developing this trajectory based in natural law further, Alphonsus Liguori in the eighteenth century declared that such pleasure was not only permissible but to

be recommended. Nature does nothing in vain, he pointed out. A wife's orgasm during coitus, he argued, probably would benefit any child so conceived. (Still, digital and oral stimulation of the clitoris or vagina, even as "foreplay," remained strictly forbidden because they might trigger an orgasm apart from coitus, which alone was potentially procreative.) In the nineteenth century, the bishop of Philadelphia, Patrick Kenrick, taught that there was a positive obligation to pursue the wife's orgasm. According to Kenrick, a husband sinned venially (by omission) if he failed to remain sexually active until his wife climaxed. Most remarkably, he argued that if she had not experienced orgasm during coitus, she had the right to bring herself to orgasm "by touches" afterward (see Peter Gardella's review of this teaching in *Innocent Ecstasy: How Christianity Gave America an Ethic of Sexual Pleasure* [New York: Oxford University Press, 1985], 9.) The Second Vatican Council recognized the goodness of sexual pleasure within marriage, and those who worked at tracing the moral implications of that teaching include: Rosemary Radford Ruether in her 1964 essay, "Birth Control and Ideals of Marital Sexuality," reprinted in *Readings in Moral Theology No. 8: Dialogue about Catholic Sexual Teaching*, ed. Charles E. Curran and Richard A. McCormick (New York: Paulist Press, 1993), 138–152; Philip S. Keane, *Sexuality Morality: A Catholic Perspective* (New York: Paulist Press, 1977); and Margaret Farley, "Sexual Ethics," *Encyclopedia of Bioethics,* ed. William Reich (New York: Free Press, 1978), 4:1575–1589. To my knowledge, though, the first serious effort by a Roman Catholic theologian to defend at length the moral goodness of women's sexual delight and to explore some of the ethical implications of that goodness was made by Christine E. Gudorf, *Body, Sex, and Pleasure* (Cleveland, Ohio: Pilgrim, 1994).

2. Gudorf, *Body*, 30.
3. John C. Ford and Gerald Kelly, *Contemporary Moral Theology: Marriage Questions* (Westminster, Md.: Newman, 1963), 2:211.
4. Gudorf, *Body*, 32.
5. Ford and Kelly, *Contemporary Moral Theology*, 196, emphasis mine.
6. Ibid., 224.
7. Ronald Lawler, Joseph M. Boyle, Jr., and William E. May, "Masturbation," in *Catholic Sexual Ethics: A Summary, Explanation, and Defense*, ed. Ronald D. Lawler (Huntington, Ind.: Our Sunday Visitor Press, 1985), 187–195, reprinted in Curran and McCormick, *Readings in Moral Theology*, 361– 371.
8. Gudorf, *Body*, 139.
9. Marie M. Fortune, *Love Does No Harm: Sexual Ethics for the Rest of Us* (New York: Continuum, 1995), 120.
10. Gudorf, *Body*, 108.
11. Ford and Kelly, *Contemporary Moral Theology*, 199.
12. Christiane Northrup, *Women's Bodies, Women's Wisdom* (New York: Bantam, 1994), 246.
13. Gudorf, *Body*, 142.
14. Gudorf, *Body*, 149.
15. For example, for Augustine, pleasure was linked only with concupiscence. As the driver for potentially reproductive activity in men, it clearly exceeded the

parameters of that requirement and hence acquired a reputation as unruly. While Thomas Aquinas noted in the *Summa Contra Gentiles* (III: 123) that sweet bonds of mutual affection sometimes developed between spouses as a result of the pleasures of copulation, the gifts of such mutual delight and love were not viewed as morally normative.

16. Beverly Wildung Harrison and Carter Heyward, "Pain and Pleasure: Avoiding the Confusions of Christian Tradition in Feminist Theory," in *Christianity, Patriarchy, and Abuse: A Feminist Critique*, ed. Joanne Carlson Brown and Carole R. Bohn (New York: Pilgrim, 1989), 148–173, reprinted in James B. Nelson and Sandra P. Longfellow, eds., *Sexuality and the Sacred: Sources for Theological Reflection* (Louisville, Ky.: Westminster/John Knox, 1994), 142.

17. Harrison and Heyward, "Pain and Pleasure," 147.

18. While respecting her work, I disagree with Lisa Sowle Cahill (*Sex, Gender, and Christian Ethics* [Cambridge: Cambridge University Press, 1996], 10) when she writes that "Christian sexual ethics today . . . has been quite effective in addressing the human suffering caused by legacies of negativity and even oppression concerning sex." Cahill's assumption that an appreciation for the goodness of women's sexual pleasure has been adequately integrated into our cultural ethos is mistaken. Furthermore, it is too simplistic to claim that "it is only when the reading of experience is individualistic—even adolescent—that the discovery of sex is the discovery of pleasure [alone]" (111, addition mine, implied by context). Such a remark—even when interpreted as primarily against a reductionistic, exclusive focus on pleasure—remains problematic. It implies that (1) the experience of sexual pleasure arrives unbidden, like the routine onset of menses for most women during their adolescence, (2) pleasure is normally a private, individual (rather than say personal, possibly mutual, and certainly socially constructed) experience, and (3) the (re)discovery of pleasure by women is regressive or developmentally arrested behavior.

19. Gudorf, *Body*, 89.

20. These findings were based on the 1992 National Health and Social Life Survey of a randomly selected sample of 1,749 women and 1,410 men, regarded by researchers in this field as the most comprehensive study of sex in the United States since the Kinsey reports of the early 1950s.

21. Pepper Schwartz and Virginia Rutter, *The Gender of Sexuality* (Boston: Pine Forge, 1998), 56.

22. Mary D. Pellauer, "The Moral Significance of Female Orgasm: Toward Sexual Ethics That Celebrates Women's Sexuality," *Journal of Feminist Studies in Religion* 9/1–2 (spring–fall 1993): 161–182, reprinted in Nelson and Longfellow, eds., *Sexuality and the Sacred,* 149–168.

23. Edward O. Laumann, Anthony Paik, and Raymond C. Rosen, "Sexual Dysfunction in the United States: Prevalence and Predictors," *Journal of the American Medical Association* 281/6 (February 1999): 537–544.

24. For more on this tendency, see Philip E. Slater, "Sexual Adequacy in America," *Intellectual Digest,* December 1973, 132–135, quoted in Janet Shibley Hyde and John DeLamater, *Understanding Human Sexuality,* 6th ed. (Dubuque, Iowa: McGraw Hill, 1997), 261.

25. I do not want to deny that for some women in precisely such an unreformed cultural context as ours the nonpursuit and nonvaluation of sexual pleasure may be necessary for their individual survival and hence may be personally a morally appropriate response. It must be said as well, however, that this response might also be rooted in a deep, theologically reinforced suspicion of all that springs from the flesh. It would be silly to think of women as exempt from the morally formative power of this traditional Christian hermeneutic. It cannot help but be shocking and seem very dangerous for women to associate grace and moral goodness with their bodies and its passions. Whatever might be said about the Christological purposes of the doctrine of the virgin birth, the Catholic emphasis on the perpetual virginity of Mary symbolizes the Church's ongoing inability to come to terms with the goodness of female sexual pleasure.

26. Naomi Wolf, *Promiscuities: The Secret Struggle for Womanhood* (New York: Random House, 1997), xxiv.

27. Michael S. Kimmel, *Manhood in America: A Cultural History* (New York: Free Press, 1996).

28. Schwartz and Rutter, *The Gender of Sexuality*, xv, emphasis mine.

29. Hyde and DeLamater, *Understanding Human Sexuality*, 353.

30. Schwartz and Rutter, *The Gender of Sexuality*, 44.

31. Wolf, *Promiscuities*, 143.

32. Even today, some evolutionary biologists theorize that women's sexual desire must peak at ovulation. But as reasonable as this hypothesis may be, it fails as a theory to prove comprehensive of all the relevant data. "Some studies found no increase in sexual interest during ovulation, peaks well before ovulation, and no variation in interest at all." See Schwartz and Rutter, *The Gender of Sexuality*, 7.

33. Wolf, *Promiscuities*, 146, 149.

34. Ibid., 148.

35. Ibid., 149.

36. Cahill, *Sex*, 198.

37. Cited in Pellauer, "The Moral Significance of Orgasm," 150.

38. Wolf, *Promiscuities*, 154.

39. Pellauer, "The Moral Significance of Orgasm," 154.

40. See Margaret Miles, *Practicing Christianity: Critical Perspectives for an Embodied Spirituality* (New York: Crossroads, 1988). For Augustine, even sex in marriage was (mortally) sinful if sought for pleasure only. Only if engaged for procreative purposes, or perhaps as a remedy for one's spouse's lustful desires, could sex be saved from sin. As he saw it, sex was not fundamentally for love, because women were not equal to men. There are of course notable qualifications of, if not true exceptions to, this pattern. For Thomas Aquinas, sex for pleasure alone was sinful, but if conjugal and procreative, the enjoyment of pleasure was not sinful. Indeed according to Aquinas sexual pleasure was muted by original sin. In paradise, our increased rationality will actually enhance our pleasures. See John Giles Milhaven, "Thomas Aquinas on Sexual Pleasure," *Journal of Religious Ethics* 5 (fall 1977): 157–181.

41. Barbara H. Andolsen, "Whose Sexuality? Whose Tradition? Women, Experience,

and Roman Catholic Sexual Ethics," in *Religion and Sexual Health, Ethical, Theological, and Clinical Perspectives,* ed. Ronald M. Green (Boston: Kluwer Academic Publishers, 1992), 56.

42. See Julian W. Slowinski, "Sexual Adjustment and Religious Training: A Sex Therapist's Perspective," 137–154, and William S. Simpson and Joanne A. Ramberg, "The Influence of Religion on Sexuality: Implications for Sex Therapy," 155–165, both in *Religion and Sexual Health: Ethical, Theological, and Clinical Perspectives,* ed. Ronald M. Green (Boston: Kluwer Academic Publishers, 1992).

43. Susan A. Ross, "Extravagant Affections," in *In the Embrace of God,* ed. Ann O'Hara Graff, (Maryknoll, N.Y.: Orbis, 1995), 109, 114. See as well Ross's "The Bride of Christ and the Body Politic: Body and Gender in Pre-Vatican II Marriage Theology," *Journal of Religion* 71/3 (July 1991): 345 –361.

44. Schwartz and Rutter, *The Gender of Sexuality,* 56.

45. Pellauer, "The Moral Significance of Orgasm," 160 –161.

46. Historically, such a foundational modus operandi has been especially problematic for women, as noted earlier. Even when its focus is expanded so as to include female experience, the dangers of physicalism loom large. The physical is always just one ingredient of human being. For both men and women, this turn to the body tends to eclipse other interpersonal and spiritual dimensions of human experience historically associated with the "order of reason." The more personalist approach, popular now with many Catholic moral theologians, aims to avoid the distortions associated with a physicalist reduction. Yet, as many revisionists themselves have pointed out, such personalism runs the risk of ignoring the body.

47. William R. Stayton, "A Theology of Sexual Pleasure," in *Christian Perspectives on Sexuality and Gender,* ed. Adrian Thatcher and Elizabeth Stuart (Grand Rapids, Mich.: Eerdmans, 1996), 335.

48. Of course, it is not the absolute good some flawed accounts claim it to be. It is just one of the many goods we ought to serve. As Thomas Aquinas noted in reflections on pleasure apart from his discussion of sexuality, delight is requisite for human happiness but accompanies human fulfillment in a much broader sense. Women know quite well that the pursuit of pleasure alone will not prove satisfying. Women know that sexual delight can be wrong in several ways: its pursuit can be inappropriate to the situation; it can be enjoyed at the expense of the dignity and well-being of both ourselves and others; or what we experience as delightful can be warped by the way our sexual relationships are constructed. There is no question that the pursuit of sexual pleasure can be manipulative and harmful.

49. In a provocative essay, Kathleen M. Sands accuses such pro-sex feminists of being naive about society's tremendous power to maintain its negative construction of sexuality in accord with the values of patriarchy. Her point about the way sexuality might continue to be used as a weapon against women is well taken. Yet apart from such alternative (re)visions of it, there is no hope of reforming the sexual practices and institutions that devalue women's sexual delight. See Kathleen M. Sands, "Uses of the Thea(o)logian: Sex and Theodicy in Religious Feminism," *Journal of Feminist Studies in Religion* 8/1 (spring 1992): 7–35.

50. Audre Lorde, "Uses of the Erotic: The Erotic as Power," excerpted from the 1984 *Sister Outsider* and reprinted in Nelson and Longfellow, eds., *Sexuality and the Sacred,* 77, 78.

51. Lorde, "Uses of the Erotic," 75.

52. Pellauer, "The Moral Significance of Orgasm," 162.

53. The point here is not to reduce sexual pleasure to a value of instrumental worth only. For example, I aim not to treat it as good because it serves to attract people into and cement relationships. Like self- and other-love, sexual enjoyment remains simultaneously both intrinsically worthwhile and linked to these other goods. The nature of the association among values need not be linear or hierarchical. One good need not be of value merely because it supports another.

54. Pellauer, "The Moral Significance of Orgasm," 160.

55. Harrison and Heyward, "Pain and Pleasure,"141.

56. Gudorf, *Body*, 115.

Seven   Beyond Compulsory Motherhood

1. I included this story in "Of Gardens and Theology: Women of Faith Respond," in *The Power We Celebrate. Women's Stories of Faith and Power*, ed. Musimbi R.A. Kanyoro and Wendy S. Robins (Geneva: World Council of Churches, 1992), 5–18.

2. The groundbreaking recognition of the importance of women's role in the labor force can be seen in Elizabeth Souza Lobo, *A Classe Operária Tem Dois Sexos. Trabalho, Dominação, e Resistência* (São Paulo: Brasiliense, 1981).

3. June Nash, "A Decade of Research on Women in Latin America," *Women and Change in Latin America*, ed. June Nash and Helen Safa (South Hadley, Mass.: Bergin and Garvey, 1986), 4.

4. A recent study in Brazil shows that the average monthly wage of a white male is R$881 and of a black male is R$423. (The Brazilian real is worth about one U.S. dollar.) White females earn, on average, 35 percent less than white males. See *Zero Hora*, August 27, 1998, 16.

5. Eva Alterman Blay, "Mulheres e Movimentos Sociais Urbanos no Brasil: Anistia, Custo de Vida, e Creches," *Encontros com a Civilização Brasileira* 26, 3/8 (1980): 63–70.

6. Delegacias da Mulher are police stations created by the Brazilian government in 1988, staffed by women in order to attend women, especially in cases of domestic violence, sexual abuse, and harassment. They were set up based on the experience that most women, when coming to regular police stations to denounce violence, were accused by law enforcers of causing the violence to happen, as opposed to being the victims of it.

7. This study was carried out by Population Action International; see *Jornal da Tarde*, July 25, 1995, 9B.

8. Kevin Neuhouser, "Sources of Women's Power and Status among the Urban Poor in Contemporary Brazil," *Signs: Journal of Women in Culture and Society* 14 (spring 1986): 690.

9. Ivone Gebara and Maria Clara Bingemer, *Maria, Mãe de Deus e dos Pobres. Um*

Ensaio a Partir da Mulher e da América Latina (Petrópolis: Vozes, 1987). In the case of Guadalupe, the Virgin appeared to a young indigenous boy called Juan Diego, on December 9, 1531, and she asked that a church be built on the hill where she appeared. Aparecida is the name given to the image of Mary fished out of the Paraiba River. Due to the dark color of the water, the image also became dark, and since then Aparecida has been identified as the black virgin.

10. In the research carried out by Datafolha, 2,052 questionnaires were answered. Of the people interviewed, 979 were male and 1,073 female. Of those who identified their racial group, 1,104 were white, 722 mulatto (mixed race), and 190 black. In terms of marital status, 1,153 were married, 678 single, 120 widowed, and 98 separated. In terms of religion, 1,438 identified as Roman Catholic, 202 as Pentecostal, 75 as Protestant, 73 as Spiritistic, 103 as other religion, and 154 as having no religion. This research was published in "Caderno Mais!" *Folha de São Paulo,* January 18, 1998.

11. Janice G. Raymond, *Women as Wombs: Reproductive Technologies and the Battle over Women's Freedom* (San Francisco: Harper, 1993), 6.

12. This technique consists of the insertion of a needle, with the help of ultrasound, into the selected fetus and the injection of a chemical solution (*cloreto de potassio*) that makes the heart stop beating. Until the eleventh week of gestation, the mummified fetus may be absorbed, but after that it will be expelled at the time of labor. *Isto É,* August 14, 1996.

13. Gisela Farias, "Cuando los Progenitores son Anonimos," in *Procreación: Nuevas Tecnologías,* ed. Susana E. Sommer (Buenos Aires: Atuel, 1996), 115.

14. Raymond, *Women as Wombs,* 9.

15. Farias. "Cuando los Primogenitores son Anonimos," 115.

16. Raymond, *Women as Wombs,* 8.

17. "Gravidez de Risco Matará 565 Mil.," *Jornal da Tarde,* July 25, 1995, 9B.

18. "Aborto em SP custa de R$150 a R$2,000," *Folha de São Paulo,* August 29, 1997, 3

19. "Aumenta o Número de Mães Adolescentes no Brasil," *Zero Hora,* August 2, 1998, 36.

20. Octávia E. Martin Danziato, *Seele Revista de Psicanálise* 1/1, at http://www.roadnet.com.br/seele/numero1/1octavia.htm.

21. "Aumenta o Número de Mães Adolescentes no Brasil," 36.

22. "Aborto em SP," 3.

23. Alejandro Moreno Olmedo, *El Aro y la Trama: Episteme, Modernidad, y Pueblo* (Caracas: Centro de Investigaciones Populares, 1993).

24. Cristina Buarque, "A Culpa Como Matéria de Desconstrução do Feminismo," *Mandrágora* 4/4 (1997): 77–83.

25. "Caderno Mais!"

26. Carolina Teles Lemos, Yone da Silva, and Dagmar Silva Pinto de Castro, "Bóias-Frias: Os Ritos Cotidianos do Não," in *Corpo: Meu Bem, Meu Mal,* ed. Rosângela Soares de Oliveira and Fernanda Carneiro (Rio de Janeiro: ISER, 1995), 110.

27. "Caderno Mais!" The data referring to religious groups were not found in the published version but were kindly made available directly through its research institute, Datafolha.

28. Maria Betânia Ávila, *Direitos Reprodutivos: Uma Invenção das Mulheres Reconcebendo a Cidadania* (Recife: SOS, 1992), 23.

29. An example of such biblical interpretation is Bárbara Huefner and Simei Monteiro, eds., *O que Esta Mulher está Fazendo Aqui?* (São Bernardo do Campo: Editeo/Imprensa Metodista, 1992).

30. See, for instance, Nancy Cardoso Pereira, "Ah! . . . Amor em Delícias!" *Revista de Interpretação Bíblica Latino-Americana* 15/2 (1993): 47–59; and Elsa Tamez, *Un Nuevo Acercamiento al Cantar de los Cantares: Los Juegos de Erotismo del Texto* (Heredia, Costa Rica: Universidad Nacional, 1985).

31. A more comprehensive analysis of this text can be found in Wanda Deifelt, "Entre o Direito e o Dever: A Crise dos Direitos Reprodutivos ou a Maternidade como Opção e Não Como Obrigação," *Mosaicos da Bíblia* 16 (1994): 11–15.

Eight   Buddhism on Sexuality and Enlightenment

1. See Isaline Blew Horner, *Women under Primitive Buddhism* (New York: Dutton, 1930), and works such as Diana Y. Paul, *Women in Buddhism* (Berkeley: University of California Press, 1985); and Rita M. Gross, *Buddhism after Patriarchy* (New York: State University of New York Press, 1993).

2. See an interesting treatment of the relationship between the understandings of immortality and the roles of women in Hinduism and Buddhism in Patrick Olivelle, "Amrta: Women and Indian Technologies of Immortality," *Journal of Indian Philosophy* 25 (1997): 427–449.

3. For an exploration of the emphasis on "person" in Hinduism and on "self" in Buddhism, see ibid., 429–431.

4. Palisuttanta-pitaka,Atthaga-nibatha,Tutiyapannast, Khotami-vagga, *The Siamese Tripitaka* (Bangkok: B.E.2530), 23:312–318.

5. This issue of the initial reluctance of the Buddha to allow ordination for women has been a hot subject for debate among feminist scholars of Buddhism. Some are too eager to prove the feminism of the Buddha by emphasizing his permission; others are too eager to criticize the Buddha for being a patriarch by emphasizing his reluctance. Please see examples in the works cited in note 1. However, a more balanced view has been presented, for example, in Alan Sponberg, "Attitudes toward Women and the Feminine in Early Buddhism," in *Buddhism, Sexuality, and Gender,* ed. Ignacio Cabezon (New York: State University of New York Press, 1985), 3–36. I argue, on the other hand, that the Buddha's decision to allow full ordination to women is indicative of his respect for the human rights of women. Detailed arguments are presented in Suwanna Satha-Anand, "Truth over Convention: Feminist Interpretations of Buddhism," in *Religious Fundamentalisms and the Human Rights of Women,* ed. Courtney W. Howland (New York: St. Martin's, 1999), 281–291.

6. The other three *vinayas* whose violation requires permanent expulsion are stealing, killing, and boasting of one's spiritual achievement. It should be noted here that the terms *sex* and *sexuality* as used in this chapter indicate heterosex and heterosexuality. The issue of homosexuality is not addressed.

7. Many of the works on women and Buddhism cited in the preceding notes seem not to have started from this distinction.

8. Anguttara Nikaya, 20/2–7/1–2.
9. Palisuttanta-pitaka, Anguttara-nikaya Panjakanitbat, Panjama-pannyast, 226/6, *The Siamese Tripitaka* (Bangkok 2530), 22:299.
10. Vinaya-pitaka, book 1, Mahavibhanga Pathombhak, *The Royal Siamese Tripitaka* (Bangkok: 2514), 1:31.
11. There are three main bodies of text in the Tripitaka (literally, the three baskets)—Sutta (teachings), Vinaya (rules for monks and nuns), and Abhidhamma (metaphysics)—which are considered most authoritative. The Jataka tales and the commentaries are supportive literatures. In connection with the questions of whether or which of the disparaging statements about women are probably words of the Buddha, please see a much-quoted research article, Kajiyama Yuichi, "Women in Buddhism," *Eastern Buddhist* 15/2 (autumn 1982): 53–70.
12. Khutaga-nikaya, Jataka 28/300/98.
13. Chateauguay-nikaya, Jataka 27/235/66.
14. Quoted in Paul Williams, "Some Mahayana Buddhist Perspectives on the Body," in *Religion and the Body,* ed. Sarah Coakley (Cambridge: Cambridge University Press, 1997), 210.
15. These comparisons are quoted in Steven Collins, "The Body in Theravada Buddhist Monasticism," in Coakley, ibid., 191.
16. Please see a discussion on this type of meditation method and its relationship to the Buddhist enlightenment in Suwanna Satha-Anand, "The Body and Enlightenment," in *Revealing Body, Concealing Form,* ed. Paritta C. Kauanantakul (Bangkok: KobFai, B.E.2541), 51–62.
17. Please see an interesting discussion on the issue of whether or not an *arahat* still emits semen and a related issue of whether an ordinary lay person may enjoy sexual pleasure, in *The Siamese Tripitaka,* 37:261–275.
18. Gross, *Buddhism after Patriarchy,* 214. This observation is, of course, debatable, as it would seem to reconfirm the perception that Buddhism is otherworldly. However, I think that although withdrawal may look like a giving up, it does carry transformative possibility for society, as the community of monks are still very much in contact with the secular world. Their exemplary life can serve as a critique as well as an ideal for existing societies.
19. The five duties of wives are: applying good (domestic) management, taking good care of a husband's relatives, being faithful, saving a husband's belongings, and being diligent. The five duties of husbands are: honoring her as wife, showing no contempt, being faithful, delegating household decision making to her, and giving her dresses and ornaments. Sinkalgha-sutta, Dhiganikaya, Patigavagga, 11/201/170; 11/200/170.
20. The eight *gurudhammas* include: (1) a nun who has been ordained even for a century must show proper signs of respect to a monk ordained just for one day; (2) a nun must not spend the rainy season in a residence where there is no monk; (3) every two weeks, a nun should seek two things from the monk order—the asking of the date of the observance day, and the coming for exhortation of a monk; (4) after the rainy season, a nun must bring to the attention of both orders in respect of three matters, namely, what was seen, what was heard, and

what was suspected; (5) a nun, if she committed a major offense, must undergo disciplining procedures for half a month before both orders; (6) after having been trained in the six rules for two years, a probationer should seek ordination from both orders; (7) a nun must not use abusive language or revile against a monk in any way; and (8) admonitions of monks by nuns are forbidden, while admonitions by monks are not forbidden.

21. "Mutta-theri," *Therigatha* (Bangkok: Pathum-vanaram Royal Temple, B.E.2539), 13.
22. Ibid., 18. Her name is Atthagasi-theri.
23. Ibid., 36. Khematheri here is later accorded the honorable position of being the female chief disciple of the Buddha who was praised for her wisdom.
24. Ibid., 73–77.
25. *The Siamese Tripitaka* (Bangkok: 2530), 37:267. The Abhidhamma section is a collection of commentaries on the original teachings of the Buddha. They are not considered direct words of the Buddha.
26. Ibid., 268.
27. Ibid., 274.
28. Sanghasopanasutta, Anguttara-nikaya, Jatukkanibata 21/7/8.
29. "Ubonvanna Theri," Pra Dhamma-pathatthagatha-plae, part 3 (Bangkok: Mahamakut Rajavidhyalai, B.E, 2500), 227.
30. Anguttara-nikaya, Ekanibata 20/164–166/35–36.
31. See a more detailed discussion of the various requirements for each position in Parichart Nontagananda, "Views on Women in Buddhism" (master's thesis, Chulalongkorn University Graduate School, B.E. 2523), 84–99.
32. Yuichi, "Women in Buddhism."
33. The eight prerequisites are: being human, being male, having accumulated great merits, having met a buddha, having been ordained, having great meditative achievement, having achieved great givings, and having an intense wish for enlightenment. *Attagatha-atthasalinee* (Bangkok: Umpolvidhya, B.E.2506), 87. Quoted in ibid., 85.
34. *The Siamese Tripitaka*, Dhiga-nikaya, Patikkavagga, book 11, 158–159.
35. Please see Paul, *Women in Buddhism*, for more detailed discussion of this issue in Mahayana Buddhism.
36. For a good discussion of the multivocality of Buddhism toward women, please see Sponberg, "Attitudes toward Women."
37. This observation is part of a study conducted by Karen Christina Lang quoted in Aloysius Pieris, "Women and Religion in Asia: Towards a Buddhist and Christian Appropriation of the Feminist Critique," *Dialogue* (NS) 19–20 (1992–1993): 153–154.

Nine   Authority, Resistance, and Transformation

1. Mary E. Hunt, "Good Sex: Women's Religious Wisdom on Sexuality," *Reproductive Health Matters* 8 (November 1996): 97–103.
2. Ibid., 97.
3. Only 50 percent of U.S. Jews are affiliated with any particular religious movement

within Judaism. Of that 50 percent, 80 percent are non-Orthodox. This means that, to varying degrees, they accept the notion of Judaism as an evolving tradition that must adapt itself to changing historical and social circumstances.

4. Cf. Judith Plaskow, *Standing Again at Sinai: Judaism from a Feminist Perspective* (San Francisco: Harper and Row, 1990), 18–21.

5. I have in mind such works as Daniel Boyarin, *Carnal Israel: Reading Sex in Talmudic Culture* (Berkeley and Los Angeles: University of California Press, 1993), and *Unheroic Conduct: The Rise of Heterosexuality and the Invention of the Jewish Man* (Berkeley and Los Angeles: University of California Press, 1997); Howard Eilberg-Schwartz, *People of the Body: Jews and Judaism from an Embodied Perspective* (Albany, N.Y.: State University of New York Press, 1992); Mark Biale, *Eros and the Jews: From Biblical Israel to Contemporary America* (New York: Basic Books, 1992); and Michael Satlow, *Tasting the Dish: Rabbinic Rhetorics of Sexuality*, Brown Judaic Studies 303 (Atlanta: Scholars Press, 1995).

6. This was a central and recurrent theme in all our Good Sex conversations, as many chapters in this volume bear witness.

7. Adrienne Rich, "Compulsory Heterosexuality and Lesbian Existence," *Signs: Journal of Women in Culture and Society* 5/4 (1980): 631–660.

8. The Talmud is a compendium of Jewish law and lore, taking the form of a commentary on the Mishnah, a second-century code of Jewish law. Since the Mishnah was the center of study at rabbinic academies in both Palestine and Babylonia, there are two Talmuds. The Babylonian Talmud is fuller and is considered the masterwork of rabbinic Judaism.

9. For some introductory material on these issues, see Rachel Biale, *Women and Jewish Law* (New York: Schocken, 1984), 192–197; and Rebecca Alpert, *Like Bread on the Seder Plate: Jewish Lesbians and the Transformation of Tradition* (New York: Columbia University Press, 1997), 25–34.

10. Gayle Rubin, "The Traffic in Women: Notes on the 'Political Economy' of Sex," in *Toward an Anthropology of Women*, ed. Rayna R. Reiter (New York: Monthly Review, 1975), 179–180.

11. Mary Daly, *Beyond God the Father* (Boston: Beacon, 1973), 12.

12. Rachel Adler, "I've Had Nothing Yet So I Can't Take More," *Moment* 8/8 (September 1983): 24.

13. On the Mishnah, see note 8.

14. Miriam B. Peskowitz, *Spinning Fantasies: Rabbis, Gender, and History* (Berkeley and Los Angeles: University of California Press, 1997), 35.

15. Saul Olyan, "'And with a Male You Shall Not Lie the Lying Down of a Woman': On the Meaning and Significance of Leviticus 18:22 and 20:13," *Journal of the History of Sexuality* 5/2 (1994): 185.

16. Bradley Artson, "Gay and Lesbian Jews: An Innovative Jewish Legal Position," *Jewish Spectator* (winter 1990–1991): 11.

17. It is remarkable how little has been written criticizing the Jewish insistence on marriage from other than gay and lesbian perspectives. See Laura Geller and Elizabeth Koltun, "Single and Jewish: Toward a New Definition of Completeness," in the first anthology of Jewish feminist work, *The Jewish Woman: New Perspec-*

tives, ed. Elizabeth Koltun (New York: Schocken, 1976), 43–49. Also see the section "Being Single" in Debra Orenstein, ed., *Lifecycles: Jewish Women on Life Passages and Personal Milestones* (Woodstock, Vt.: Jewish Lights, 1994), 99–116.

18. I am very grateful to the group conversation at the Good Sex meeting in Amsterdam for pushing me to be clearer about the ways in which Jewish feminists have moved beyond simply resisting women's traditional roles to creating new forms of practice, identity, and community. Mary Hunt's concept of imagination in her chapter in this volume is a helpful way of naming this dimension of feminist method and practice.

19. Sharon D. Welch, *Communities of Resistance and Solidarity* (Maryknoll, N.Y.: Orbis, 1985).

20. Daly, *Beyond*, chapter 1.

21. See Daniel Boyarin, "Justify My Love," in *Judaism Since Gender*, ed. Miriam Peskowitz and Laura Levitt (New York: Routledge, 1997), 131–137.

22. Phyllis Trible, "Eve and Adam: Genesis 2–3 Reread," in *Womanspirit Rising*, ed. Carol P. Christ and Judith Plaskow (San Francisco: HarperCollins, 1979), 80.

23. This theme of concealment and revelation kept coming up in our Good Sex conversations, in relation to recovering women's history and experiences in many traditions.

24. Alpert, *Like Bread on the Seder Plate*, 29–34; Bernadette Brooten, *Love Between Women: Early Christian Responses to Female Homoeroticism* (Chicago: University of Chicago Press, 1996.)

25. Alpert, *Like Bread on the Seder Plate*, 33.

26. Lisa A. Edwards, "A Simple Matter of Justice" (sermon, April 29, 1993).

Ten   The Sex of Footbinding

1. Charlotte Furth, "Rethinking Van Gulik: Sexuality and Reproduction in Traditional Chinese Medicine," in *Engendering China*, ed. Christina Gilmartin, Gail Hershatter, Lisa Rofel, and Tyrene White (Cambridge: Harvard University Press, 1994), 126. Furth argued that Dutch sinologist Robert H. Van Gulik's classic history of sexuality in China, *Sexual Life in Ancient China* (Leiden: Brill, 1974), is a product of his Victorian attitudes toward sex. She also cautioned against a common misconception among modern readers that Taoism is more woman friendly than the "misogynist" Confucianism. "The classic bedchamber manuals teaching Taoist secrets of longevity portray an aristocratic and lavishly polygamous society where very young women were exploited as sexual handmaidens—the stereotype of a royal harem." (Furth, "Rethinking Van Gulik,"145–146.)

2. Rey Chow, *Woman and Chinese Modernity* (Minneapolis: University of Minnesota Press, 1991), 123, emphasis mine. Chow disagrees with Chinese and Western critics who argue that psychoanalytic theories are foreign in origin, hence do not apply to the study of modern Chinese literature. Denying the applicability of psychoanalysis is to deny that the Chinese have psychic lives. I am pushing Chow's arguments further by suggesting that premodern Chinese psychic lives should also be subjected to feminist analysis.

3. Personal communications.

198 Notes to Pages 142–146

4. Anthropologists have conducted interviews with footbound women in the nineteenth and twentieth centuries, and many spoke of the pain of binding or the lack thereof. These voices cannot be used, however, to reconstruct the bodily experiences of footbound women before the modern era, which, I maintain, are forever lost to us. For a sample of these interviews, see Howard Levy, *Chinese Footbinding* (Taipei: Southern Materials Center, 1984), 203–285.

5. Daly mentioned the criticisms of Audre Lorde in her preface to the 1990 edition of the book but countered by saying that "*Gyn/Ecology* is not a compendium of goddesses." Mary Daly, *Gyn/Ecology: The Metaethics of Radical Feminism* (Boston: Beacon, 1990), xxx. Page numbers in parentheses that follow in the text refer to this source.

6. Julia Kristeva, *About Chinese Women* (New York: Marion Boyars, 1986), 83–85. Kristeva and Daly both used the ethnic Other to launch a radical self-critique of the West. But the parallel ends here; their means of deploying the other and their readings of footbinding are radically different. Kristeva visited China in 1974, but even as she saw them, the bound feet remained unknowable to her as a foreigner: "I can still see them, in Peking or in the provinces, these elderly women all dressed in black, with tiny babies' feet that I hardly dared to look at, let alone photograph. It doesn't help to know that this tiny foot exists, and that it is very tiny: it is perfectly unimaginable" (85). Rey Chow saw in this idealization and distancing an example of sexualizing a foreign culture by making it the feminine and primitive Other, hence "repeating the metaphysics she wants to challenge." Chow, *Women and Chinese Modernity*, 7.

7. Daly, *Gyn/Ecology*, 136.

8. Much of Daly's vocabulary is Andrea Dworkin's: sadism, necrophilia, planetary, 1000 years. Andrea Dworkin, *Woman Hating* (New York: Plume, 1974).

9. Daly, *Gyn/Ecology*, 151.

10. Daly was perhaps not aware that her radical view of the physical body as the gateway to truth and transcendence is close to that of Taoist women saints, as discussed by Suzanne Cahill. See Cahill's "Discipline and Transformation: Body and Practice in the Lives of Taoist Holy Women of the Tang Dynasty," in *Women in Confucian Cultures in Premodern China, Korea, and Japan*, ed. Dorothy Ko, Jattgur Kim Haboush, and Joan Piggott (Berkeley: University of California Press; forthcoming).

11. Daly's stance on her own privileged position as a Western intellectual is complicated. In a curious passage, she recognized the destructive power of imperialism but ascribed hegemonic power to the West as a result: "Virtually all of modern patriarchal society has been influenced/shaped profoundly by the West, becoming a sort of Total Westworld" (*Gyn/Ecology*, 96). I wonder if she did not ascribe too much power to the West. In another instance, she seemed oblivious to her own location in insisting that "haggard criticism should enable women who have been intimidated by labels of 'racism' to *become sisters* to these women of Africa—naming the crimes against them and *speaking on their behalf*—seeing through the reversal that is meant to entrap us all. . . . Beyond racism is sisterhood" (154, 172; emphases mine). Daly seemed unaware of or unconcerned

with the tension between identifying with African women (becoming sisters) and speaking for them.

12. Tonglin Lu, ed., *Gender and Sexuality in Twentieth-Century Chinese Literature and Society* (Albany: State University of New York Press, 1993), 12.

13. Zhong Xueping, "Sisterhood? Representations of Women's Relationships in Two Contemporary Chinese Texts," in Lu, *Gender and Sexuality,* 171–172.

14. Ibid.

15. Lionel Jensen, *Manufacturing Confucianism* (Durham, N.C.: Duke University Press, 1997)

16. Daly, *Gyn/Ecology,* 138.

17. The sexually explicit descriptions of a man biting the bound foot or rubbing his penis against it, or the confessions of "Lotus Knower" cited by Daly (137–138), are in fact products of the nineteenth and twentieth centuries. In the premodern period, it was unthinkable to write about the sex of footbinding in such explicit terms. Indirection is key even for erotic novels, in which fondling the foot was a euphemism for sexual intercourse. See Keith McMahon, *Misers, Shrews, and Polygamists* (Durham, N.C.: Duke University Press, 1995).

18. Che Ruoshui, *Jiaoqi ji,* 20a, in *Qinding Siku quanshu (The four treasuries) zibu* 10, *zajia lie* 3 (author's translation).

19. Whereas the meaning of finality for males is unequivocal, there is always a tension for females in a patriarchal and patrilineal family system. Upon marriage, the daughter has to transfer her loyalty from her parents to her in-laws. Susan Mann and Du Fangqin have discerned a historical shift in the official interpretation of finality for women: in medieval times the filial duties of daughters were an orthodox concern, as evinced in such classics as the *Book of Filial Piety for Women.* In late imperial times, women were increasingly expected to lodge their loyalties with in-laws and gain recognition as wives and mothers. Marital fidelity and sexual purity became the dominant demands, hence the late-imperial chastity cult. "Competing Claims on Womanly Virtue in Late Imperial China," in *Women in Confucian Cultures in Premodern China, Korea, and Japan,* ed. Dorothy Ko, Jattgur Kim Haboush, and Joan Piggott (Berkeley: University of California Press; forthcoming).

20. Furth, "Rethinking Van Gulik," 133.

21. One familiar trope of male desire in lyrics is the male poet's quest for the goddess, which is a quest at once for religious transcendence and erotic love. See Suzanne Cahill, "Sex and the Supernatural in Medieval China: Cantos on the Transcendent Who Presides over the River," *Journal of the American Oriental Society* 105/2 (1985): 197–220.

22. Tonglin Lu, *Rose and Lotus* (Albany: State University of New York Press, 1991), 26.

23. I have written about this discourse of the natural body in "Footbinding as Female Inscription," in *Rethinking Confucianism: Past and Present in China, Japan, Korea, and Vietnam,* ed. Benjamin Elman, John Duncan, and Herman Doms, Asia Pacific Monograph Series in International Studies (Los Angeles: University of California; forthcoming).

24. Rey Chow contends that conventional class analysis is not good enough, for the

speaking intellectual committed to universal justice is not likely to reflect on her own privileged position. "This means that we can, as we must, attack social injustice without losing sight of the fact that even as women speaking for other women, for instance, we speak from a privileged position." Rey Chow, "Against the Lure of Diaspora: Minority Women, Chinese Women, and Intellectual Hegemony," in Lu, *Gender and Sexuality,* 36–37. Chow's critique of an overzealous commitment to universal justice certainly explains the pitfalls of such radicals as Mary Daly, who had no qualms about speaking on behalf of African women. But is it an inherent weakness of class analysis? It seems to me that it is an inattention to global class formation that leads to a facile commitment to universal justice.

25. Ibid.

26. Wanyan Yunzhu, comp., *Guochao guixiu zhengshi ji* (Correct beginnings: Poetry of ladies from our dynasty) (n.p.: Hongxiang guan, 1831–1836), 9.5b–6a. The poet Hu Shilan's emphasis on gentility accords with the editorial purposes of Yun, as analyzed by Susan Mann in *Precious Records* (Stanford, Calif.: Stanford University Press, 1997), 94–117. Other female-authored poems depict shoes as mementos of female friendship, mediums of exchange in a sentimental economy.

27. Given how famous Veblen's theory of footbinding is, it is curious that he mentioned it only in passing. Equating the "constricted waist . . . of the Western culture" with "the deformed foot of the Chinese," he regarded both as products of a particular stage of economic evolution in which "conspicuous leisure is much regarded as a means of good repute, the ideal requires delicate and diminutive hands and feet and a slender waist." Thorstein Veblen, *The Theory of the Leisure Class* (New York: Penguin, 1994), 148–149. Whereas Veblen's evolutionary view of economic development is questionable, his insights that standards of feminine beauty are conditioned by changing economic conditions merits attention. The logical conclusion of his theory, however, would put thirteenth-century China at the same stage of economic development as Victorian England.

28. On Wanyan Yunzhu and her work, see Mann, *Precious Records.*

29. Daly, *Gyn/Ecology,* 4–5.

30. Timothy Mitchell, *Colonising Egypt* (Berkeley and Los Angeles: University of California Press, 1991), xiii. This bifurcating colonizing episteme also manufactured new forms of personhood and spatial configurations.

Eleven   Just Good Sex

I am deeply grateful to my colleagues in this project, especially Rebecca Alpert, Pinar Ilkkaracan, Ayesha Imam, and Patricia Beattie Jung, whose insightful comments enhanced this work.

1. Solveig Anna Boasdottir, "Violence, Power, and Justice: A Feminist Contribution to Christian Sexual Ethics" (Ph.D. diss, University of Uppsala, Sweden, 1998), builds on the work of Marie M. Fortune and others. Boasdottir establishes the need to take the terrible reality of male battering of women as a starting point for feminist sexual ethics. Beverly Wildung Harrison, in her landmark volume *Our Right to Choose* (Boston: Beacon, 1983), makes the case for women as moral agents with bodily integrity, capable of making their own decisions on reproductive health and other issues.

Despite widespread opposition by some churches and conservative Christian theologians, there is a strong movement among progressive Christian theological ethicists to establish homosexuality in all of its sexual fullness as a moral good in accord with social scientific and biological studies. See, for example, Carter Heyward, *Staying Power: Reflections of Gender, Justice, and Compassion* (Cleveland: Pilgrim, 1995); Mary E. Hunt, *Fierce Tenderness: A Feminist Theology of Friendship* (New York: Crossroad, 1991); Marvin Ellison, *Erotic Justice: A Liberating Ethics of Sexuality* (Louisville, Ky.: Westminster/John Knox, 1996).

2. "Kyriarchy" is Elisabeth Schüssler-Fiorenza's word for "interlocking structures of domination [i.e. kyriarchal, elite males, relations of ruling *(Herr-schaft)]*," literally, structures of lordship. See her *But She Said: Feminist Practices of Biblical Interpretation* (Boston: Beacon, 1992), 8. The Roman Catholic Church in its institutional form is a kyriarchy in structure and governance. The Women-Church movement, by contrast, is based in the radical equality of its adherents.

3. Laura Donaldson, *Decolonizing Feminisms: Race, Gender, and Empire Building* (Chapel Hill: University of North Carolina Press, 1992), 135, quoted by Elisabeth Schüssler-Fiorenza, *Sharing Her Word: Feminist Biblical Interpretation in Context* (Boston: Beacon, 1998), 193.

4. Patty Crowley's story is in Robert McClory, *Turning Point: The Inside Story of the Papal Birth Control Commission and How Humanae Vitae Changed the Life of Patty Crowley and the Future of the Church* (New York: Crossroad, 1995).

5. Cf. Carmel McEnroy, *Guests in Their Own House: The Women of Vatican II* (New York: Crossroad, 1996).

6. "Women's Lives in a Changing World," *Interhemispheric Resource Center Newsletter,* January 1995, 2 (Box 4506, Albuquerque, N.Mex. 87196–4506).

7. David R. Loy describes market forces on religion in "The Religion of the Market," *Journal of the American Academy of Religion* 65/2 (1997): 275–290.

8. Diana L. Eck, "Neighboring Faiths," *Harvard Magazine* 99/1 (September–October 1996): 44.

9. Ibid., 41.

10. Cf. Boasdottir, "Violence, Power and Justice," for a comprehensive treatment of the literature.

11. The French Canadian bishops published a report condemning violence against women that was years in translation to English because the contents were judged so controversial. *A Heritage of Violence? A Pastoral Reflection on Conjugal Violence* (Montreal: Social Affairs Committee, L'Assemblée des Evêques du Québec, 1989).

12. Joan M. Martin, "The Notion of Difference for Emerging Womanist Ethics: The Writings of Audre Lorde and bell hooks," *Journal of Feminist Studies in Religion,* 9/1–2 (spring/fall 1993): 39.

13. Mary E. Hunt and Frances Kissling, "The New York Times: A Case Study in Religious Feminism," *Journal of Feminist Studies in Religion,* 3/1 (spring 1987): 115–129.

14. One useful discussion of the issues is in the Chilean feminist journal *Con-spirando* 25 (September 1998), focused on the theme "Derechos Humanos: Que Derechos? Derechos de quienes?" (Human rights: What rights? Rights for whom?).

15. The language of the "U.N. Universal Declaration of Human Rights" (1948) is clear: "a common standard of achievement for all peoples and all nations, to the end that every individual and every organ of society, keeping this Declaration constantly in mind, shall strive by teaching and education to promote respect for those rights and freedoms and by progressive measures, national and international, to secure their universal and effective recognition and observance, both among the peoples of Member States themselves and among the peoples of territories under their jurisdiction."

16. See, for example, David Hollenbach, *Claims in Conflict: Retrieving and Renewing the Catholic Human Rights Tradition* (New York: Paulist, 1979).

17. Rosemary Radford Ruether, "Women and Culture: The Case for Universal Rights," *Conscience* 16/4 (winter 1995/96): 13–15.

18. Ibid., 15.

19. Daniel C. Maguire, "Population, Consumption, Ecology: The Triple Problematic," in *Christianity and Ecology*, ed. Dieter T. Hessel and Rosemary Radford Reuther, Cambridge: Harvard University Press for Harvard Center for the Study of World Religions, 2000, 403–428.

20. Audre Lorde, "Uses of the Erotic," in *Sister Outsider* (Trumansburg, N.Y.: Crossing, 1984).

21. Cf. Karen Lebacqz, "Justice," *Dictionary of Feminist Theologies*, ed. Letty M. Russell and J. Shannon Clarkson (Louisville, Ky.: Westminster/John Knox, 1996), 158–159. Lebacqz refers to Carter Heyward with regard to "right relation."

About the Contributors

REBECCA T. ALPERT is assistant professor of religion and codirector of women's studies at Temple University, Philadelphia. She is the author of *Exploring Judaism: A Reconstructionist Approach* and *Like Bread on the Seder Plate: Jewish Lesbians and the Transformation of Tradition.*

RADHIKA BALAKRISHNAN is an associate professor of economics and international studies at Marymount Manhattan College. She is the author of several articles on reproductive health and population, global justice and ethics, and feminist economics, and the editor of a five-country study entitled *The Hidden Assembly Line: Gender Dynamics of Subcontracted Work in the Global Economy.* She is currently on the international advisory board to the Margaret Sanger Institute.

WANDA DEIFELT is a professor at Escola Superior de Teologia in São Leopoldo, RS, Brazil, where she holds the chair of feminist theology. She has published many articles on the topics of ethics, hermeneutics, and women's rights, most of them in Portuguese.

MARY E. HUNT is a Catholic feminist theologian who is cofounder and codirector of the Women's Alliance for Theology, Ethics, and Ritual (WATER) in Silver Spring, Maryland. She is an adjunct faculty member of the women's studies program at Georgetown University and author of *Fierce Tenderness: A Feminist Theology of Friendship.*

PINAR ILKKARACAN, a psychotherapist, researcher, and activist, is co-founder and coordinator of Women for Women's Human Rights in Istanbul, Turkey. She has worked as an activist, writer, and trainer around issues of migrant women, women's sexuality, racism, and violence against women. She is author of *The Myth of the Warm House: Domestic Violence and Sexual Abuse* and director of the film *It's Time to Say No!* a documentary on domestic violence in Turkey.

AYESHA M. IMAM, a Nigerian who resides in Lagos, is coordinator of the Western Region (Africa and the Middle East) of the International Solidarity Network of Women Living under Muslim Laws. She has written many articles and coedited several books on women in Africa and in Muslim societies.

GRACE M. JANTZEN is a Quaker feminist philosopher of religion, and the John Rylands Professorial Fellow in the department of religions and theology at the University of Manchester, England. Her most recent books are *Becoming Divine: Towards a Feminist Philosophy of Religion* and *Power, Gender, and Christian Mysticism.*

PATRICIA BEATTIE JUNG is professor of moral theology at Loyola University Chicago. She and her husband, Shannon, have enjoyed each other's company for over twenty-five years and have been blessed with three sons: Michael, Robert, and Nathan. She coauthored with the late Ralph F. Smith *Heterosexism: An Ethical Challenge.*

DOROTHY KO is Chinese by birth, and was made a British subject but chose to become a U.S. citizen. She has spent twenty years in her native Hong Kong, sixteen years in the United States, five years in Japan, and un-counted time wandering between worlds. A historian at Rutgers University in New Jersey, she has found a home in New York City. Through her journeys, she has taken refuge in books, including the one she wrote, *Teachers of the Inner Chambers: Women and Culture in Seventeenth Century China.*

JUDITH PLASKOW is professor of religious studies at Manhattan College and a Jewish feminist theologian and activist. She is author of *Standing Again at Sinai: Judaism from a Feminist Perspective.* She cofounded, and for ten years coedited, the *Journal of Feminist Studies in Religion.*

SUWANNA SATHA-ANAND is an associate professor and former chair of the philosophy department, Chulalongkorn University, Bangkok. She has published several books and many articles in the fields of Buddhist philosophy and of religion and social change. Her most recent paper is "Truth over Convention: Feminist Interpretations of Buddhism."

Index